FOOTBALL, EUROPE AND THE PRESS

LIZ CROLLEY and DAVID HAND

The Manchester Metropolitan University

FRANK CASS

LONDON   PORTLAND, OR

First published in 2002 in Great Britain by
FRANK CASS PUBLISHERS
Crown House, 47 Chase Side, Southgate, London N14 5BP

and in the United States of America by
FRANK CASS PUBLISHERS
c/o ISBS, 5824 N.E. Hassalo Street
Portland, Oregon 97213-3644

Website: www.frankcass.com

British Library Cataloguing in Publication Data

Crolley, Liz, 1966–
    Football, Europe and the press. – (Sport in the global
    society; no. 24)
    1. Soccer – Social aspects – England 2. Sports journalism –
    England 3. Nationalism and sports – England 4. Soccer –
    Social aspects – France 5. Sports journalism – France
    6. Nationalism and sports – France 7. Soccer – Social aspects
    – Spain 8. Sports journalism – Spain 9. Nationalism and
    sports – Spain
    I. Title II. Hand, David
    306.4′83′094

            ISBN 0-7146-4957-0 (cloth)
            ISBN 0-7146-8017-6 (paper)
                ISSN 1368-9789

Library of Congress Cataloging-in-Publication Data

Crolley, Liz, 1966–
    Football, Europe, and the press / Liz Crolley and David Hand.
        p. cm. – (Sport in the global society, ISSN 1368-9789; no. 24)
    Includes bibliographical references.
    ISBN 0-7146-4957-0 – ISBN 0-7146-8017-6 (pbk.)
    1. Soccer–Europe–Cross-cultural studies. 2. Soccer–Press
    coverage–Europe–Cross-cultural studies. 3. National
    characteristics–Europe–Cross-cultural studies. I. Hand, David, 1960–
    II. Title. III. Cass series–sport in the global society; no.24.
    GV944.E8 C76 2002
    796.334′094–dc21

                                            2001008545

2275135l

Printed in Great Britain by MPG Books Ltd, Bodmin, Cornwall

Liz:
To Hannah and Kathryn, born on the eve of a new red dawn

David:
To Christopher and George, both born with a blue moon rising

Contents

Acknowledgements

We would like to thank many people for help and support offered in a variety of ways: to Frank Cass; to J.A. Mangan, for not throwing our book proposal in the bin and Jonathan Manley, for being (very) patient while we wrote; to the Department of Languages at The Manchester Metropolitan University, for supporting our work as researchers; to Aidan Coveney and Richard Waller, for information on the PCC; to Paul Darby, for perceptive comments on some of our earlier work; to the Fédération française de football, for kindly supplying data; to Ralf Jeutter, for contributing material on Germany; to José del Olmo at the Centro de Investigaciones de la Historia y la Estadística del Fútbol Español, for helping during the early stages of the project; to the Public Relations Department of the Real Federación Española de Fútbol, for pointing us in the right direction when seeking information; to Matthew Screech, for help with Asterix; and finally to our families and friends, for living the project with us.

Series Editor's Foreword

Lately, in the mornings, he would read only the sports section, concentrating his full attention on the pages at the back where box scores and statistics were carefully charted and updated each day. He somehow found the columns of numbers and percentages comforting. They were clear and concise, an absolute order in a disordered world.[1]

The quotation is by way of a promissory note. *Football, Europe and the Press* makes good the note's promise. It is concerned with community reassurance and the sporting press in modern Europe.

At the outset, it must be recognised that despite sometimes desperate parochial patriotic declamations – in reality, more often than not, 'cultures are not discrete, sealed entities; ideas have scant regard for political boundaries; individuals belong to more than one culture, and the life of the mind is intently cosmopolitan'.[2] This is bravely and up to a point, wisely said. Consequently, while there is certainly no single European history, there are 'multiple histories that overlap and intertwine with each other'.[3] It remains true, however, that most Europeans inhabit national cultural 'bastions' with the doors more often closed by the steady winds of national language, customs and tradition than blown open by the occasional draughts of cross-cultural linguistics, customs and traditions. Thus there is clearly logic in commentators giving their attention to the life carried on within a given culture which is defined in largely linguistic terms.[4] This is mostly the cautious practice in sports studies. It is all the more refreshing, therefore, that sometimes, as in *Football, Europe and the Press* the authors prove to be bolder.

In my introduction to *Tribal Identities: Nationalism, Europe, Sport* I wrote:

In the period of national reassertion in Eastern Europe, and, to an extent, in no way to be exaggerated, national non-assertion in Western Europe, and in an era when sport, transmitted instantly and widely by the media, can graphically and powerfully reach huge audiences, its role in the making and unmaking of national, cultural and social allegiances merits the most serious inquiry ... it is far more than a national and international entertainment: it is a source of political identity, morale, pride and superiority. It also sustains political antagonisms, hatreds and prejudices.[5]

I see no need to revise the statement five years on. *Football, Europe and the Press* supports me in my original belief.

Perhaps the cynical Richard Vinen is right:

> It is highly questionable whether what are now defined as 'European values' have had much influence on most Europeans in the twentieth century, or whether they are incarnated by the political institutions of the European Union. Perhaps in a few years historians will regard all histories of Europe as value-laden and artificial constructions that should be confined to the academic dustbin along with histories of the 'Anglo-Saxon race' of 'Western civilisation'.[6]

I suggested later in *Tribal Identities* that three fascinating questions were yet to be answered about sport in Europe:

> To what extent can it be used to sustain smaller national identities within that larger community? To what extent will it serve to deny attempts at a European community with a common identity? Can it and should it be used, calculatedly, to merge the nations in Europe into a new corporateness which could claim a meaningful communality?[7]

Football, Europe and the Press goes some way to providing answers.

Since 1995 much has changed in Europe, at least, by way of intention. Ambitions have now moved on. It is within the framework of recent and future circumstances that these questions must now be posed. Football, and its press, knowingly or unknowingly, follow in the wake of politics. European politics are in massive flux:

> Three great changes have been interconnected. In reverse order, it was the collapse of communism that allowed the reunification of Germany that precipitated the Treaty of Maastricht. The shock-wave moved from the east to the centre to the west of Europe. But causes and consequences remain distinct. The outcomes of these processes obey no single logic. More than this: to a greater extent than in any previous phase of European integration, the impact of each is quite uncertain. We confront a set of ex ante indeterminacies that, adopting a Kantian turn of phrase, might be called the three amphibologies of post-Maastricht politics. They pose much more dramatic dilemmas than is generally imagined.[8]

Such revolutionary happenings in time will have intriguing consequences for European sport, its press and its sports' politics.

Nevertheless, when the proverbial chips are down, will much actually change within the national cultural bastions? Possibly not. And if this is the case, football and the football press will play a more than insignificant part. At present football both unites and divides the continent of Europe and 'the accent is placed [by an influential press] upon difference, upon that which divides rather than unites'.[9] Will it be a case of *plus ça change, plus c'est la même chose*? In football stadiums there is every chance of it! War, at least without weapons, between nation states will continue. Unflattering stereotypes will continue to be peddled – racial, sexual, regional and national – all reflecting history. One of the present roles of the European press, as Crolley and Hand remark, is to reinforce, if not inculcate, myths of national character which are deep rooted in the political, diplomatic and cultural past. In their attractive turn of phrase, football writers in Great Britain, France and Spain constantly 'play the identity card'[10] – a card that is the same. Partisan passion rules.[11] Time to call in the post-Maastricht spin doctors?

J.A. MANGAN
International Research Centre for Sport, Socialisation, Society
University of Strathclyde

Introduction:
Football, Europe and the Press

Europe is the centre of gravity of Planet Football. The modern game's origins may be traced to mid-nineteenth century England, while the organisation of international competitions, such as the World Cup and the European Championships, as well as the founding of the institutions that regulate the game globally, such as FIFA, owe much to the pioneering spirit of the French. Europe still attracts the sport's greatest players and offers them the best financial rewards, particularly in Spain and Italy, while the continent's most prestigious domestic championships, such as the English FA Premiership, the German Bundesliga and, indeed, the Italian Serie A and the Spanish Primera Liga, are widely held to be the most competitive and most attractive competitions of their type in the world. Finally, football's importance as a social and economic phenomenon within Europe itself cannot now be disputed. Some 20 million men and women are registered as players in over 50 national football associations, while the professional game, benefiting (at the apex, at least) from large injections of private capital and increasingly business-like in its approach, continues to attract ever-mounting attention from Europe's media.

The relationship between football and television and, to a lesser extent, radio has been well documented elsewhere.[1] It is the coverage of football in the print media, in particular the 'quality' daily press, that will be the focus of the present volume. Football is certainly an important element of print media discourse. As the socio-economic importance to Europe of sport continues to rise, it becomes ever more unthinkable that a publication claiming the title of 'newspaper' could survive commercially without increasingly extensive and successful coverage of sport in general and of football in particular. Indeed, the attention received by football is, in part, reflected by the considerable amount of space devoted to it by European newspapers. It is our contention, however, that when Europe's newspapers report on football, they do far more than merely give accounts of the game's technicalities. Match reports, for instance, do not contain only dry facts: A passed to B, B shot and scored, 1–0. European print media discourse on football may also be said to play a significant part in the construction of national, regional and group identities. For linguistic and commercial reasons that will be touched upon shortly, match reports and related articles frequently take on the characteristics of literary narratives in which the characters (players and clubs, domestic or national) are pitted against each other in moments of crisis and conflict (football matches and competitions) that form the central plot and they may be read, therefore, partly at least, as weaving a story about how Europeans interact with each other and how they reflect upon their own national, regional and group identities. The present study seeks precisely to analyse the representation[2] of identity in the print media of some of Europe's most dominant footballing nations with the aim of understanding the mechanisms at work in reflections in the sports media of the key issues of national and regional identity, as well as those of ethnicity and gender. It offers empirical findings that are related to a broader interpretative and conceptual framework and, in a modest way, will stimulate further debate in the field. Before explaining the methodology of the study and presenting our analyses of the data researched, we shall devote some time to a review of the history of European football journalism, particularly in the 'quality' press, and to an examination of the principal features of its distinctive writing style. Important theoretical considerations regarding the processes of identity construction will then also need to be taken into account in order fully to appreciate the ideological significance of such writing.

The history of the involvement of the press with football, at least in its professional form, is a lengthy one and is generally marked by continual expansion in terms of coverage and considerable change in reporting styles.[3] In any review of this type, honourable mention must be made of the specialist, Manchester-based *Athletic News* and of Liverpool's *Football Echo*. The weekly *Athletic News*, dating from 1875 and part of the Edward Hulton stable of publications, provided coverage of matches in the early days of the English Football League. Widely regarded as the authoritative voice of football, the paper reached circulation figures of 180,000 plus at its height and could be considered as the forerunner of modern European football journalism. The *Football Echo* was founded only slightly later, in 1888, and is noteworthy as the first ever football edition of a local newspaper. It was the Edwardian era, at the beginning of the twentieth century, though, that saw the first great wave of expansion in national press coverage of football in Great Britain, as the more general daily papers devoted more time and space to the game. By the 1930s coverage of football, which had by then established itself as the national winter sport, was becoming important in the increasingly fierce circulation wars in which the popular press found itself engaged. There had also been something of a revolution in reporting styles too. Breakthroughs in photography and improved printing processes allowed the fast reproduction of good quality photographs which now accompanied the text of match reports and related articles. Although much reporting, notably in *The Times*, was still of a rather basic, factual nature, focusing more on description rather than interpretation and comment, football was beginning to be treated as a glamorous activity with an increased accent on personalities, gossip and action. These trends continued in the 1940s and beyond and saw the advent of sensationalist feature writers in the popular press concentrating on the darker aspects of the game, such as corruption and scandal. The 1940s and the 1950s are also particularly important from the perspective of this volume as they mark the second wave of expansion in the press coverage of football in Britain, this time led by the 'quality' dailies. As a consequence of football's increasing status and widespread appeal, British broadsheets such as *The Times* and the *Guardian* could no longer merely give scant attention to the domestic game (although the 'quality' press still proved adept at largely ignoring international competitions such as the FIFA World Cup and the first European Cup in 1955). In turn, coverage of the domestic game in the 'qualities' further raised the status of football and lent it an intellectual respectability that it might be felt to have lacked up to that point. The 1960s then presented a new challenge to the press in its coverage of football: the advent of television. Newspapers responded by broadening their own coverage still further, adding interviews with players and managers, transfer speculation, match previews and other types of feature article to the mainstay match reports that had been their preserve for so long but which now were being challenged for currency and immediacy by televised match highlights and, latterly, games being shown live on television. Finally, the 1980s and the 1990s confirmed the place of pre-eminence occupied by football even in the 'quality' British press, which had taken so long to embrace it but which now was leading yet another period of expansion of coverage. It could be argued that the most significant development of the last 15 years in this area has been precisely the growth of the sports pages in 'quality' dailies, with football occupying a now fully secure and central place in that significantly expanded coverage. The 'quality' British press, it seems, has realised the importance of sport in driving sales figures and has also responded to changing trends in its readership – which is now less interested in politics and current affairs and more concerned with lifestyle issues, leisure activities and sport.

In European countries other than Great Britain the trajectory of press coverage has, by and large, been similar but not identical.[4] In France, for instance, football was not played professionally until 1932 but coverage of the game still featured initially in the 1910s and the 1920s in specialist sporting publications such as *Sporting*, *La Vie au grand air* and *Le Miroir des sports* (at which many of the journalists were former players).[5] The baton has been carried more recently by *L'Equipe*, founded in 1946 as the descendant of *L'Auto-Vélo*, established in 1900 by Henri Desgrange, founder of the Tour de France. *L'Equipe* is a specialist sports newspaper which devotes about 40 per cent of its space to football, claims almost two

million readers a day (374,000 copies sold on average per day in 1997) and
vies with the general newspapers *Le Parisien* and *Le Monde* for the title of
France's best-selling daily paper.[6] Moreover, not unsurprisingly, the day
after France's victory in the 1998 World Cup final *L'Equipe* went into the
record books by selling more than 1.7 million copies, the single biggest sales
figure for any edition of any daily newspaper in France.[7] France also has a
respected biweekly publication devoted exclusively to football: *France
Football* celebrated 50 years of publishing in 1997, sells some 300,000
editions per week and basks in the nickname of 'the Bible of football' thanks
to its authoritative coverage and extensive statistics on the French, European
and world games. The coverage of football by France's general daily papers,
though, was somewhat slower in taking off than that by the specialist press
but was, by the 1970s, a firmly established if still somewhat peripheral
element of the portfolio of national dailies such as *France-Soir*, *Libération*
and *Le Monde*. The last, in particular, tended to cling to its rather serious if
not dour persona and the amount of space devoted to football was still not
great, usually amounting to little more than one page per week on average.
Progress made on the pitch by French club sides in Europe, such as Saint-
Etienne's reaching the European Cup final in 1976, and, especially, by the
national team, winners on home soil of the 1984 European Championships
and World Cup semi-finalists in 1982 and 1986, provided considerable
impetus for the expansion of the press coverage of the sport, a trend
confirmed by the extensive reporting in French dailies of Euro 96, France 98
and Euro 2000. At France 98, for instance, every major French daily carried
a football supplement and even the staid *Le Monde* sent over 40 writers to
cover the competition; they joined the press corps of some 11,000 reporting
on the event in over 150 different languages.

    The model of football journalism in Italy is similar to that in France with,
perhaps, an even greater emphasis on specialist publications. The football
weekly *Il Calcio Illustrato* appeared from 1930, while the much revered,
Milan-based *Gazetta dello Sport* dates from even earlier – 1896 – when its
prime focus was on cycling, and now enjoys its position as one of Italy's
most popular daily papers. Two other national sports dailies are widely read
and, like the modern *Gazetta*, also devote about 70 per cent of their space to
football: *Corriere dello Sport* (based in Rome) and *Tutto Sport* (from Turin).
Germany, however, has tended to follow the British model of a relatively
limited, specialist, sporting press, with football mainly being covered by
general newspapers. A football weekly, the rather serious *Kicker*, founded as
early as 1919, still circulates today but readers requiring coverage of the
game continue to turn in the main to newspapers such as the *Süddeutsche
Zeitung*, Germany's best-known, liberal daily.

    In Spain, the end of the nineteenth century saw the first information
about sport appearing in the generalist press, probably influenced by French

and English models. However, some publications dedicated to sport already existed. *El Cazador*, edited in Barcelona in 1856/57, is considered to be the first Spanish publication devoted to sport.[8] The earliest publication on sport which is still produced today is *El Mundo Deportivo*, also printed in Barcelona, which dates back to 1906 when it appeared weekly and which became a daily paper in 1929. Today's best-selling, daily sports paper, *Marca*, established in San Sebastián in 1938, with publication being transferred to Madrid in 1942,[9] leads the market in daily sports publications and enjoys around 62 per cent of total sales (sales of over 420,000), followed by *As* with 15 per cent, *Sport* with 13 per cent and *El Mundo Deportivo* with 10 per cent. Indeed, sales for *Marca* are now greater than those for Spain's most widely read, general daily, *El País,* which records sales of just under 400,000.[10] The role of *Marca* in particular was significant in the early promotion of football in Spain. However, during the Civil War (1936–39) the paper also became heavily politicised and earned a reputation for supporting centralism as well as favouring Madrid over the rest of Spain, accusations that still persist today.[11] During the latter half of the twentieth century coverage of sport in the press was shared between daily, general newspapers and specialist publications. General newspapers such as *ABC* and *El País* tend to devote between 7 and 10 per cent of their coverage to sport, and of this, during the football season, an average of 70–80 per cent is dedicated to football.[12] During two key periods recently, namely the European Championships and the World Cup, both *ABC* and *El País*, like many of their counterparts in other countries, considerably increased their coverage and carried special daily supplements.

As more and more column inches or, rather, centimetres (Brussels *oblige*) are devoted in Europe's daily newspapers to the coverage of football, the language employed by journalists in this section of the press is increasingly worthy of attention. It has been noted that football journalists work under considerable pressure to produce copy quickly and that this can, at times, lead to excesses variously described as 'over-familiar clichés' and 'part melodrama, part slop'.[13] There is, however, also no doubt that a range of writing styles has developed that is distinctive, rich and diverting. Hopcraft, himself a football journalist, has noted that football writing has developed into 'an entertainment in its own right' and asserts that, 'While football matches are sometimes dull, sports pages can never afford to be.'[14] Media sport is, in other words, a valuable consumer commodity which has to be packaged in an attractive and therefore marketable linguistic form, which, partially at least, accounts for the highly imaginative and inventive metaphors employed by European football writing examples of which were examined by Jeutter and the present authors in a previous study.[15] One of the techniques used by journalists writing about the game that has been widely observed and discussed is the propensity to employ military metaphors and the vocabulary of warfare.[16] The physical, adversarial nature of sport lends itself readily to this sort of treatment, of course, and it cannot be denied that much football writing is replete with facile references to troops and battles, soldiers and raids, hard-fought victory and defeat, tactics and territory, conquest and combat, heroism and leadership. The analysis of the language of European football writing that follows, however, aims to go far beyond the simplistic cliché. The richness of the corpus studied is such that the themes and images deployed in this section of the press prove to be many, varied and complex. Above all, much may be learned about the construction of European identities from such a survey, and it is to this aspect of the study that attention is now turned.

It has long been recognised that sport can inform the popular memory of communities as well as offer a source of collective identification and expression of local community for those who follow it.[17] Football, in particular, is an important site for the affirmation of regional and local identities. The increasing commercialisation of European football, the transformation of many of its clubs into public limited companies (especially in Spain and England) and increased media company ownership (especially in Italy and England, but also, increasingly, in France) might be threatening to weaken the links between football clubs, supporters and their local communities,[18] but it cannot be denied that those links are still strong and pertinent. A football match is a public event and, as such, cannot be dissociated from the oral and written descriptions and interpretations that surround it. These commentaries take many forms, of course, but two of the most fruitful from the point of view of research involve football 'fandom' and media coverage of the game. Many fans still regard their chosen club as the representative of a local or regional community. They see in its characteristics, especially in its reputed style of play, a reflection of a specific, collective identity and football does more than simply permit this sense of belonging or identity to be recorded or classified. It allows it to be verbalised or recounted. Through their chants, songs, banners and, latterly, fanzines and other publications, fans recount their own local allegiances and verbalise their own regional affiliations. Initiation into such rituals for new supporters is also an initiation into the values upheld by a town, city or region, values which might draw upon distinctive local characteristics or, indeed, upon the social and political relationships the locality in question has with others.[19] The strong sense of local identity that may be observed in supporters of, say, Liverpool FC, Olympique de Marseille or FC Barcelona, derives not only from the emotional bond between the fans and the clubs which are seen as representatives of a city or, indeed, of a whole region. It is also bound up with wider issues of identity that exist outside the game: Liverpool's sense of uniqueness in England, Marseille's particular involvement with the Paris–province divide in France, and Barcelona's status as the principal focus of Catalan nationalism in Spain. As well as the fans' own commentaries, football matches are also accompanied by the interpretations of professional wordsmiths, the journalists whose job it is to describe, analyse and comment upon football. Of particular interest from the perspective of the present study is the way in which media sport, to use Boyle and Haynes's terms,[20] reproduces and amplifies elements of the identities associated with fans, clubs and the cities or regions in which they are based. The media play a not insignificant role in the fostering of the sense of collective, local identity that already exists both within and outside the football context. The language of the print media in particular which can never be dull, for reasons already explored, typically plays with strong images and deals in the emphatic and the striking rather than the subtle and the understated. Print media discourse finds, therefore, a rich source of inspiration in pre-existing, already defined, local and regional identities and, in particular, in marked local and regional antagonisms. The nature of some of these identities and the ways in which they are narrated by football journalism will be explored in some detail in Chapters 2, 5 and 8 below.

If media sport is noteworthy because of the insights it offers into local and regional identities, then another driver in the upsurge of academic interest in this field is the pressing agenda set by issues surrounding ethnicity and gender. Part of the power of the media is their ability to contribute to the shaping of public opinion. In representations of certain sections of society they often do this by reducing complex and diverse groups into a set of simplistic characters with specific characteristics. When the groups involved are ethnically- or gender-based, questions need to be raised about the validity of the portrayals and the effects these potentially disturbing discourses have in society as a whole. The growth of the African-Caribbean community in Great Britain, for instance, has found its parallel in the increasing number of blacks working in football as players, managers and officials. How are black footballers operating in England represented by the press? Can the African-Caribbean community readily identify with the portrayals? Has negative racist stereotyping truly disappeared? As we shall see in a case study presented in Chapter 2, the representation of black players taken as a group is still largely based upon traditional and potentially damaging appreciations of 'racial' differences and upon outmoded perceptions of the role of African-Caribbeans in British culture, perceptions which themselves do not necessarily derive from within football but rather from the wider legacy of Britain's imperial and colonial past. Similarly, Chapter 6 offers an initial analysis of the representation of women in a section of Europe's 'quality' daily press, this time in France. Despite their increasing involvement in French football both as players and fans, women still tend to be largely absent from press coverage of the game in that country. When they do appear, it might be felt that the way in which they are represented does more to uphold the patriarchal values of male dominance and female subordination than to challenge them. In short, football writing would appear to be a conservative domain for the framing of representations of gender.

Football writing in Europe is also an arena for the representation of national identities and it is this issue that will constitute the largest part of the study. The metaphorical descriptions and emotive vocabulary which are, as we shall see, so prevalent in football journalism in Europe's 'quality' daily press are not merely ingenious stylistic devices affording attractive literary qualities to the prose in question. Sport is a major economic, cultural and political phenomenon that is primarily consumed through the media. As such, media sport communicates information not just about itself but about culture as a whole. In short, a press report on a match involving the England national team, for instance, might take the form of an article on the world of international sport, but its content is inextricably bound up with wider psychological, cultural and ideological processes, and it therefore also provides information about concepts of Englishness itself. Football is, then, often appropriated to communicate information about national identity. It becomes 'indexical'[21] in that it is used to represent perceived national characteristics about which it apparently presents direct evidence. As Blain and Boyle state: 'The way in which sport is written about ... becomes a source of information about our beliefs, opinions and attitudes as cultures.'[22] An integral element of these beliefs is, of course, a sense of our own collective, national identity and an awareness of other nations' supposed characteristics. Indeed, the role played by media representations of football in the construction of national identities cannot be overestimated. A 'culture of nationality'[23] is developed, shaped, even inculcated by the media in this respect which, therefore, contribute to the maintenance of a set of shared cultural values which serve to reinforce a consensual perception of national unity. National identity is, above all, a shared identity; it is not innate, it is rather a cultural product, an idea that has become a force through its mediation by important vectors such as political institutions, educational systems, television, radio and the press. Concepts of national identity are then perpetuated, or, to use Debray's term,[24] transmitted through time to become powerful, heritage-laden, collective notions offering shared points of reference that help to bind individuals into a national community. At this point in such discussions it is almost obligatory to quote the work of Anderson.[25] We do not intend to disappoint in this respect. For Anderson, a nation is more than simply a geopolitical entity with specific political institutions. It has subjective as well as objective qualities. It is vitally an 'imagined community', a unified group of people whose sense of nationhood depends upon their recognition of a common bond founded upon shared descent, interests, concerns and references. This sense of national identity is a powerful force in the collective imagination and that imagination is frequently fuelled or fed by media representations that both define a nation inwardly in terms of its own history, invoking familiar, indigenous cultural traditions, and outwardly in terms of its difference from other nations. In this way the abstract concept of the nation is brought into focus and becomes coherent, homogeneous, almost monolithic. As we shall see in what follows, football in Europe offers a particularly rich source of material for the analysis of the role of the 'quality' daily press in these processes of definition and transmission of shared notions of national identity.

There is a long-standing tendency to read football as the expression of the societies in which it operates and this is particularly true of national teams which are frequently seen as representing facets of national identity in their reputed style of play. The styles often become sources of national pride and function in opposition to other national styles.[26] This identification with the style practised by a particular team is, therefore, also an affirmation of a specific, collective national identity. The universal practice of football is 'indigenised',[27] with the effect that certain playing styles are seen as unique and essential to the nation concerned, as well as representing values that are deemed important in that nation. Notions are widespread, then, of English fighting spirit and virility, French flair and style, and German mental strength and efficiency. These concepts, among many others, will be studied in some detail in Chapters 1, 3, 4, 6, 7 and 9.

As Bromberger notes, however, 'national styles do not always correspond to the reality of the game as practised by players, far from it, but rather to the stereotypical images, embedded in time, that a nation attributes to itself and that it wishes others to see'.[28] We are dealing, then, not so much with the way in which people actually play football but rather with the way in which they are represented when playing it. Such representations frequently take the form of stereotypes, especially at the hands of supporters and media commentators.[29] Stereotypes may be regarded as social constructs or shared cultural artefacts. Part of their power and one of the reasons for their longevity is that they resonate as markers of identity across many domains within a given culture, passing unchanged, unhindered and frequently unchallenged from, say, sport to the cinema and from literature to politics and back again. That is, they are iterative, capable of being repeated from text to text or from cultural product to product. They are, then, 'recognisable and well accepted conventions of representation',[30] a form of cultural shorthand in that they are invariably over-simple, reducing, in this case, a nation to a limited set of supposedly typical characteristics. Indeed, stereotypes are particularly useful devices for the perpetuation of a national identity, given that, as Anderson and Weymouth note, 'One characteristic of a mythical, imagined community is its tendency to overgeneralisation'.[31] In this way, then, stereotypes speedily affirm group membership as well as identity and serve to classify human diversity into a set of instantly recognisable and largely reassuring categories.

Some commentators read the robust survival of national stereotypes as one expression of a desire to hold on to what is traditional and familiar in an increasingly globalised environment which is ever more complex and uncertain.[32] Globalisation is certainly an important feature of contemporary society. Its effects are increasingly apparent as, with the development of multinational companies, global mass-media marketing and the potential offered by the Internet, a world economy with increasingly standardised consumer habits takes shape. Politically, too, many states are being subsumed (some kicking and screaming) into wider, supranational bodies such as the European Union, while even militarily nations are participating in broader, global organisations. In this respect, the proposed European Rapid Reaction Force might be added to the long-standing example of NATO. Sport, too, and football, in particular, of course, is also increasingly globalised in terms of media exposure as well as the growing attachment to transnational commercialisation and sponsorship by multinationals. Caution needs to be exercised, however, in judging the extent to which globalisation might be eroding distinctive national (and local) identities. Football, and its mediation by television, radio and the press, might well provide a salutary lesson that globalising forces are not erasing nor homogenising these identities and that, indeed, they are being expressed with considerable force, partly as a reaction against globalisation. As D. Rowe *et al.* note:

> Even if we accept ... that nation states are in decline after only a brief flowering ... there is no reason to believe that nationalism as an ideological and cultural force is also on the road to oblivion ... In fact, the reverse is the case – the more that national-political, economic and military sovereignty is undermined, the greater the need for states to construct a semiotically potent cultural nation. There is surely no cultural force more equal to the task of creating an imaginary national unity than the international sports-media complex.[33]

One of the aims of the present study, then, is precisely to explore some of the ways in which the European print media continue to construct potent national identities through football writing and, in this respect, the familiar national stereotype remains a favoured recourse.

Much light has been shed on national stereotypes in the football context by Archetti's exploration of the concept of 'essentialist' identity.[34] Essentialist national identity is the ideal displayed by a 'typical' style of play and represented by 'mythical teams' and 'model players'. Key values that appeal to a nation's sense of collective belonging are exemplified by 'great' teams, 'great' heroes and the 'great' games of the past in which they played. A process of representation ensues that creates a stock of values, events and meanings that form the symbolic capital lying at the heart of definitions of the 'essence' of national character. Events on the field are recounted in such a way by players, coaches, fans and journalists that an entire historical narrative is produced recording the valued image of a specific national identity. The 'essence' of Argentine football, for example, according to Archetti, is that technical virtuosity and individual brilliance provide the unexpected on the pitch. Moreover, this 'essence', which is reflected in accounts of the style of play of a given national team, has an origin, a foundation in a specific event which is frequently held up nostalgically as the first, best example of the exemplification of the identity in question. Archetti's example focuses on the 'foundation myth' of the emergence of a national style in the run-up to Argentina's participation in the 1930 World Cup final, during which Argentine teams were widely credited with technique, elegance and openness, factors that continue to define Argentina's footballing identity to the present. Generally the essentialist desire is to preserve the 'essence' of national identity as expressed through football, which is why apparent changes of tactics or styles of play can meet with fierce resistance. If key values are being sacrificed, a sense of decay is felt along with a loss of self-identity. Changes can be accepted but only if key values are maintained. Continuity counts. To add to Archetti's remarks on Argentina, we might note the criticism in the French press before the 1998 World Cup of manager Aimé Jacquet's team selections and tactics (see Chapter 4). Considered from this standpoint, these criticisms might be read as the outward expression of a deep-seated fear that Jacquet's team was somehow in danger of betraying continuity and tradition and, therefore, of contributing to a dangerous loss of 'essential' Frenchness. This incident, of course, raises the further question of the extent to which national identity can be dynamic rather than static and is one to which we shall return. Indeed, for all the importance of familiar stereotypes and essentialist identities, it might be felt also that the European print media contribute to the on-going process of the (re)shaping of identities. As we shall see, particularly in Chapters 1, 4 and 7, national identities are, in varying measures, in the process of evolution, they are being renegotiated, and, as such, are never complete.[35]

Archetti's location of the foundation myth of essentialist identity in the footballing setting is valuable though. Certainly it cannot be denied, for instance, that archetypal myths of English footballing heroism were regenerated by England's victory in the 1966 World Cup and those of French flair and 'champagne football' by France's triumph in the 1984 European Championships. Both of these events have left in their particular countries a legacy of 'essential' identity that successive English and French teams have had to live up to (or be castigated for if they fall short). However, it is our contention that the origins of certain myths of national identity are not located only within football itself. Despite the ease with which they can be applied to football and for all their conventional, reductionist qualities, stereotypes of national identity are clearly rooted in wider objective realities. They are founded upon events or developments in political, cultural, socio-economic and military domains and, therefore, connect with issues other than the sporting. Throughout this discussion, then, we shall attempt to highlight some of the origins of the stereotypes and images in question. This 'discursive paralysis we call stereotypification'[36] will be seen to operate through football writing in all the countries studied rather than in England alone and, consequently, notions of national identity tend to be continually evoked across the European continent. What this study attempts is to isolate and describe these notions in Blain, Boyle and O'Donnell's terms of 'autotypification' (how nations perceive themselves) and 'heterotypification' (here how Europe's dominant football nations are perceived by others).[37] In this way we hope to make explicit the mechanisms by which media sport in general and football journalism in particular contribute to the (re)construction of national identities in Europe.

Given the role played by media sport in the construction of identity, then, it was felt important to examine in some detail the coverage of football in a representative sample of Europe's 'quality' daily newspapers. From Great Britain we mainly studied *The Times*, the right-of-centre daily tracing its ancestry back to the eighteenth century. We have, however, also included many examples from other 'quality' dailies where appropriate, such as the *Guardian*, the *Daily Telegraph* and *The Observer*. The French newspapers considered are two of those that appeal to the educated élite: *Le Monde*, a prestigious left-of-centre daily, founded in 1944, which has an international reputation for being a reliable, serious source of in-depth news coverage, and the slightly more popular *Libération*, founded in 1973. Finally, in Spain, the newspapers examined are *ABC*, a historically right-wing, tabloid-size daily, and *El País*, a left-of-centre publication generally considered biased towards Spain's socialist government in office between 1982 and 1996. The newspapers studied are all major dailies in their several countries. Moreover, it is worth noting that, according to an opinion poll conducted by Ipsos-RSL,[38] many of them are among the dailies most likely to be read by Europe's decision-makers: the politicians, diplomats, business leaders, media personnel, civil servants, scientists and culture chiefs. *Le Monde* and *El País* came top of the league in their own circulation areas, while *The Times* was second only to its more specialist sister publication the *Financial Times*. (The German newspaper, the *Süddeutsche Zeitung*, which we shall also have occasion to quote, came second only to the *Frankfurter Allgemeine Zeitung*.) In other words, given their general importance and especially given their readership, the 'quality' European dailies examined here are clearly very influential and, therefore, worthy of study. Admittedly, different political biases operate in these newspapers and our findings must be read with some caution in this light. A research opportunity awaits, for instance, for a comparative study of media sports texts produced by, say, two newspapers from the same country but of opposing political convictions. The number of papers studied here (and their political orientation) may vary, then, but the amount of column inches analysed is approximately the same from country to country, ensuring that the sample sizes from each nation were roughly equal.

The mediation of football by the tabloid press has not been considered in detail. There are several reasons for this. First, the tabloids have already been studied to a considerable extent.[39] Secondly, as has already been noted, the expansion of the coverage of football by the 'quality' press has been one of the most significant developments in journalism in the last ten to 15 years and it is, therefore, intrinsically worthy of attention as a study in itself. Finally, and possibly most importantly, our analysis is cross-cultural. The 'particular quality–popular dichotomy'[40] so characteristic of Great Britain, and based on the contrast between the writerly style of the former and the somewhat cynical, reader-driven reporting of the latter, is largely absent on the continent. Given that there is simply no fully comparable, mainland European equivalent of the British tabloid press, it would have been an error to try to compare British tabloids with continental European 'qualities', since, to be fruitful, comparisons should be effected on a like-for-like basis. (For similar reasons, we have not included examples from continental Europe's specialist sporting press, since, once again, there is no real equivalent in Great Britain.) Having said this, we have, nonetheless, still, on occasions, drawn on some British tabloids, including the *Sun*, the *Daily Star* and the *Daily Express*, where examples of the discourse employed by them were particularly appropriate and relevant to the discussion as well as when their input into the debate about European identities simply could not be ignored, as with the *Daily Mirror*'s rather special contribution to Anglo-German relations during the 1996 European Championships (see Chapter 1).

In studying the ways in which the press represents national, regional and group identities in Europe, we have focused primarily on the coverage of England, France, Germany, Italy and Spain since they are unquestionably Europe's most dominant footballing nations. By the end of the 1999/2000 season these countries had won eight of the 16 FIFA World Cups so far and seven of the 11 European Championships played to date, while, at club level, teams based in them had won almost four-fifths of all the major European trophies contested (90 out of 115).[41] On a more subjective and broader note, there is also widespread agreement that these five countries are among those world-wide where football is played at its best and most competitive levels.

Gérard Houllier, now Liverpool's manager, notes, for instance, that 'The great football teams come from those countries that have top quality domestic leagues. Football's G7 is made up of five European nations (England, Italy, Spain, Germany and France) plus Brazil and Argentina' (*Libération*, 14 July 1998).

Next, to provide a manageable and compact chronological focus for our analysis, the data studied were drawn from the years 1996 to 1998 inclusive and specifically from the 1996 European Championships held in England, the 1997/98 domestic campaigns in the English FA Premiership, the French Division 1 and the Spanish Primera Liga, and the 1998 World Cup contested in France. Furthermore, examples of the print media discourse employed by match reports and related articles from earlier periods are also quoted where appropriate and, given that, at the time of writing Euro 2000 had just taken place, we have also included some preliminary findings from our initial analyses of the press coverage of that tournament. For the most part, we have successfully resisted the temptation to quote other researchers' data (but we are more than happy to acknowledge those occasions when we do). Almost all of the media sports texts quoted here have been researched by the present authors who have studied several hundred match reports, analyses and related articles from Great Britain, France and Spain (although it is not claimed that the survey was exhaustive). Moreover, in the case of foreign language sources (primary or secondary), the translations into English are our own as are, therefore, any consequential errors, imperfections or omissions.

Finally, when considering sports journalism, it is useful to bear in mind the typology established by Rowe.[42] *Hard news* is the ostensibly objective record of facts and events including match analyses; *soft news* is made up of gossip, scoops, exclusives, biography, hero worship and 'infotainment' largely contributing to the construction of celebrity status for footballers; *orthodox rhetoric* is avowedly subjective punditry, the presentation of an authoritative viewpoint, judgement or criticism deriving from the experience, fame or status of the journalist or columnist in question; and *reflexive analysis* addresses the problematic of sport by questioning the writer's own involvement with and relationship to it. Our analyses of European football journalism in 'quality' daily newspapers focus almost exclusively on the categories of hard news and orthodox rhetoric, although occasionally examples are drawn from soft news. (Reflexive analysis, as understood by Rowe, is rare in newspaper sports journalism, being far more likely to be encountered in popular football book writing and fanzine literature.)

It should be stressed at this point that the interpretations outlined in the study are, of necessity, subjective and our readings are, therefore, clearly open to further comment. We are also aware that there is a view that the type of discussion that follows 'can descend to a fairly sterile semantic debate involving, as it does, rather too many "reflecting" chickens and "reinforcing and constructing" eggs'.[43] Apart from answering 'cluck, cluck', we would contend that it is the very nature of European football journalism to be both the cause and the consequence of the circulation of images of collective identity, whether national, regional or group and that the linguistic and discursive mechanisms by which this is achieved are themselves worthy of study. Furthermore, as has been noted and as will be demonstrated, those images of identity are grounded in objective realities in the wider social and political spheres and cannot, therefore, be fully appreciated without reference to the latter. This is no media-centric chicken-and-egg debate then, but rather one which regards the print media as one important agent in the process of identity formation within the complex interplay of social, economic, political and historical factors by which identity is ultimately determined. As such, it raises important questions. In what ways do the vocabulary and imagery employed by European football writing contribute to the construction of collective identities? Are Europeans' perceptions of national character as mediated by the press the same from country to country? Are discourses of national and local identity as well as those of ethnicity and gender so deeply embedded in European society that the mediation of football by its 'quality' daily press functions as a (re)producer of traditional views of the world?

Identity is certainly a central and currently fashionable question debated by researchers working in the post-modern, post-structuralist world. As linguists (as well as football players and fans) operating in the field of cross-cultural studies, we contend that identity is constantly being reproduced through the cultural activities of daily life, such as sport, and that language has a primary role within this process as a major determinant of perceptions of the world and one's place in it. It is principally through language that human beings create and reinvent their world. Social identities are represented, enacted and negotiated via language.[44] The discourses of European football, the language used to describe it and the narratives recounted about it, are inseparable from the many social identities that make up European culture as a whole. In order to engage with and understand that culture, it is imperative to investigate the ways in which it is represented discursively in the media. Let us discover, then, what the language of football writing says about perceptions of identity in Europe.

PART ONE:
ENGLAND

1

The Bulldog Spirit

Football was born in England. In the early nineteenth century students and teachers in public schools would play an early version of the game but without common rules, especially on the handling of the ball, or standard equipment. In 1848, at Trinity College, Cambridge, agreement was finally reached between the public schools (with the exception of Rugby) on a definition of the rules of 'the dribbling game' and these rules formed the basis on which the Football Association (FA), founded in 1863, organised and developed the sport nationally. From its public school beginnings and with the growth of professionalism in the 1870s, football expanded both geographically and socially to encompass the industrial, 'working-class' heartlands of London, the Midlands and the North. By the end of the century and little more than 30 years after the creation of the FA, football had firmly established itself as a major element of English culture.[1]

As the social and economic significance of football in the country grew in the twentieth century, so media coverage of it expanded rapidly (see the Introduction). It is our contention, though, that the media do far more than report the outcome of football matches and explain the technicalities of the game. Football is mediated as an extension of social structures and values; it becomes 'indexical' in that it is appropriated to communicate information about society itself and is used to represent the perceived characteristics of a given group, region or nation's identity.[2] When the daily press reports on the fortunes of the England national team, for instance, the discourse employed connects with a wider view of 'Englishness' which is founded on a relatively limited set of simplistic beliefs about what it is to be English. The picture of 'Englishness' painted in the football writing under consideration tends towards a stereotype and is probably best summarised by the phrase 'the bulldog spirit'. A brief explanation of this symbol follows, then, along with a detailed examination of the discursive and linguistic techniques deployed by football writing in a representative of the British 'quality' press, *The Times*, which shape and perpetuate an idealised portrait of the patriotic, determined and battling English people.

Although frequently qualified as 'British', the bulldog has become a symbol *par excellence* of the English and, as such, appears in a variety of manifestations from politics to cartoons, and from advertising to sport. Arthur Reece's music hall song of the late Victorian era, 'Sons of the Sea,

All British Born', popularised the expression 'the bulldog breed' which associated the tenacious and pugnacious qualities of the hound itself with the patriotic and belligerent spirit of the British at a time of increasing military rivalry with the German Empire.[3] The elevation of this animal to the status of unofficial national symbol consequently presents these traits as typically British virtues to be praised. Indeed, the bulldog was, for a time, specifically but also somewhat controversially associated with the English national team. The dog was chosen as the official mascot of the England team competing in the World Cup finals in Spain in 1982 at a time when the extreme right-wing political party, the National Front, had also adopted it, valuing its connotations of strength and power and distorting its symbolic patriotism into narrow nationalism and xenophobia. The bulldog also found its way on to football paraphernalia during the 1990 World Cup finals held in Italy and was, in particular, brandished on the tee-shirts of the fringe of England followers overtly displaying their nationalistic and aggressive tendencies in violent confrontations with other countries' supporters.[4] By the late 1990s, then, the image of the bulldog had been somewhat tarnished and its role as symbol of England in a footballing setting seems to have been taken over by that other emblematic beast, the lion. As we shall see, in football writing the highly valued attributes of the typical England team (bravery, courage, tenacity) are conveyed by vocabulary and imagery which evoke both animals, by name in the case of the lion and implicitly with the bulldog, whose spirit, at least, if not its form, survives in media sports text portrayals of 'Englishness'.

The overriding themes of the press reports of English football studied are those of patriotism and combat, with the supposedly typical English sporting virtues of commitment, power and, above all, fighting spirit being highly prized by the media discourse examined. Regarding a sporting contest, especially a football match, as an arena for the affirmation of combative patriotism is a feature of British society which has been noted on numerous occasions. As Critcher remarks, 'it is difficult to specify anything, other than war and royalty, which articulates national identity quite so powerfully as the England team competing in the latter stages of a World Cup',[5] and these patriotic, even nationalistic sentiments are both reflected and fuelled by the media in their coverage of such events. To develop Critcher's point further on the strength of our analyses, the principal characteristics of England's imagined identity are, indeed, frequently communicated metaphorically by the media's drawing upon the language of war and, as we shall see later, royal motifs. A television news broadcast during the 1998 World Cup finals held in France, for example, began its report of England's victory over Tunisia in the opening group game by asserting that 'The players entered the arena like gladiators. They sang the national anthem with pride. The coach led from the front.'[6] So, the England team represent the whole country and 'fight gladiatorially' on behalf of the entire nation. This bond is also firmly anchored by the discourse of print media match reports and articles examined here. Referring to Alan Shearer's return for the pre-France 98 friendly against Portugal, *The Times* stressed the link between team and nation in the following vein: 'The most comforting gift *a nation* can be granted this close to the World Cup finals is confirmation that *its leader* is back, sound in mind and body and spirit' (23 April 1998, our italics). Similarly, the need for England to get back into the game after going 2–1 down against Romania at France 98 is described by *The Times* as 'the cause' (23 June) and a report of the defeat at the hands of Argentina in the same competition prompts the following enjoinder: 'Let us take pride in the collective bravery and the discipline shown by the depleted side. They did the country proud' (*The Times*, 1 July).

Kelly notes that 'Patriotism has always been a hallmark of Fleet Street, whether describing war, diplomatic negotiations or sport' and that 'There ... remains an assumption that Britain – or England – is the best.'[7] Indeed, on occasions, patriotism turns to chauvinism as footballers from other countries are denigrated as inferior and even demonised in less than subtle ways by the language used even in the 'quality' daily press as well as in the tabloids. A match in the 1997/98 English domestic season, for example, was described as a 'muck and bullets game in the depths of an English winter' which Sheffield Wednesday's Italian players would not be able to dominate because of their weak 'theatrical temperament' (*The Times*, 6 October). Later in the season, the same Italians, Paolo di Canio and Benito Carbone, were qualified as 'white-booted fairies' who need someone 'to smack a bit of life into' them (*The Times*, 25 June 1998). Again, returning to the 1998 World Cup and England's defeat by Argentina, we note that Michael Owen won a penalty in the game by demonstrating 'the artfulness of a Latin rather than an English footballer' (*The Times*, 2 July). The implication is clear: typically, Latin players resort to trickery and deception while English players do not (usually) as they are expected to be honest in their demonstration of the superior values of fair play. By the same token, non-English opponents are often demonised in the press even (or especially) when it is they who display superior technique. For example, Roa, the Argentinian goalkeeper who saved Paul Ince's spot kick in the penalty shoot out in the France 98 encounter, is described in less than complimentary fashion as 'a lank-haired Latin who could easily play one of the bad guys in a spaghetti western' (ibid.).

The jingoistic denigration of foreigners in football writing became a major issue, of course, during the 1996 European Championships held in England. Much controversy and condemnation were sparked by newspaper headlines such as the *Daily Mirror*'s 'Achtung Surrender! For you, Fritz, ze Euro 96 Championship is over' (24 June) before England's semi-final meeting with Germany. The headline was also accompanied by photographs of the England players Stuart Pearce and Paul Gascoigne sporting superimposed army helmets. The whole, replete with further crude references to the Second World War, prompted widespread criticism of its jingoistic and xenophobic approach to the Germans in what was supposed to be, after all, an amicable, sporting contest. The British Press Complaints Commission (PCC), the voluntary, self-regulating body set up in 1991 which acts as the watchdog of the press, acknowledged at the time that many people found such use of language and imagery tasteless and liable to cause offence and the parliamentary National Heritage Select Committee also criticised this 'xenophobic, chauvinistic and jingoistic gutter journalism', thereby countering the *Daily Mirror*'s editor's assertion that this was simply tabloid humour not intended to cause harm.[8] If a certain English attitude of insecurity when faced with the significant European 'Other' is exemplified by the offending article, itself written in a more general climate of British Euro-scepticism towards the increasing integration favoured by most in the European Union, then the German reaction to this incident also reveals much about that country's self-image. A correspondent from England wrote to the main liberal German newspaper, the *Süddeutsche Zeitung*, apologising for the *Mirror*'s behaviour. The German daily accepted the apologies, but far from agreeing with the correspondent and all those indignant newspapers which stressed the *Mirror*'s bad taste and the potential damage done to Anglo-German relations, it sided with the *Mirror*'s editor. It accepted 'kraut-bashing' as a British national pastime, rather like cricket, greyhound racing, darts and bingo, all of which must certainly seem strange to German eyes, but since they originate in the mother country of sport, everything must be well. The *Daily Mirror*'s piece was considered as real life satire, an example of the British sense of humour, with which, according to Germany's manager Berti Vogts, the Germans 'are very familiar' (*Süddeutsche Zeitung*, 26 June 1996). The paper even felt sorry for the *Mirror*, which now had to endure so much criticism in its turn, although the writers for that paper should be considered 'humorists'. It would have been easy for the German newspapers to exploit this situation, to show moral outrage and, as the injured party, acquire some moral kudos from it. But the opposite occurs. Perhaps the Germans recognise themselves in all the politically-correct condemnations of the British tabloids by the high-brow press and well-meaning citizens, in their highly principled assurances that these views on Germany are not shared by the majority, and especially in Bobby Charlton's confession of 'shame' over the incident, with which he trespassed on to German territory, since this part is usually played by the 'good', repentant Germans who have to bear the guilt stemming from the previous generation's involvement in the war. It seems that the German newspaper enjoys the political incorrectness and frivolity of the British press, something in which German public discourse is so badly lacking, and which can, therefore, be found and appreciated only outside Germany. This is the lack of comic relief from which the Germans are reputed to suffer and for which England is so well known, liked and admired. Any remorse from the English, then, is something genuinely disappointing for the *Süddeutsche Zeitung*.

Before the 1998 World Cup, with the bad taste still in the mouth and bad blood still abroad (though not, remarkably, in Germany itself, as we have just seen), Lord Wakeham, chair of the PCC, appealed to newspapers not to repeat the jingoistic tone of the Euro 96 coverage 'nor to foster any form of xenophobia'.[9] This appeal came in response to the *Daily Star*'s announcement that the 'Frogs need a good kicking' in the style of Agincourt and Waterloo because of the alleged mishandling of ticket sales for France 98 (2 March 1998), but, unfortunately, it has to be said that the appeal did not prevent the 'quality' press from indulging in the sort of belittling stereotypification of foreigners that we have outlined and which, we would contend, is linked to a wider belief in Great Britain's historical superiority over its European neighbours. Qualifying players of ethnically Latin origin as weak 'fairies', 'lank-haired bad guys' prone to cheating is only marginally less offensive than describing the French as 'slimy continentals' (*Daily Star*, 2 March 1998) or the Germans as 'greedy Krauts' (*Sun*, 26 April 1996) and tends in the same direction. The broadsheets' engagement with such stereotypes might appear more subtle than the blunt, one-dimensional treatment typically found in the tabloids, but it is just as potent in perpetuating preconceived notions of the supposed deviousness of foreigners as the tabloids' more pejorative approach to questions of national identity. In this respect, we would support Anderson and Weymouth's notion of the 'dominant interpretation' of print media discourse. Commercial considerations might dictate that the press, especially the tabloids, deal with a certain range of topics but these themes are 'underpinned by clear and recurring ideological boundaries indicating and delineating only a limited range of possible interpretations'.[10] When print media discourse refers to 'frogs', 'krauts' or, indeed, '[Italian] fairies' the interpretations of it cannot be so varied as to extirpate sentiments of xenophobia. In this case, despite the protestations of editors to the contrary, 'There is here only a dominant xenophobic reading available and ... consumers are encouraged to read such texts for their dominant interpretation potential.'[11] It is our contention that even in British broadsheets such dominant interpretations do underpin many football match reports and related articles and serve to perpetuate what Carrington calls

The notion of the hard-working, industrious and 'honest' Englishman [who] is contrasted with the skilful foreigner who only ever beats the

English by luck – penalties, unfair dismissals – or cheating – hands of God, play-acting – thus leaving England with the perennial 'we would have won but for ...'[12]

Foreigners are quite simply portrayed in a negative light throughout the British press as the inferiors of the superior, honest, upright and brave English.

Bravery is, indeed, a supposedly typical virtue of the English footballer and, as such, is often praised in the press, occasionally with a little irony.

> We are, you see [explains *The Times*], a courageous nation. Bravery is perceived in the image of Paul Ince in Rome [in] October [1997], battling on, his head swathed in bandages. The blood seeping through was the red badge of courage, so terribly British. (25 May 1998)

The commitment, energy and sheer power behind the courage of English footballers are also much vaunted by media sports texts, which might be read, therefore, as contributing further to the maintenance of a cultural definition of insular 'Englishness' which Critcher has noted is partly based upon 'an aversion to theory or fancy ways [and] ... a sustained belief that foreigners have little or nothing to teach us'.[13] For instance, Tony Adams, England's captain at the 1996 European Championships, is described as 'the epitome of English footballing determination [who] made a rousing call to arms to his team-mates' (*The Times*, 8 June), while his colleague David Platt is praised for being 'courageous' and 'heroic' in a match against Spain in the same tournament (*The Times*, 24 June). Similar values are perceived and duly reported in certain domestic matches which are portrayed as representative of English football as a whole. Thus, in the Chelsea–Bolton Wanderers match, *The Times* notes that 'The relentless motion of English football precludes time for thought and consideration' (11 May 1998), and that the earlier Leicester City–Bolton game was played on 'an afternoon when the passion of the British game left onlookers breathless' (24 November 1997). The insularity of Britain in this respect is frequently mentioned. *The Times* was happy to reproduce without challenge the views of the former Blackburn Rovers manager Roy Hodgson on his team's game with Chelsea: 'It was a very English contest ... It must have been a remarkable game for an outsider, difficult to comprehend in the sense that there was very little time on the ball because both teams closed down so quickly' (ibid.). Indeed, for our newspaper, this is the classic 'British approach' manifesting the 'traditional values' of players who are 'very fit and physically imposing' and who achieve 'victory [through] effort and strength' (ibid.), rather than technical skills. Combined with the tendency to chauvinism noted earlier, the perceived uniqueness of the English game, high on effort, low on technique, is, somewhat perversely, regarded as a source of pride. Reporting on the Leeds United–Coventry City game towards the end of the 1997/98 season, *The Times* appears delighted that 'Probably in no other country could an end-of-season game on which so little rested have produced such ferocious commitment, such high tempo endeavour ... or such chronic defending ... But, what the heck, if the quality was low, the excitement was undeniable' (27 April).

National identity, even in the case of England, is, however, not necessarily always fixed; it can change through time, although, as we shall see, the type of stereotypification prevalent in football writing, which falls into Blain, Boyle and O'Donnell's category of 'discursive paralysis',[14] is resistant to change and demonstrates time and again its own longevity as a favoured recourse in sports media discourse. The England teams participating in the major international tournaments of the late 1990s (the 1996 European Championships, the 1997 Tournoi de France and the 1998 World Cup finals), successively managed by Terry Venables and Glenn Hoddle, were, for a while, regarded as personifying a modification of the typical English game which might be felt to connect with wider developments in British culture at the time. The coming to power in politics of 'New Labour' (1 May 1997) coincided with the 'Cool Britannia' fad in fashion, design and the arts. Similarly, the England football team, almost always mediated as an extension of the nation's dominant values, was said to have come out of 'the dark ages' as a result of 'English football ... becoming more and more sophisticated' with 'Venables and Hoddle ... successfully [adapting] the traditional qualities of the English game – passion, pace and power – to the more refined needs of the international stage' (*The Times*, 1 June 1998).

It does not require much, however, for football writers to return to more familiar portrayals of England. Stereotypes, unlike hot potatoes and clangers, it would seem, are particularly difficult to drop. Courage, determination, tenacity and sheer fighting spirit are still the values most lauded by the sports media in this country. Thus, 2–1 down to Romania in a France 98 group game, England '*still* did not give up' and 'rallied furiously' to 'the cause' (*The Times*, 23 June; our italics). Even though such effort may ultimately prove to be in vain in terms of the result, it will be made because this is the English way. Defeat can, then, be tolerated (just) so long as the team has gone down fighting, battling to the last with all guns blazing. What Orakwue terms 'the happy-loser mentality dominating English culture'[15] then allows those who have lost to be transformed by the media into heroes.[16] This is why the recruitment to the ITV squad to cover France 98 of Bobby Robson and Terry Venables (losing England managers at Italia 90 and Euro 96, respectively) is regarded as such a coup by *The Times*: their teams, both coincidentally eliminated at the semi-final stage by Germany in penalty shoot outs, were defeated honourably and, therefore, their managers' 'valiant near misses seem to command ever greater affection in the hearts of the sentimental British public' (*The Times*, 8 June 1998).[17]

No better example of this process can be found, though, than the exuberant media coverage of England's elimination from the 1998 World Cup finals, following defeat, again by penalty shoot-out, this time at the hands of Argentina. Despite the game's ending in 'a sickeningly familiar tale of heroic failure', it provided 'a story of defiance to the point of absolute inspiration' (*The Times*, 1 July). *The Times* urges us to wonder at the 'fitting display of camaraderie in adversity' shown by the English players and the 'almost superhuman strength of the ten left behind' (ibid.) following *that* sending off. Moreover, patriotic pride is satisfied because, even in defeat, every man in the England team, as expected, did his duty and fought to the end:

> The heart thrilled at the resolve of Tony Adams and swelled at the application of Alan Shearer ... It marvelled at the strength and courage of Michael Owen and, *most of all*, it raced at the indomitability of Paul Ince who played as if he was three men. (ibid., our italics)

Reporting in this vein is by no means unique to *The Times* nor, indeed, to the print media. Television also played a significant part in the perpetuation of this mythical England, tenaciously fighting to the bitter end and heroic defeat. In the ITV coverage of the Argentina game,[18] the commentator Brian Moore noted that the support given to the team by the England fans in the Geoffroy-Guichard stadium in Saint-Etienne 'epitomises English spirit' and, employing exactly the same vocabulary later, affirmed that the display of players such as Ince 'again epitomises English spirit as well'. Similarly, Moore stated that, in extra time with ten man England locked at 2–2 with the Argentines, that 'The true spirit of English football is being shown here' and, immediately after the game, asked 'Has there ever been a more glorious exit from a tournament than this?' Not wishing to be left out, the co-commentator, former England captain and future manager Kevin Keegan just loved the fact that the players 'have shown all the qualities of English football, the bulldog spirit and all that' (a rare example of England's erstwhile canine mascot being explicitly mentioned by name in recent media discourse on the game). ITV then ended its coverage with a remarkable and, in view of our analysis, highly revealing sequence. As the credits rolled, the television audience was treated to a series of shots of England players toiling valiantly to the strains of the patriotic hymn to the words of Blake's poem 'Jerusalem', the nearest thing the English – as distinct from the British – have to a national anthem. The myth is preserved. The status quo is intact. The imagined identity of the English nation is confirmed. In all of the examples cited of the media discourse used to comment upon and interpret the performance of the English footballers in the France 98 match against Argentina, then, it is clearly not concepts such as sophistication, refinement, technique or 'coolness' which are being vaunted. Rather the virtues emphasised and praised are those of patriotism, defiance, resolve, application, strength, courage, indomitability and fighting spirit, which are, thereby, represented as the prerequisites of true English heroism.

That resolve, courage and fighting spirit are essential English qualities is clearly never doubted by sports journalists. However, preliminary analysis of the press coverage of Euro 2000 suggests that England's elimination at the group stage prompted something of a re-evaluation of those qualities and a realisation that, although they are the right stuff of (English) heroes, alone they are no longer sufficient for success. The then manager, Kevin Keegan, for instance, was widely quoted as saying after the defeat by Romania which led to England's exit: 'If it was about endeavour and honesty, we would have won the tournament' (for instance, *Guardian*, 21 June 2000). Even before the championships had begun, the *Daily Express* issued a warning that ultimately proved prophetic:

> But there is the little matter of dealing with the sophisticated side of the game. The days of relying on pride and passion, bulldog spirit, the Three Lions or the words, for that matter, of Henry V, are long gone. Yes, those *traditional English qualities* can be an asset, but there has to be finesse. (12 June 2000, our italics; Shakespeare's patriotic play *Henry V* is England defender Tony Adams's favourite pre-match read, apparently)

When that finesse was not forthcoming and England were sent home, ignominiously this time, there was much soul-searching in the press. England remains 'synonymous with failure in major international tournaments' lamented the *Guardian* (21 June 2000) while another piece on the same day reflected that, 'In terms of technique and tactics [English football] is still stuck in a deadly time warp' (ibid.).

The favoured virtues and potential shortcomings of the English sporting stereotype are not only conveyed explicitly by name in the press, football writing also communicates them metaphorically, most notably via imagery relating to one of England's national symbols, the lion, and to one of the country's almost perennial activities, warfare.

The lion as a national symbol came to the fore with Richard I ('the Lion-Heart', 1157–99). His military exploits on the Third Crusade made him a medieval legend which his death in battle against the French did much to enhance. He was the prototype brave, courageous, English lion heart, who, as we shall see, provides the implicit model for football journalists reporting on the England team's exploits. Furthermore, Richard's heraldic red shield incorporated three golden lions to represent the kingdom of England. As such, this shield still appears on the Royal arms today (alongside Scottish and Irish emblems) which, since 1603, have been supported by a crowned lion and a unicorn. Given its origins, history and current use on the monarch's arms, the English lion must be read politically as connotative of royalty in addition to its more overt communication of the qualities of power, bravery and courage. In a sporting context, too, the king of the beasts is often associated with English football. It has long been the emblem of the FA, for instance, and, as such, appears in triplicate on the shirts of the England national team. Similarly, the commercial mascot of the 1966 World Cup, held in England, was, of course, a lion, 'World Cup Willie' (who somewhat incongruously sported a shirt with a Union Flag in its design rather than the more specifically English red cross of St. George). The lion symbol was thrown into further prominence at Euro 96 when the song 'Three Lions (Football's Coming Home)', performed by David Baddiel, Ian Broudie and Frank Skinner, was adopted by supporters as the tournament's unofficial anthem and proved very popular with the public.[20] It is not altogether surprising, then, that the patriotic, royalist symbol of the lion should be so extensively employed as a metaphor by football journalists reporting the England team's exploits. Following England's 2–0 defeat of Scotland at Euro 96, for instance, the midfielder and goal-scorer Paul Gascoigne was qualified by the *News of the World* as a 'lion-heart' (16 June 1996), while after beating the same opponents in the first leg of the Euro 2000 qualifier play-off, the entire team were described as 'lion-hearted stars' (*Sunday People*, 14 November 1999). The use of this metaphor is not restricted solely to the tabloids, however, but is also widespread in *The Times*. Against Germany in the semi-final, for example, England benefited from the presence of 'young lions such as McManaman, Anderton, Barmby' (27 June 1996) while, in earlier matches, Tony Adams was 'the lion-heart ... diving in with a tackle' (24 June 1996) and Alan Shearer was 'a lion-heart in the English mould of Lofthouse, Milburn, Smith' (19 June 1996). Collectively, too, the English team's perceived qualities are often conveyed by this metaphor. Against Holland at Euro 96, 'the lions were rampant' as 'England roar into the quarter-finals' (*The Times*, 19 June 1996). This now-familiar imagery resurfaced during the 1998 World Cup finals where Paul Ince's performances in the group games were felt to represent 'the England of the roaring lion, the acceptable, admirable face of English pride and aggression' (*The Times*, 20 June). Similarly, following the celebrated 'heroic' defeat by Argentina, Glenn Hoddle, in a previous incarnation as England manager, was quoted as saying of his team, 'They defended like lions' (*The Times*, 2 July), while one report of the game itself carried the headline 'England's lions keep fighting to the bitter end' and began: 'A lion-hearted England team plunged out of the World Cup in Saint-Etienne last night' (*The Times*, 1 July).

Finally in this exploration of English autotypification through the discourse of football writing, we note the prevalence of military metaphors which are used both in a general sense and specifically to (re)construct the notion of the English fighting spirit.

J.A. Mangan has noted the importance of warfare in British culture and rightly asserts that 'War, symbolised in the metaphors of war used so widely and so frequently, is deeply embedded in our institutions, thinking, recreations.' Indeed, he goes on to demonstrate the links between militarism and sport particularly in the Victorian and the Edwardian era. In the days of the British Empire, war was regarded as a national duty; it was the necessary instrument by which superior British values were exported around the world. It required of its participants patriotism, disciplined aggression, courage, leadership qualities, physical strength and self-sacrifice. These virtues were extolled in the prose, poetry and painting of the imperial era, especially that aimed at young men in the public schools upon whom was placed 'an expectation of aggressive assertion'.[22] A culturally endorsed ideal of manhood developed, then, and grew into a 'martial mythology of masculinity'.[23] Of great importance from our point of view is the vital role played by sport in the propagation of this ideological warrior ethos. Mangan notes the frequent parallels drawn in the British culture of a century or so ago between the qualities demanded of the colonial soldier and the virtues acquired through sport. The bond between the two was so great that war itself came to be portrayed as a sport in which 'colonial battlefields [became] exotic versions of the playing fields of Eton'. In the football writing of the late twentieth century the parallels between sport and a militaristic mode of thinking, which itself might be considered the legacy of the imperial era, are still highly active, with the result that the language of football is imbued with military metaphors and references which, thereby, connect football with a broader, socio-cultural and historically-determined perception of a typically aggressive and virile form of 'Englishness'.

Military metaphors employed generally can range from the clichés noted by numerous observers (see the Introduction), in which a game of football is seen as a 'battle' between 'enemies', 'fought out' by the players described as 'troops' (for instance, *The Times*, 12 March 1998) to a rather more imaginative usage of lexis and imagery to convey the battling attributes of the England team as a whole and, at times, of representative individuals within it. Thus, against Germany at Euro 96, England were said to have played 'combative football' with Steve McManaman being 'the flag-bearer of [their] assaults' (*The Times*, 27 June). Similarly, a pass by Teddy Sheringham in the game against Holland at Euro 96 was released 'as if out of a catapult' (*The Times*, 19 June), while runs by the full-back Graeme Le

Saux in a friendly against Portugal were depicted as his 'launching raid after raid down the left' (*The Times*, 23 April 1998). Again, the striker Michael Owen's style of play during the 1998 World Cup was likened to 'some sort of arrow that wings inexorably on towards its target, nothing deflecting its trajectory, nothing slowing it down until it hits its mark' (*The Times*, 12 June), while, in a Euro 2000 qualifier, he was 'a frightening weapon' (*Sunday People*, 14 November 1999) as his colleagues at the back 'built an impregnable defensive fortress around [the goalkeeper] Seaman' (ibid.).

As well as these general images of combat and warfare which illustrate one of the favoured virtues of the English sporting stereotype, the data we have analysed also provide many examples of specific historical and cultural references reflecting the same myths. As with other countries' newspapers' usage of the same technique (see Chapters 4 and 7), this type of reference demands of its reader some familiarity with European history in order for its full cultural significance to be appreciated. By way of example, *The Times* report of a victory over Scotland may be cited: 'England's finest moment, never mind the hour, of Euro 96 has already taken place' (17 June); as may the review of England's performances at France 98 in which Le Saux's experience of the World Cup was qualified as 'not one of his finest hours' (*The Times*, 2 July). Both of these examples, of course, evoke the famous 'this was their finest hour' passage in Winston Churchill's 1940 Battle of Britain speech and thereby situate England's performances on the football field in a socio-historical context of victory in war (and sport), requiring fighting spirit and the sheer will to win against a technically superior enemy. Moreover, we see once again a representative of the 'quality' daily press employing the same references as some of its tabloid homologues. Before Euro 96, for instance, the *Sun* claimed that this tournament 'should be our finest hour', in addition to evoking Nelson's speech before the Battle of Trafalgar: 'England expects every fan to do his [*sic*] duty ... Let's be proud of our country and our flag' (8 June).[25]

In a similar vein, striker Alan Shearer's exploits in the pre-World Cup friendly against Portugal were reported by *The Times* in terms evoking yet another period of British military history, namely the aggressive foreign policy of the mid-nineteenth century: 'Portugal were like a man-o-war holed beneath the waterline and England ... were revelling in their centre-forward's own brand of gunboat diplomacy' (24 April 1998).

Finally in this respect, as we have already seen, defeat in a match can be honourable, heroic even, so long as the defeated players, whether a club side or the national team, can be said to have proved their qualities of tenacity and defiance by fighting to the last. Considering yet another defeat for his team, for instance, the then Barnsley manager Danny Wilson told *The Times*: 'If we have to go down, we will go down with a damn good fight' (10 November 1997), while Liverpool's exit from the UEFA Cup following a

3–2 defeat by the French club RC Strasbourg was qualified as a 'heroic failure' with 'some honour restored' because they went 'down with guns blazing' (*The Times*, 5 November 1997), that is, at the deciding home game Liverpool almost wiped out the three-goals deficit inherited from the first leg of the tie. Again, reflecting on Crystal Palace's impending relegation from the Premiership, *The Times* could still find praise for the club because 'At least they are going down with a fight, even if rescue seems remote' (12 March 1998).

When it is the England national team which is involved in 'heroic failure', the vocabulary and imagery employed by press articles and match reports are also overtly militaristic. The term 'gallant' and its cognates, so often used to describe (male) soldiers, of course, are frequently found. In the Euro 96 semi-final defeat by Germany, England were 'Gallant' (*The Times*, 27 June), apparently, and, similarly, against Argentina at France 98, the team 'held out gallantly' only to suffer a 'gallant and unlucky exit' from the tournament (*The Times*, 2 July). Moreover, the same article further reported on the now legendary encounter in Saint-Etienne by speaking of the English supporters' 'gathering pride tinged with astonishment, as the England defence ... held out against the odds' and remarked that this game was 'surely one of the finest rearguard actions in the long history of the England team' (ibid.), which last phrase implicitly connects English football with military history in that memories of famous 'rearguard actions' from Rorke's Drift in 1879 (during the Zulu War) to Dunkirk in 1940 live on in the country's psyche as defining features of a national identity which has as a major characteristic the ability to transform a disappointing and costly defeat into a cause for a celebration of patriotic defiance and a heroic refusal to surrender to a potentially overwhelming opponent. 'Heroism' on the football field, then, is portrayed as ranking alongside 'great' events from military history. Moreover, the former is described in terms of the latter thereby discursively binding the two in an almost symbiotic relationship.

To conclude, the representations of English national identity offered by the media in their reporting of English football and, especially, of the England national team are based upon a cluster of perceptions which, we would contend, derive from and feed into wider assumptions in the national imagined community dating from the imperial era that serve to define 'Englishness'. The mediation of football, particularly but not exclusively by *The Times* articles analysed here, perpetuates notions of English patriotism and endeavour[26] which, themselves, are made up of related stereotypical characteristics and supposedly traditional virtues: bravery, combativeness, determination, tenacity, commitment, honesty and hard work. Discursively, these values are communicated both explicitly, by name, in the lexis of football writing and metaphorically in its imagery which typically draws upon the connotations of the national royal emblem, the lion, and military terminology and history for its inspiration. The portrait of 'Englishness' painted is rather familiar and, as with any stereotype, limited and exclusive from the point of view of accuracy and applicability, not least of all in its dependency on traditionally constructed, male values of virility and aggression. So, a certain type of 'Englishness' is represented with which many English people would find it uncomfortable if not impossible to identify: overtly nationalistic and militaristic, implicitly chauvinistic and royalist. As Perryman asserts, 'repainting our symbols of Englishness' would seem to be a necessity if we are to construct a more widely acceptable English identity for the twenty-first century.[27] Unless or until a radical re-evaluation of 'Englishness' is undertaken, then, not only by journalists but also by that part of the population whose views they shape and reflect, the 'British bulldog' will continue to growl tenaciously and the 'English lion' roar regally in the pages of this island's football writing.

2

This Green and Pleasant Land

The English question is on the agenda. For centuries notions of Englishness have tended to be linked primarily with the politically and economically dominant white 'middle class' of the Home Counties. Political and social developments in the 1980s and the 1990s, however, have started to raise awareness of the real complexity of English identities in what is an increasingly diverse and multiethnic nation and a re-evaluation of Englishness itself is now urgently required. Englishness might be felt to operate in a new framework, decentred from its traditional base and expressing a wide range of voices and viewpoints. It is timely and appropriate, then, to examine how notions of English identity are communicated by media sports texts. Has football writing, in particular in the 'quality' daily press, responded to social and cultural change in contemporary England or does it still cling to static perceptions rooted in the past which tend to stereotype the English regions as well as deny the right of full expression and representation to non-white voices?

Among the most enduring myths about England is that it is, in the words of Blake's poem 'Jerusalem', essentially a green and pleasant land blighted by the arrival of dark, Satanic mills, which may be read as a metaphor for the industrial, 'working-class' North.[1] The mythical greenness of England, with its metaphorical associations with former glory, as well as a certain vision of the North are two traditional notions which are, even today, reflected in football writing in *The Times*. At a time when newspapers in France were analysing the technical qualities of the turf laid at the newly-built Stade de France, for instance, the journalists of *The Times* preferred to focus on the lush appearance of the grass at Wembley, symbol of English national sporting endeavour and, by extension, of the country itself. A friendly against Portugal, for instance, was played out on 'Wembley's fine field' (23 April 1998), while an interview with Geoff Hurst, another icon of English sporting greatness thanks to 1966 and all that, was said to have been conducted 'on the green sward of Wembley stadium' (13 June 1998). Similarly, before the Euro 2000 tournament held in Belgium and Holland the press explicitly invoked the 'Jerusalem' metaphor with its nostalgic connotations of England's former beauty and glory: 'After 34 years of hurt' the *Daily Express* appealed to England's footballers with reference to the last and only time a major trophy had been won, 'we want a green and pleasant land fit for heroes' (12 June 2000).[2]

The cosy world view of the green and pleasant land lying at the core of a deep-seated nostalgia for past glories might be one cultural myth which, traditionally at least, links all English people in a common bond. A sense of decline engendered by Great Britain's retreat from Empire and fall from economic world dominance has been a major theme in national identity since the Second World War and finds its parallels in sports media discourse, especially when the latter is centred on the national football team and on the national stadium, scene of the triumph of 1966 which still looms large in the English football mind.[3] However, as Hill and Williams note, 'Understanding Englishness requires appreciation of what divides, as well as what unites, those who regard themselves as English.'[4] In this respect, the North has acquired an imagined identity which is quite distinctive and specific, setting it apart, especially from the South-East and generating 'powerful resonances in English cultural life'.[5] The characteristics of typically northern identities may, in part, be traced to the Industrial Revolution which not only greatly enhanced the importance of the North to the British economy but also created a set of beliefs about Northerners' capacity for hard work and endeavour as well as their reputed qualities of determination and toughness. The economic decline of the post-war period and the recessions of the 1970s and the 1980s generated the belief that the North of England was becoming impoverished while the South retained its prosperity and further served to fuel the concept of the North–South divide. Even in the 1990s the debate still retained its currency. Miall's only semi-humorous account of the English noted that:

> The English have a natural distrust of the unfamiliar and nowhere is this more clearly seen than in their attitude to the geography of their own country. Since time immemorial there has been a North–South divide in England. To the southerner, civilisation ends somewhere around Potter's Bar (just north of London).[6]

Again, a remark in the *Daily Telegraph* by the writer Anne McElvoy that she feels 'a prickle of recognition and unaccountable excitement' (1 February 1996) when seeing a road sign bearing the words 'The North' prompted a reader to respond that such signs do more harm than good by postulating not so much a geographical direction as an identity and encourage further the popular awareness of a cultural as well as a socio-economic divide between North and South, while a phone-in programme on BBC Radio 5 Live was devoted to the issue on 30 November 1999 as the Prime Minister was about to embark on a short tour of the North-West, during which he tried to convince audiences in Chester, Manchester and Liverpool that there was, in fact, no North–South divide at all. Whether these ideas of a divide have any validity in reality is not the issue here. We are much more concerned with the notion of the North being 'as much a state of mind as a place'[7] and with the ways in which football writing recycles many of the deep-rooted popular conceptions of northern English identities.

The first preconception reflected by the match reports and articles analysed is that the North is a remote place populated by people whom it is permissible to define as deviations from the southern norm. During the 1996 European Championships, for instance, *The Times* commented on the games taking place in Group B, 'stuck out as it is in Newcastle and Leeds' (8 June). Clearly, in the southern English view of the world echoed here, northern cities may, indeed, be regarded as far-flung places, remote from the true centre of the universe that is London. Furthermore, the inhabitants of such localities also find themselves on the receiving end of a certain amount of disdain displayed in the 'quality' daily press. Barnsley fans, for example, were mocked by *The Times* report of a match at Liverpool by a farcical attempt to convey a Northern accent in print: ' "We're staying oop", the travelling supporters sang' (24 November 1997). Examples of this type are, moreover, not new. The same attitude was displayed by the *Sunday Telegraph*'s report of the 1965 FA Cup final between Liverpool and Leeds United: 'Skywards soared the chant from the rain-soaked Liverpool end: "We'll be running round Wembley with the Coop" ' (2 May). It is, perhaps, also worth noting that natives of the Midlands suffer the same fate as northerners in this respect. The long-serving Wolverhampton Wanderers striker Steve Bull was quoted as giving an interview 'in his treacle-thick accent', for instance (*The Times*, 3 April 1998). But no patronising or derisory comments about South-East accents can be traced in the data studied ...

Images of England north of the Watford Gap as remote and rough are, indeed, a long-standing feature of sports media discourse and the press articles in the last years of the twentieth century may be read, therefore, as perpetuating, only slightly more subtly, the sorts of view expressed by the much-quoted *Pall Mall Gazette* report of Blackburn fans' threatening descent on the capital in 1884: this was 'an incursion of northern barbarians ... sharp of tongue, rough and ready, of uncouth garb and speech. A tribe of Sudanese Arabs let loose in the Strand would not excite more amusement and curiosity' (31 March 1884).[8] When we read of Newcastle United fans being described as 'the black and white hordes [who will] descend on the capital next month' (*The Times*, 21 February 2000) and of Liverpool supporters being qualified as 'The Liverpool hordes [who] commandeered [London's Selhurst Park] stadium' (*The Times*, 17 April 2000), we are forced to note that the distance travelled since the 1880s by the southern English press in its perception of menacing, uncivilised Northerners is depressingly short.

To focus the analysis of sports media representations of northern English identities more sharply, it would be appropriate to consider two specific and revealing examples: the cases of Merseyside and Yorkshire.

The imagined identity in English culture of Merseyside in general and of Liverpool in particular is well established. First, Liverpool is represented in the press as a community apart, a city which is self-reliant and independent to the point of rebelliousness. During the 1998 World Cup finals, for example, *The Times* attempted to introduce the French host cities to its readers by indicating points of comparison with English cities. In this respect Marseille was described as the French equivalent of Liverpool, wilfully 'different' from the rest of the country with its football team being 'as much a tribal temple as Liverpool are to Liverpudlians – a force against the ruling capital' (12 June 1998). In similar vein, two years later, but in stark contrast to the proud signs on the M62 motorway that welcome visitors to 'Liverpool Maritime City', another 'quality' daily portrayed Liverpool somewhat patronisingly as 'a port town' manifesting a 'kind of provincial independence' as well as a 'bullish identity' (*Observer*, 2 July 2000). The latter aspects of the city's identity are ones which many of its inhabitants actively foster, of course, and, therefore, feature both in autotypification and heterotypification. The Liverpool supporter and football writer Andy Thompson, for example, claims that one of the reasons why the new manager Gérard Houllier is so popular there is because he 'plots a lone course that strikes a chord with the passionately independent city of Liverpool'.[9] Similarly, more than one observer, at home and abroad, has recognised in Liverpool FC's own slogan, 'You'll never walk alone', a symbol of the spirit of togetherness and the cohesion of the Liverpool community,[10] while Thompson, again, praises Houllier because, like Bill Shankly some time before him, he has 'harnessed this intense local spirit and channelled its energy through the team'.[11] The togetherness of Merseysiders has also been emphasised many times in football journalism both in the past and recently. As Boyle and Haynes note, 'in Liverpool it appears that football occupies a less divisive position in the cultural life of that city, and instead it provides a specific city identity which is placed in opposition to other regional and English national identities'.[12] When, for instance, in 1906, Liverpool won the league and Everton the cup, the *Liverpool Daily Post and Echo* carried a cartoon portraying the captains of the two teams arm in arm, symbolising a football city united in common triumph.[13] Again, in 1986, when the two teams met in the first all-Merseyside FA Cup final, much comment was made of the unity of the supporters who 'mingled together ... red and blue ... on the terraces ... [in] the friendly final' and sang 'Merseyside, Merseyside' in unison (*Sunday Times*, 11 May 1986). It is difficult, indeed, by way of contrast, to imagine, say, Manchester City supporters displaying such camaraderie towards their neighbours from Stretford.[14]

Second, but rather less fortunately, Liverpool would also seem to have attracted a reputation as a city of crime and illegal dealings. The decline of its traditional industries, notably the docks, and the subsequent rise in unemployment were misrepresented by the dominant political viewpoint of the 1980s, which automatically equated poverty with criminal activities to strengthen the air of illegality surrounding this city's image. So, when *The Times* stated that Liverpool 'has never been the home of the goody-goody' (3 November 1997), it might be felt to be doing more than simply commenting on the conduct of some of the players who have worn the red (white, green or yellow) shirt down the years, in that the phrase would connect with and reinforce pre-existing images in the popular consciousness of Liverpool being the home of shady dealings and suspect activities, images which have been nothing if not fuelled by successive television situation comedies and dramas from 'Boys from the Blackstuff' and 'Bread' of the 1980s, to 'Liverpool One' of the 1990s.

Finally, the people of Liverpool are, apparently, renowned for their wit and humour. Or rather these are human characteristics which football writers feel a pressing need to mention frequently in connection with Merseysiders. The *Times* report of the 1997/98 Everton–Liverpool Derby match, for instance, predictably trotted out comments about the sharp wit of the crowd which displayed 'Revelry at its wickedest' (20 October 1997). Precisely what constituted this wicked revelry? Such rib-tickling quips as 'You should've put that bandage over your mouth, Ince', 'You've emptied the pie shop, Ruddock' and that great side-splitter 'Can we play you every week?' (ibid.). The fact that such fare is only mildly amusing at best as well as being commonplace on the football terraces throughout the country escapes the journalist who deems it essential to bring out in this way the reputed good humour of the Merseyside crowd which, therefore, preserves intact the image of Liverpool wit. There is no reliable evidence to suggest that its inhabitants are any more or less humorous than those of other British cities, despite the best efforts of certain professional Scousers who consciously try to affirm the opposite in their work in the media and the entertainment industry; and yet the image persists and is, indeed, long-standing in the football press as a final example illustrates: 'It was not a spectacularly colourful Wembley, but the humour of the Liverpool contingent more than enlightened the gloom' (*Liverpool Football Echo*, 1 May 1965).[15]

Turning to Yorkshire, football clubs playing in England's largest county are seen as representative of its reputed qualities of bluntness, hospitality and 'grit'. For example, *The Times* reported that a week or so before the 1998 World Cup match between England and Argentina, David Batty had been asked whether he would take a penalty in the game: 'the *Yorkshireman* gave a *typically forthright* reply. Not a chance' (1 July; our italics).[16] The supposed bluntness of Yorkshire people does not prevent them from having the image of being hospitable, though, and this is frequently reflected in the match reports and articles studied in our data. Barnsley, for instance, is portrayed as 'the centre of a coalmining community, one of warmth and hospitality' (*The Times*, 29 June 1998), while the hospitality on offer at Sheffield Wednesday's ground must have proved so remarkable to the journalist covering a game there that it warranted a special mention: there were, apparently, 'enough fast-food outlets and bars on the Hillsborough concourses to satisfy a small army' (*The Times*, 27 October 1997). On one occasion, the famed Yorkshire hospitality was used as an ironic contrast to the rather dull spectacle offered on the playing field, by the end of which Leeds United had proved 'generous to a fault' in handing victory to their visitors:

> As mine hosts, Leeds United are unsurpassed ... The hospitality begins with the provision of enough parking space to meet the demands of a busy airport. Out on the pitch, cheerleaders dance in the centre circle before kick off and a male singer, complete with pony tail, performs ... songs to the uninterested crowd ... Half-time allows Leeds another chance to play the obliging hosts. Not for them dehydrated triangles posing as sandwiches. Instead the gratis fill-up in the press room is a savoury hot meal ... On the way out ... a smart young man in a club blazer bids everyone a fond farewell. Leeds United: wonderful manners, shame about the football. (*The Times*, 22 September 1997)

Finally, portrayals of Yorkshire sides in action (whether or not they actually contain any players born or bred there) almost inevitably alight on the county's traditional qualities of determination, endeavour and 'grit'. Barnsley, for instance, 'the Yorkshire club', reduced to ten men in a cup quarter final, still 'fought on, brave to the end' (*The Times*, 9 March 1998), while the same team's victory in the league over Tottenham Hotspur provided further grist to the mill of the debate about the contrasting identities of the North and the South: 'Fat cats shamed by dogged spirit' ran the headline to the match report in *The Times* (20 April 1998). While Spurs players were described as 'pampered', Barnsley had their 'spirit and their heart, their decency and their honesty' to carry them to victory (ibid.). Here Tottenham, which was, it is not irrelevant to note, the first British football club to become a public limited company (in 1983), represents the bloated, prosperous, effete south of England to be contrasted with the hard, tough, spirited North symbolised by Barnsley.

Football, then, especially as it is mediated by the press, retains its power to confirm a sense of being from a specific place, its power to shape affiliations to a locality, such as Liverpool, or to a region, such as Yorkshire, a power which is essentially that of constructing and perpetuating myths through time.[17] The arrival on the football scene in England of players from ethnic minorities, particularly African-Caribbean blacks, has, as we shall see, generated a set of myths of a rather different order.

    The first black professional footballer in England was Arthur Wharton,
who played for Preston North End and Stockport County, among others, in
the 1880s,[18] and a number of black players featured in the game in the 1920s
and the 1930s too.[19] It was, however, the 1960s and the 1970s that saw the
beginning of the expansion of the number of blacks playing in the top flight.
By the end of the 1970s there were approximately 50 black professionals,
one of whom, Viv Anderson, became the first black player to win a full
England international cap (against the former Czechoslovakia in 1978).
Further breakthroughs in the professional game occurred when Edwin Stein
became the first black team manager (at Barnet) in 1993, when Ruud Gullit
became the first black to manage a top flight team in English football
(Chelsea) in 1996, and when Uriah Rennie, a year later, became the first
black referee in the FA Premiership. Estimates vary of the number of black
footballers operating in England in the 1980s and the 1990s from about 12
per cent of the total number of professionals, to 25 per cent.[20] What is
certain, though, is the scale of racist abuse that these players have had to
endure, with the case of John Barnes's treatment at the hands of certain
Everton followers in 1987 providing a high-profile example.[21] It was only
belatedly, then, that the Professional Footballers' Association (PFA) decided
to join forces with the Commission for Racial Equality (CRE) in 1993 to
mount the campaign entitled 'Let's kick racism out of football'. The
initiative was relaunched in 1997 as 'Kick it Out', with the twin ambitions
of combating racism in football and encouraging more supporters from
ethnic minorities to attend matches. A report by the newly formed
Government Football Task Force in March 1998, however, indicated just
how far there is to go in these respects, since only about 1 per cent of the
fans in a typical Premiership crowd are from ethnic minorities and racism,
in a variety of forms, permeates the game at all levels. A straw poll
conducted by BBC journalist Stephen Lyle has revealed that the top two
issues of concern in this respect are racist abuse on and from the terraces and
racist stereotyping in the media.[22] As the data gathered for our study indicate,
in so far as the British press is concerned, stereotyping of black footballers
is not solely the preserve of the tabloids.
    The first element in the portrayal of black footballers by the press articles
and match reports that we have studied concerns psychological attitudes.
Blacks are often perceived as laid-back and lacking in seriousness and
application. Orakwue traces this stereotype back in the footballing context
to at least as far as the 1970s[23] and examples were still apparent in the late
1990s: reporting on a Chelsea–Derby County game, *The Times* noted that
'Paolo Wanchope may be a magician on occasions, but at Stamford Bridge
he simply disappeared' (1 December 1997), while the same player's efforts
in a later game were dismissed as 'the ephemeral fripperies of Wanchope'
(*The Times*, 30 April 1998). Similarly, the Everton winger Danny

Cadamarteri was said, in one game, to have run at the Arsenal defence 'with joyous glee' skipping past them 'almost with a chuckle' (*The Times*, 29 September 1997). Indeed, it is not only Cadamarteri's supposedly happy-go-lucky style which is commented on by the press report under consideration. He is implicitly portrayed as the black deviation from the white norm by the article in that it highlights 'the unusual amalgamation of letters that form his surname' (unusual that is, presumably, because when combined they do not spell Smith or Jones) and his 'exotic ancestry' (ibid.; he was, in fact, born in Yorkshire). Cadamarteri is, then, the unusual, exotic, chuckling black, a member of a group, black footballers, described perceptively by Orakwue as 'outsiders who have to contend with attitudes no white player comes up against. People who are judged not on the basis of their individuality but on the basis of concocted group characteristics enshrined in mythology.'[24]

A further characteristic which is frequently ascribed to black footballers as a group is that of physical power. Their strength is frequently commented upon, with references to their physique being commonplace. Viv Anderson, the first black full England international, was described by the *Daily Express* as 'the supremely athletic Nottingham Forest right back' (28 November 1978), for instance, connecting with a stereotype of the congenitally athletic black, which was still circulating some 20 years later when Stan Collymore's athleticism was described as 'natural' by a report in *The Times* (6 October 1997). Furthermore, when black players are tall, their build as well as their fabled power becomes a focal point for the media discourse employed. Paolo Wanchope, for example – now of Manchester City – was described in one match report as 'loose-limbed, long-legged, unorthodox and unpredictable' (*The Times*, 3 November 1997) and Arsenal's Patrick Vieira in another as 'the long striding midfield enforcer' (*The Times*, 1 December 1997). In the latter case, a black's build is, once again, linked to physical power and it is noteworthy how many times media sports texts alight and comment upon this aspect. A clear research opportunity awaits to complete a thorough stylo-statistical survey of the vocabulary used in the press to describe black footballers, but it is definitely our impression so far that certain items of vocabulary are used far more frequently to qualify black players than white. The following list is by no means comprehensive but it is indicative of the main trend at work:

> battle – 'Ekoku battled into the Derby area' (*The Times*, 23 October 1997);
> burst – 'Hasselbaink burst to the by-line' (ibid., 10 November 1997);
> force – Julian Joachim 'forced his way' through (ibid., 27 October 1997);
> lunge – 'Ferdinand, lunging in ... beat his own goalkeeper' (ibid., 10 November 1997);

sear – Jimmy Floyd Hasselbaink's 'searing pace' (ibid., 16 March 1998);

robust – Dwight Yorke was 'robust throughout' (ibid., 27 October 1997);

fierce – Joachim's 'fierce shot' (ibid.); and

bulk – 'Noel Blake was a bulky nuisance' (ibid., 1 December 1997), Michael Duberry's 'intimidating bulk [was] an essential contrast to complement Frank Lebœuf's composed distribution' (ibid.).

If our impressions are correct and words such as these are more often used to describe black footballers than white, then the discourse in which they operate functions ideologically in that it perpetuates one of the most enduring myths of white, Western civilisation, that of the naturally athletic, strong, powerful, aggressive and frightening black male. The origins of this myth may be traced to the colonial era when media accounts and cultural representations of blacks portrayed them as aggressive, potentially savage and uncivilised, providing the spurious moral justification for colonisation. Moreover, the stereotype forever associating blacks with the body is often brought into sharper focus by modern media sports texts' insistence on contrasting black footballers' physical attributes with their implicitly superior white colleagues' disciplined intellectual capacities. Indeed, the reduction of the black subject to his or her body plays an important part in the maintenance of perceived 'natural' differences between 'races', emphasising and playing on, as it does, the belief that blacks are closer to nature than the 'more intellectual' whites. Quite simply, in English football as mediated even by the 'quality' daily press, blacks provide the brawn, whites the brain. By way of example, we have already seen how the black Duberry's 'intimidating bulk' was contrasted with the white Lebœuf's 'composed distribution'. The example is not isolated. 'If only [the black] Collymore had half the gumption that [the white] Hartson possesses' laments a report in *The Times* (1 December 1997), while the Derby County manager Jim Smith also brings out the same contrast with his after-match comments to the same newspaper: 'you talk about Wanchope but Baiano is instrumental ... he's bright, he's clever' (3 November 1997). Presumably, a black South American cannot be as intelligent as a white European. Just as the vocabulary of physical power and strength is made to work overtime in sections of match reports and articles describing black players, it is conversely the vocabulary of discipline, control and the intellect that features highly when white players are discussed. While blacks jostle and burst, whites are thoughtful and intelligent. While Ian Wright, for instance, is 'an errant devil' (*The Times*, 1 December 1997), David Batty displays '*controlled* aggression' (*The Times*, 27 November 1997, our italics). While Jimmy Floyd Haisselbank 'burst to the by-line' (*The Times*, 10 November

1997), Roberto di Matteo 'sprinted towards the by-line' (*The Times*, 27 November 1997). Paolo Wanchope is 'unorthodox and unpredictable' (*The Times*, 3 November 1997), Peter Beardsley is 'incisive ... cunning' and has 'cranial power' (*The Times*, 15 October 1997). While Ian Wright 'jostled', Denis Bergkamp was 'elegant' (*The Times*, 20 October 1997). Most telling of all, perhaps, is the discursive dismissal of the notion that a black footballer might actually be intelligent offered by a report of a match between West Ham United and Southampton in *The Times*: 'No offence to Palmer [*sic*] ... but it is not the same as being beaten by a genius' (27 April 1998).

In the match reports and articles of *The Times*, then, the stereotypical portrayal of the black male footballer is complete. He is naturally athletic, generally big and powerful; he can be smiley, happy-go-lucky or, by virtue of his unpredictable temperament, he might be fierce and aggressive. In either case, intelligence would seem to be only an optional extra. If *The Times* is not untypical of British sports media discourse as a whole, we are faced with a widespread but over-simple and damaging portrait of a significant and increasingly important group in our society, the African-Caribbean community. The black population merits media representations which allow it full and equal expression, which portray blacks as well as whites as complex, multifaceted personalities rather than as unidimensional stereotypes, representations which, above all, employ a vocabulary and imagery which no longer give rise to fears dating from the colonial era when blacks were perceived to inhabit what Orakwue calls a 'dark, unstable, unfathomable world'.[25]

In conclusion, our analysis of the vocabulary and imagery deployed by match reports and related articles in the press in general and in *The Times* in particular has revealed the propensity of media sports texts to revel in a discourse which is both reductionist and static. Groups in English society, whether they are geographically based – Yorkshire, Liverpool, or ethnically defined – black African-Caribbeans, are reduced to a limited set of purportedly typical characteristics, largely rooted in traditional cultural perceptions. These essential characteristics coalesce into recognisable stereotypes which are then constantly reiterated by the texts we have studied, from the 1997/98 English Premiership season, and through time, as is evidenced by the examples from earlier periods. The result is that, although on occasions the language used in the late 1990s might be more subtle, less blunt, the images portrayed remain largely the same static representations of English regional and black identities which fail to take account either of the complexity of human nature or of the evolving dynamism and diversity of England as it moved into the twenty-first century. We have seen how football writing in *The Times* and in other newspapers still portrays the north of England as a remote, rough and ready region, populated by humorous, hospitable and hard-working people. In this way, sports media discourse both connects with widely held views about the North in English society outside football, as well as providing further proof of the fact that notions of place, locality and region are still strong inside football, even in the modern, commercialised, globalised and Bosmanised game.[26] By focusing on clearly defined and recognisably northern imagined identities in the way it does, football writing in the press at once reflects and fuels what Russell calls 'one of the game's central dynamics' and further contributes to 'the symbolic conflict between north and south, provinces and metropolis, that remains a potent feature of English culture'.[27]

Finally, with regard to the representation of African-Caribbeans in English football, we have noted a somewhat depressing tendency to cling to outdated and essentially inaccurate stereotypes of the typical black footballer who is generally portrayed as physically strong but lacking in the characteristically white attributes of discipline and intelligence. The days may be long gone when a black footballer could be described in print as 'the coloured man from Mozambique' (*Daily Telegraph*, 27 July 1966) or as 'the coffee-coloured king of the wing'.[28] However, the examples of stereotyping from the late 1990s that we have isolated are nonetheless denigrating and, as such, need to be challenged. The language may be more subtle but this simply renders its effects more insidious. The new racism of the 1990s has, indeed, been seen as a 'coded, sophisticated reconfiguration of racist attitudes'[29] which is able to cloak itself in a respectability its more aggressive and overt predecessor never could. It is certainly not our intention to label the users of the language analysed here as racist; this would, in any case, serve no useful purpose. What is important here is not to attempt to ascribe racist motivations to the originators of a certain type of sports media discourse but rather to consider the impact of that language on its intended audience. The perceptions of football fans and of general readers alike will be shaped by their reading of football match reports and articles. It is our contention that it is surely dangerous for what Moran aptly calls 'that grinning, singing, shuffling, all-sporting prowess, no brains stereotype'[30] of blacks to continue to circulate in this way and that no real appreciation of the full contribution to society made by the black population can be made while it still does.

English regional and ethnic identities mediated by football writing would, then, appear to remain grounded in the archetypal English foundation myth of the green and pleasant land where sophistication, refinement and intelligence are narrowly asserted to be southern, white qualities. In short, embedded in the language of late-twentieth-century sports media texts there remain notions of southern and white superiority over northern regions and over black communities, notions which are no more than demons from the industrial and colonial past that must be exorcised if England is to progress as a nation in the twenty-first century.

An Englishman's Home …

How are foreigners in English football portrayed? How are England's European neighbours represented in football writing, especially in the 'quality' daily press? These are important questions if we are seeking to understand the mechanisms at work in heterotypification, the formulaic characterisation of the Other in discourse. The questions are particularly apposite where Great Britain is concerned. Britain's insularity is not only geographical but also, many would argue, psychological as well and, within Britain, the English in particular have a reputation for distrusting the unfamiliar and the foreign. Miall, for example, asserts (humorously?) that 'xenophobia is the English national sport – England's most enduring cultural expression', while Perryman concurs that 'The English, more than most, do have a problem with things foreign.'[1] It is, then, very much part of the process of constructing Englishness to focus on the contrasts provided by representations of foreigners and their nations with the accent placed especially on their difference, their alterity. Given this context, let us briefly consider the increasing presence of foreign footballers in the English game before, most importantly, moving on to examine the ways in which they and their countries are represented in football writing.

Footballers from abroad have been playing in the English game since the early years of the twentieth century. The first non-British player to operate in England was Max Seeburg, a German, who played for Tottenham Hotspur in 1908/9.[2] He was followed by other foreigners, several of whom earned a certain celebrity owing to their exploits on the pitch, notably Seeburg's compatriot Bert Trautmann, the prisoner of war who stayed in England to become Manchester City's goalkeeper and who, famously, helped the Manchester club to win the 1956 FA Cup, despite receiving a severe neck injury in the final. Even by the 1960s, however, the number of foreign players in the English game was relatively small. In 1968, for instance, Manchester City won the old Division 1 title with a first choice line-up of 11 Englishmen, a feat which has, though, never been repeated since.[3] It was in the 1970s that the first already established, non-British internationals to play top-flight football in England arrived with Osvaldo Ardiles and Ricardo Villa, the Argentines who signed for Tottenham in 1978. By the 1980s the number and the quality of non-English footballers in the game had increased rapidly to the point where, in 1986, Liverpool became the antithesis of

Manchester City by winning the FA Cup without fielding a single Englishman in their line-up. Structural changes in the game in the 1990s, such as the *Bosman* ruling and the creation of the FA Premier League, with its massive injections of cash from the satellite television company BSkyB, served to accelerate the trend already becoming apparent in the late 1970s. In 1992/93, there were 11 overseas players in the English FA Premier League, but by 1998/99 the number had risen to 171.[4] Furthermore, in the domestic season under consideration in this volume, 1997/98, footballers from 32 different countries played in the Premiership, both West Ham United and Leeds United had internationals from eight different countries in their squads and both Chelsea and Arsenal could have fielded teams of 11 players in their correct starting positions all of whom were born outside the British Isles.[5] Chelsea, in fact, went on to make history on Boxing Day 1999 by doing precisely that: their line up against Southampton contained no British-born players at all. Indeed, recent research suggests that of the five countries considered in the present study, England is the one with the biggest percentage of foreign players operating in its top division.[6]

We have seen, then, that the foreign presence in English football is now an established and probably irreversible fact. It is, indeed, commonplace to see foreign players operating in teams alongside their English colleagues. How, though, are foreign players represented in newspaper match reports and related articles? Is the fact that they are now such a common sight translated into the discourse of media sports texts or are foreigners still marked out as such, as strangers to the English game, as outsiders in a football fortress depicted primarily as an Englishman's home?

The debate surrounding the presence of foreign players in England and, especially, their impact on home-grown footballers is being increasingly aired in a number of forums. Much may be learnt about a certain English attitude to foreigners from our study of the language employed by the print media when reporting on football. In December 1997, for example, *The Times* spoke of 'the high-profile *horde* of *foreigners* [who] have *invaded* the FA Carling Premiership in recent seasons' (1 December), while in the 1999/2000 season, *Match of the Day* magazine commented on 'the *invasion* of *ball-juggling* foreigners' and 'the *droves* of imports in the Premiership' (April 2000, our italics), highlighting a theme reiterated elsewhere by the comment in the otherwise reputable *Guinness Book of Football* that 'foreign players increasingly infiltrate British shores'.[7] The image is (re)constructed of an island nation, a fortress country threatened with invasion from attacking foreigners, an image which resonates throughout British history, of course, and which clearly indicates the negative role of foreigners in that history. As has been noted, the role of foreign players in the English game has increasingly been the focus of debate. Opinions are divided as to whether the quality and the development of home-grown players are being adversely affected by the presence of foreigners. Writers in *The Times*, however, cannot be accused of sitting on the fence in this respect since it noted that English players are 'still ... being groomed ... even if so many foreigners are around to block their progress' (14 May 1998). Once again, the role of the foreigner as perceived in England is negative and obstructive.

Already on the receiving end of negative comments about their general presence, foreign footballers find no escape into anonymity in the discourse of football writing as the one element which is precisely and almost invariably evoked is their specific status as a foreigner. Tinkler is 'the South African midfield player' (*The Times*, 24 September 1997); Petrescu is 'The Romanian' while Ribeiro, 'the stocky little Portuguese ... sent the Australian, Harry Kewell, away on a run (*The Times*, 27 October 1997); Riedle is 'the German' pulled down by an opponent (*The Times*, 5 November 1997), while Rudi is 'the impressive, composed Norwegian midfield player' (*The Times*, 24 November 1997); Wreh is 'the Liberian' selected to play up front (*The Times*, 18 May 1998) while, as a final example in a list that could be continued almost *ad infinitum*, Zola and di Matteo are 'Chelsea's gifted Italians' (*The Times*, 10 November 1997). Foreign players are quite simply marked out as deviations from the implied English norm. Moreover, the alterity of foreigners is frequently conveyed by recourse to stereotypical representations of national characteristics, as the examples from the press dealing with Italian footballers will demonstrate.

First, coverage of Italian footballers operating in England tends to centre on the supposedly typical Italian qualities of style and flair. We have already noted how Gianfranco Zola and Roberto di Matteo were described as 'Chelsea's *gifted* Italians' (our italics) and, in the same article, these players' exploits are qualified as 'elegant' and 'inspired'. Zola in particular is frequently employed as a vector for reinforcing the positive side of the Italian stereotype. In a European Cup Winners Cup match against Tromsø, his free kicks were described as 'superb' and his passing as 'polished' (*The Times*, 7 November 1997), while in the final of the competition we are invited to admire his 'Latin touchplay' as he demonstrated 'the skill of an artist' (*The Times*, 14 May 1998). The stylish technique of Zola in particular and of Italians in general is frequently remarked upon in British media football texts. The vocabulary most often used to describe Italians scoring goals is resonant with images of Italian style: 'Vialli *stroked* in the equaliser' against Crystal Palace, while 'Zola *tucked* in the second' in the same match (*The Times*, 12 March 1998, our italics). Similarly, when a Sheffield Wednesday team containing two Italians, Paolo di Canio and Benito Carbone, earned a satisfactory draw at Aston Villa, *The Times* headline to the report did little to dispel the widely held notion that the principal characteristics of Italians are style and artistic ability: 'Latin duo's dance routine completes [manager] Pleat's day' (29 September 1997). Indeed, so well ingrained is this notion that when an Italian fails to display artistic flair and skilful elegance it is felt to be worthy of comment. During ITV's coverage of the Italy–Chile match during the 1998 World Cup finals, for example, Kevin Keegan was compelled to describe Vieri as 'big, strong and powerful, not a typical Italian centre forward, more English in style'.[8] Italians are expected to be effervescent flair players; when they are not, they paradoxically almost cease to be Italian and take on the mantle of being more in the English mould. The expectation that Italians will put on an expressive display surely derives from Italy's long-standing prowess in and affection for the performing arts, especially opera. Italian footballers, then, find themselves frequently portrayed as artistic, theatrical, operatic characters. The depiction is usually implicit, a given located in the subtext of the vocabulary and imagery employed. Occasionally, though, the portrayal is explicit. In one report of the Italy–Belgium game at Euro 2000, for instance, the Italian player Stefano Fiore was described as 'thrust before the microphone and performing with all the gusto of a Pavarotti' (*Independent on Sunday*, 18 June 2000).

For all the positive elements of the Italian stereotype represented in the British media, there is, on the other hand, also a distinctly negative side. Italians are often represented in football writing as superficial, extravagant and temperamental. Despite the praise lavished on Carbone and di Canio, they were also described by the match reporter as 'highly paid, highly strung performers', 'often walking an emotional tightrope' who made 'theatrical gestures and grimaces' (*The Times*, 29 September 1997). Outbursts of emotion are expected from Italians, and when they are not forthcoming, the surprise registered by journalists is palpable: against Aston Villa, 'there was no temper, nor tantrum' from Carbone nor di Canio; shock, horror, then, as Italians fail to live up to their stereotype. Normal service was resumed, though, later in the season when the same players were castigated by successive reports in *The Times*. Against Bolton Wanderers, for instance, 'the flicks and dummies of Carbone and di Canio that had been so cute before now looked like extravagances. One wondered whether they were intent on scoring goals or on going through their repertoire of party-pieces' (16 March 1998). Similarly, when it appeared that Philippe Troussier might take over at Hillsborough in the summer of 1998, his stern and tough methods were described as 'Perfect, then to smack a bit of life into Paolo di Canio, Benito Carbone and the other white-booted fairies at Sheffield Wednesday' (25 June 1998). The subtext of remarks such as these is clear and speaks volumes about the traditional English suspicion of foreign flair with its concomitant doubts about the commitment of footballers from Latin countries. Once again, on this occasion implicitly, the typical qualities of the English norm – strength, power, commitment, 'hardness' – are accentuated by contrast with the supposed deficiencies in this respect of many foreign footballers. First analyses of the data provided by Euro 2000 suggest that the press still had little regard for Latin footballers' qualities (at least before the tournament had begun). The *Daily Express*, for instance, was happy to concur with Graeme Souness's views on Portugal ahead of the group game meeting with England:

> Portugal are *a typical Latin team* – neat and tidy. They huff and puff a lot, but they don't cause much damage ... They will catch the eye with individual skill, but once England's teamwork, directness and aggression get to work they will cave in. (12 June 2000, our italics)

Evidently the Portuguese did not read the script before the game. At 2–0 down, they caved in to win 3–2.

Occasions for national stereotyping are, then, clearly not restricted solely to press coverage of foreigners playing in England. Indeed, when the daily press does turn its attention to foreign national teams competing in international tournaments, its match reports and articles are replete with familiar portraits of some of England's nearest European neighbours.

The portrayal of Germany, for instance, is well established and connects with more widely held views about German identity found outside the context of football. Essentially the German stereotype is constructed on the basis of three characteristics: strength, efficiency and self-belief. First, the myth of German strength bordering on near invincibility is largely conveyed by military metaphors usually evoking Germany's role in the two World Wars; references to warfare are probably much more extensively made in football media discourse when describing Germany than any other team, England included, and serve, therefore, to reinforce the image of the Germans as aggressive and warlike. Players representing 'the mighty Germany' at the 1996 European Championships (*The Times*, 24 June and 1 July) make 'sorties' (*The Times*, 20 June) and 'forays' (*The Times*, 25 June); they lead 'the battle on two fronts' (ibid.) and are suspected of preparing 'some sort of ambush' (ibid.) for their opponents. Collectively, they 'regroup' (*The Times*, 3 June and 20 June), 'march on' (*The Times*, 20 June) and ensure their defence is 'a hostile zone' (ibid.). In one game at Euro 96, 'Germany were the first to advance, pressing the Czechs back with eight men garrisoned around their penalty box' (*The Times*, 29 June). Ultimately, their striker Jurgen Klinsmann, 'the blond bomber', will help them 'to conquer Europe', that is, win the trophy (*The Times*, 3 June). Even the footballer's career hazard of injury is conveyed in military terms when it befalls Germans: injured players are 'German wounded' (*The Times*, 24 June) and, with several players sidelined before the final of Euro 96, they obtained permission to 'draft reinforcements into their squad' (*The Times*, 29 June). In short, Germany's mythic strength was conveyed in politico-military terminology: it was quite simply 'the world's leading football power' (*The Times*, 2 July).

Two years later, at the 1998 World Cup finals, similar images of power, strength and militaristic aggression recurred: 'they still act as if at the wheel of a steamroller. There were treadmarks all over Iran.' Indeed, the Iranians were simply 'overpowered ... crush[ed] ... by the sheer insistence of Germany' in their group game meeting (*The Times*, 26 June). Apparently, Germany's 'old soldiers' (*The Times*, 5 July) continued to display traditional characteristics at France 98: 'Resilient, tough and stubborn. Those are certainly the unquenchable attributes of Berti Vogts' side' (*The Times*, 29 June) as they beat Mexico in the knock-out phase. The role of the Germans in encounters such as these is invariably constructed as that of the bully, victimising smaller and less powerful opponents, an image no doubt owing its origins, at least in part, to representations of German military history. The German football team at France 98, then, was said to move 'relentlessly on, spoiling innocent hopes and dreams such as those of gallant Mexico' (*The Times*, 30 June). Even when German teams are defeated, military metaphors are never far away. Defeat against Croatia in the 1998 World Cup quarter-final was attributed to the fact that, on this occasion, the Germans could muster 'no rearguard action' to save them (*The Times*, 5 July) and *The Times* delighted in repeating the Croatian coach's comments that his tactics were 'to see that the Germans ran out of petrol, just like Rommel in the desert' (7 July). It is worth noting here, though, that the use of military metaphors to describe the German team which is so widespread in the British print media (and elsewhere in Europe, see Chapters 6 and 9) is not, for obvious reasons, a luxury that is replicated in Germany itself where there is a total absence of war vocabulary (see *Süddeutsche Zeitung*). Self-glorification and militarism are still taboo in public discourse there but widely attributed to Germans by other Europeans.

Secondly, but just as apparent in the data studied, is the stereotype of German efficiency which, partially at least, derives from widely-held appreciations of the post-war economic miracle. West German reconstruction after the Second World War was swift and impressive, resulting in the economy becoming the third strongest in the world and something of a model of economic efficiency for her European partners. Popular European perceptions of Germany reinforce the point. An opinion poll was conducted by TMO/INRA surveying the attitudes of the inhabitants of 14 European Union countries (all bar Luxembourg) to other European nations. In this poll Germany was ranked top overall in the four categories of *strong economy, quality of manufactured goods, quality of industrial products* and *trustworthy/reliable people.*[9] Within this context, the imagery used in the British press to represent German efficiency constantly evokes machinery, especially automotive machinery with which the modern

German economy is inextricably identified. One can, it seems, 'always rely on Germany' (*The Times*, 10 June 1996), whose 'traditional efficiency should win them the [European Championship] title' (*The Times*, 27 June 1996), because Germany 'is a tournament machine' (*The Times*, 2 July 1996). The report on the Euro 96 group game against Russia provides further examples. Here 'Germany went about their business in the usual systematic way.' Hässler and Möller were 'a couple of midfield motorcycles who take the shortest line between them, their front-runners ... and the goal' and the German team as a whole 'typically looks as if it was manufactured in a factory by Porsche' (*The Times*, 17 June). Similarly, before France 98 *The Times* previewed Germany's chances and concluded that they were 'a role model for order, discipline and collective spirit' (8 June). Indeed, once the tournament had begun, it was these very qualities that were highlighted by successive media sports texts in the press and utterances on television. In the victory over the USA, for example, 'Germany were not rampant, just tidy and efficient' and 'the traditional German qualities of discipline and organisation remain in evidence' (*The Times*, 16 June). Again, in the game against Mexico, 'as we know, heat or no heat, the German machine grinds on inexorably' (*The Times*, 30 June), while the BBC commentator John Motson, never one to overlook the opportunity for a cliché, curiously enough, reminded us that Berti Vogts's team's preparations for the France 98 quarter-final would have been accomplished with 'typical German thoroughness'.[10] Finally, in this respect, it is worth noting once again the astonishment registered by sports journalists when a stereotype is not consistently supported by the facts. When the Germans played Yugoslavia, for instance, *The Times* reporter was amazed by their 'indisciplined performance' and concluded that they had 'betrayed their history' (22 June). Similarly, during Euro 2000, Motson could hardly believe his eyes as he witnessed Germany's disarray against Romania: 'The Germans are a shambles, I've never said this before, I never thought I'd ever say it ... This is extraordinary and most un-German like.'[11] Rather than re-evaluate the historical stereotype and accept that Germans are perfectly capable of being indisciplined, the media discourse employed prefers to preserve the traditional essentialist image and, instead, castigates the present team for being an aberration, for not fitting the template of discipline preconceived for them.

One of the reasons the British press finds it hard to drop the image of the Germans as being ultra-disciplined and efficient if a touch dull is that Germans themselves also contribute to its perpetuation. It is not that the Germans have not tried periodically to shed this image of the efficient but boring and often undeservedly lucky team. Like the New Germany, they have been keen to make friends and to please. Before the 1996 European Championship, Vogts, Germany's manager, stated that he would rather go down beautifully than win in bad style (*Süddeutsche Zeitung*, 21 June 1996), but all too readily the Germans are portrayed by their own press as well as by that in Great Britain as reverting to their traditional ways, which is playing defensively and trying to destroy whatever is creative in the opposition's game.

The national team in Germany itself tends to be represented as one without creative stars. The striker Oliver Bierhoff, for instance, was described by the *Süddeutsche Zeitung* as typically 'petit-bourgeois', emotionally repressed, rational, unspontaneous and, even after victory in the final of Euro 96, only ever cautiously enthusiastic (2 July), again confirming the most common British stereotype of the German: boring but efficient. The other uncharismatic (anti) star of the German team of the mid to late 1990s was 'Der brave Eilts' (*Süddeutsche Zeitung*, 17 June 1996) – the 'upright, worthy, honest' Eilts – the personification of Germany's dominant values: fight and tackle, work and run. 'Der *brave* Eilts', this is an adjective which alludes deliberately to the 1950s, where all the players (except, perhaps, for Rahn) could be described as good and well-behaved.[12] Is this a hint that the post-unification Germany of the 1990s has a lot in common with the post-1945 Germany? Is this a confirmation of Chancellor Kohl's status as 'Adenauer's grandson'? Does the *Süddeutsche Zeitung* think that Adenauer's post-war slogan 'no experiments' applies equally well to the New Germany? Another article in the same German newspaper (21 June 1996) also refers to the Germans as dull and unimaginative, sending home the Italian team whose manager was a 'visionary' and reports on how Kohl congratulated Vogts, his friend, after the dull, defensive performance by speaking of the German team's 'super performance' and adding: 'It's not important how one wins but *that* one wins', thereby justifying his own policy of win at all costs and 'continue as before' with the help of the people's game. The *Süddeutsche Zeitung* in this instance views political history and football together. The strategy in both appears the same: save your skin and win, regardless of the costs. This example shows how print media discourse on football reflects the dominant values of the time: there is no space in Germany for vision or experimentation, it is only success that matters and here, indeed, the Germans are champions. It is clear from these examples how critical Germany is of itself (through the eyes of the liberal press). Other Europeans have a tendency to regard the Germans as efficient but dull. The TMO/INRA poll referred to above placed Germany top of the list for *trustworthy/reliable people* but bottom in the category of *likeable/cheerful people*. The stereotypes of the Germans offered by the British media (and, as we shall see, by the French and the Spanish press, too) might well reflect widely-held appreciations of Germany but they are also interestingly confirmed by the Germans themselves.

The third typical characteristic of Germans perpetuated by football writing in England is that of self-belief. One of the reasons Germany won Euro 96 was, apparently, their 'belief, bordering on arrogant self-assertion that binds [them] again and again' (*The Times*, 2 July). Their striker, Klinsmann, was singled out as 'No one exemplifies [the German approach] more admirably' with his 'unremitting competitiveness ..., toughness of attitude' and 'battler's mentality' (*The Times*, 20 June). Similarly but more generally, to beat Russia earlier in the tournament the Germans 'drew on their collective resolve' (*The Times*, 17 June), while the semi-final meeting with England (a nation with its own brand of spirit and commitment, as we have seen) was won because Germany produced 'the competitive spirit that runs through the history of games between the nations' and displayed 'the conditioning and courage one expects from them' (*The Times*, 27 June). Once again similar themes emerged from the media coverage of Germany's performances at the 1998 World Cup. 'If Germany are still numbered among the possible winners of this World Cup,' stated *The Times* halfway through the tournament, 'it is because people are wary of the resolve that inhabits their minds' and 'It is impossible not to respect the conviction with which Germany apply themselves. Doubts and misgivings which might erode their purposefulness are eradicated' (26 June). Moreover, it is not only in the press that this theme is expounded. It reverberates in other media coverage as well. The ITV commentator at the Germany–Mexico game, for instance, pointed out that 'It's difficult to generalise in football' before proving that it is, in fact, quite easy to generalise by saying 'but you sense that when Germany are a goal down they have a better chance of getting out of it than anyone', while summariser Ron Atkinson simply refused 'to bet against Germany, never, anybody else in a white shirt, maybe, but not Germany.'[13] Similarly, during the Germany–Croatia quarter-final, John Motson made references to the 'great campaigners' and 'the German mentality' while sagely advising his audience 'don't rule [the Germans] out at this stage'.[14]

There remains a vexed question. Given Germany's unremitting belligerence, machine-like efficiency and undying resolve, how was it possible that they could be eliminated from a major tournament as early as the quarter-final as they were at France 98 (even if that elimination prompted so much joy in countries around the globe)?[15] *The Times*, at least, provides the answers. First, the Germans have, it would seem, an Achilles heel. They lack imagination and invention and can, therefore, be exposed by opponents demonstrating these qualities. Against Iran, for instance, 'Vogts' team rarely suggested that they were capable of the technique and guile that could have embarrassed their opponents' and they went on to win the game only because of their superior power: 'Dissatisfied with their display in the first half, they simply increased the aggression rather than attempt a change of style' (26 June 1998). Secondly, the team competing at France 98 fulfilled, by and large, the expectations of them in terms of aggression, efficiency and belief (to say otherwise would be to undo half a century of stereotyping, a feat which, as we have seen, the media are reluctant to perform); they could not ultimately succeed, however, because they were simply too old. Some of the team were 'approaching the bath chair stage' (ibid.), 'the spine of the team is a museum piece', 'How appropriate, then, that the venue of the quarter-final against Croatia, Stade de Gerland, is listed as a historic monument' (4 July). Obviously, 'the old soldiers' (5 July) did not die but they did fade away. There may or may not be a point in footballing terms in attributing Germany's elimination from France 98 to old age (although one doubts that this would have been such an issue had Germany's performances been better than they were); what this tack does do, however, is preserve the essentialist image of the strong, battling and determined Germans in order for it to be pressed into service at future international tournaments such as the Euro 2000 and World Cup 2002 clashes with England. For instance, following the home defeat against Germany in the World Cup 2002 qualifier, which also sparked the resignation as manager of Kevin Keegan, Glenn Hoddle, his predecessor, reiterated the perceptions of Germany held by many when he cursed 'yet again, the ruddy Germans, those infuriatingly tough and efficient Germans' (*Mail on Sunday*, 8 October 2000). Similarly, the *Manchester Evening News* preview of the earlier Euro 2000 match subverts its own amiable banner headline, 'We meet again, old friend' (16 June), with references in the text of the article itself to England's 'old adversaries', 'fierce rivals' and 'old enemy' while also speaking of the need for 'revenge' to be taken for defeats 'fought out' in previous contests. The vocabulary of adversarial conflict so often used in the media to describe matches involving Germany is once again still apparent. Indeed, references to the Second World War are never far away in this respect. On the day of the Euro 2000 encounter between England and Germany *The Times* noted that the kick-off time was 19.45 'which has to be a good sign' and, on hearing the news that Germany would host the 2006 World Cup, the same paper announced: 'Hitler's stadium will host the World Cup'.[16]

To turn to images of France in the sporting media, we may note how French players and managers operating in England are, first, invariably designated as the foreign other and, second, how they frequently become the peg on which to hang stereotypical representations of Frenchness.

The Arsenal manager Arsène Wenger, for instance, is almost always referred to as 'the Frenchman' in press coverage and his success in guiding his team to the double in 1998 was presented by *The Times* as an almost magical ability to mix a potion the essential elements of which were the supposedly typical English and French virtues: 'this Frenchman's ability [has been] to hold on to *English passion and spirit* and to lace it with *fine French technique*' (18 May, our italics). Similarly, in the season under consideration, *The Times*'s descriptions of Tottenham Hotspur's David Ginola seemed to be largely derived from a set of recognisably French characteristics based on the notions of glamour, style and aloofness familiar from other sports media representations of French footballers.[17] His performance against Newcastle United was qualified as 'charming' (6 October 1997), but later he became 'the splendidly arrogant but isolated Ginola' (10 November 1997), a 'talented enigma' (26 November 1997). Ginola's contribution to his team's victory over Bolton Wanderers prompted further comment along the same lines. His approach was 'flamboyant' as 'he inspired his struggling side' with 'beautifully weighted' passes:

> Condemned by so many for so long as a luxury player that Spurs can ill-afford in their time of trouble, written off as a man who has not got the stomach for a fight, the Frenchman responded with a performance of wonderful poise and artistry. (2 March 1998)

That these characteristics of style and artistry but with doubtful commitment are purportedly typically French is indicated in the media discourse studied not only by the many references to Ginola's nationality – which is, therefore, deemed important in the descriptions – but also by the fact that they are, indeed, more generally applied to coverage of the French national team itself.

One of the persistent myths reiterated by the press in this country is that of the French national team's flair and style. As Andrew Marr notes in *The Observer*, 'For most of British history, the educated middle classes have looked to France as a place where they live better' (20 February 2000). This concept, based on British (and French) appreciations of Gallic culture, cuisine and life style, is one that is widely held in Europe at large. The TMO/INRA survey of Europeans' perceptions of their neighbours described earlier ranks France second only to Germany for *high standard of living* and places it first for *quality of life* and *gastronomy*. These notions of France being a county where they live better are translated into sports media discourse by portrayals of France as a country where they play better: that is, with fine technique and admirable style. As Euro 96 progressed, for instance, the French continued 'to delight with their positive attitude' (*The Times*, 19 June), particularly against Spain and Bulgaria around whom they '[danced] carefully crafted rings' (*The Times*, 28 June). Notions of spectacle and of the performance arts are frequently evoked by the highly visual imagery used to describe French players in the articles studied. Youri Djorkaeff, the forward, was 'dazzling' and 'electrifying' against Spain (*The Times*, 19 June) while the same player's near miss against the Czechs provided an 'incandescent moment' (*The Times*, 27 June). The French team collectively is similarly described as 'alight' against Spain specifically (*The*

Times, 19 June) and 'dazzling in the group games' in general (*The Times*, 1 July).

The 1998 World Cup finals held in France itself, of course, provided further opportunities to re-establish the link between the concept of style and the French nation as represented by its football team. The opening match against South Africa, for example, 'should signal the start of the home pulse accelerating, but only if – this being France – style accompanies the points' (*The Times*, 12 June); 'The French nation may be looking for style as well as victory from the host team', added another article the following day, while the headline to the report of the South Africa match clearly suggested the themes the report itself would develop: 'French polish and passion proves winning mixture' (13 June). In the body of the report, we learn that:

> Here ... was the authentic flavour of French football ... the French were like piranha fish, their tackles snapping at South African heels, their advances were sweeping and vivacious, but naturally they were profligate in front of goal ... If only they could finish what they create. (ibid.)

Representations of French vivacity in the victory over South Africa were not confined to the press. 'The French do like to do things with such style, don't they?' asked Brian Moore during the ITV coverage of the game,[18] thereby increasing the longevity of the portrayal. Moreover, as France 98 unfolded, the theme could simply not be dropped by the print media either. Against Denmark, for example:

> The first 45 minutes was as entertaining as anything witnessed in the tournament so far, packed with French flair and the romantic notion that winning actually mattered, whether qualification for the second round depended on it or not. (*The Times*, 25 June)

Similarly, France's match against Croatia was said to be characterised by 'French flair and Croatian pride' (*The Times*, 8 July), with the French described as 'gifted ... They have dared to attack in every game. They have entertained through their passing, through the invention personified by Zidane' (ibid.) and, after the French victory in the final, the front page of the *Guardian* blared out the eminently predictable headline: 'On top of the world: French flair leaves Brazil stunned' (13 July).

The second element of France's stereotype in British (and French) football writing is also frequently recycled: unlike the Germans, the French lack self-belief. Both Holt and Wahl trace the historical origins of this image to French military defeats at the hands of stronger, better organised (especially English and German) opponents.[19] In the knock-out stages of

Euro 96, for instance, the French 'could not generate the flair expected of
them' (*The Times*, 27 June) because of this fatal flaw. Following the match
against Holland, *The Times* noted: 'If they possessed a belief to match their
talents, they would have won comfortably and be strong favourites to win
the European Championship' (24 June). The report then asked: 'If they can
somehow start to believe ... who knows what may be possible?' (ibid.).
Worse was to follow after defeat in the semi-final: under the headline
'France freeze in sight of Wembley' (*The Times*, 27 June), we read that the
team 'seized up' and gave a performance marred by 'anxiety' and
'fretfulness' (ibid.). Rather than focus on the players' tactics or the
misfortune of the penalty shoot-out, the combination of which surely led to
the French defeat, the reports analysed preferred to re-present the myth of
the fragile French psyche. This was a 'fear-tainted' and 'inhibited
performance' by the French who could not cope with the 'pressure of the
unknown' (*The Times*, 28 June) and who ultimately 'succumbed once more
to that affliction which seems always to grip them at major championships,
a lack of belief' (*The Times*, 1 July). The same theme resonated in both
television and press coverage of the French national team at the 1998 World
Cup. 'The French will be worried about the penalty shoot-out', shrieked
Barry Davies during the knock-out match against Paraguay, 'there's a lot of
players out there affected by nervous tension',[20] while his ITV homologue
Clive Tyldesley flirted with the boundaries of acceptability with his
sweeping comments that France is a 'very emotional country', where
'patience is not necessarily a national trait'.[21] *The Times* shared this view of
the fretful French. In the run-up to the quarter-final against Italy, 'they had
been desperately trying to persuade each other they could win' apparently,
but 'their team ... did not seem at all convinced' (4 July). The semi-final with
Croatia proved to be the high water mark of this tidal wave of preconception.
On BBC television, Martin O'Neill's preview of the game contained the
succinct but predictable 'France will be nervous', while John Motson and
Trevor Brooking's match commentary more than amply fulfilled the
prophecy as they variously described the French as 'not confident', 'edgy',
'very nervous', 'so, so worried', 'ill at ease' and 'lacking in confidence'.[22]
The following day, *The Times* delighted in re-presenting the theme. France
were full of 'uncertainties', 'terrified by nerves and emasculated by their
own caution' (9 July). The fact that France won the game to qualify for the
final then had to be presented, not so much as a victory based upon superior
technique or tactics, but as a French triumph over their own lack of resolve.
Two reports in the same newspaper towed the line to the point of employing
the same vocabulary: 'But then Thuram answered, almost as quickly as we
could ask, the question about French morale' (*The Times*, 9 July); 'When
[Thuram] scored, within 30 seconds of the Croatia goal, he answered on
behalf of the tricolour nation the question that was in our throats. How

would French morale cope with going a goal down?' (*The Times*, 10 July). France's qualification for the World Cup final on the strength of six straight victories involving a goal tally of 12 for and 2 against posed a tricky problem for sports journalists. According to the traditional stereotype, French teams usually crack and fall at the last hurdle. An explanation needed to be found, then, for this impressive French success which did not overturn decades of clichéd reporting. When that explanation came from *The Times* it was as sinister as it was discursively inconsistent. According to the newspaper's preview of the final, the mental strength displayed by the French team so far was a newly acquired trait (it had to be, of course, to excuse the fact that it had not been spotted earlier) which was attributable to the presence of black players in the squad: 'Lilian Thuram, the athletic right back who scored both goals in the semi-final victory over Croatia is another [along with Marcel Desailly] whose distinctive background has contributed to a strength of mind' (11 July). Not only, then, does the resolve of white French footballers remain in doubt but mental strength is now supposedly brought to a team by black French players, whilst the stereotype of black footballers operating in England alleges just the opposite, positing their supposed lack of commitment and application as a group characteristic (see Chapter 2).

Finally, an insight into certain perceptions of the Spanish may be gleaned from the data studied. Historically, Spain was a powerful diplomatic and colonial rival, of course, and, more recently, the suspicion with which she was viewed during the Franco years has given way to acknowledgement of her role as a full partner in the European Union. Given the strong presence of Spain on the international stage and, of course, in the footballing context, given the successes of Spanish club sides, it is expected that the national team will be successful in the international football arena. Spain's relative lack of success is thus a source of some surprise and not a little consternation in the British sports media, which often, therefore, seem obliged to qualify the Spanish as 'underachievers' (for instance, *The Times*, 20 June 1998). Spain's supposedly early exit from the 1998 World Cup finals, for instance, was described as a 'bewildering eclipse' (*The Times*, 21 June). The article in question then went on to ask exasperatedly: 'How could it be that a side so rampant, so powerful, so full of scoring potential and who many believed had the capability of going all the way had been erased from this tournament?' (ibid.). Spain's failure to live up to expectations is portrayed in Britain as an inexplicable mystery.

Next, in common with other predominantly Latin teams, the Spanish are represented in the British press as a temperamental, contrary and fearful side capable at times of playing with inspiration, 'tremendous verve' and 'brio' (*The Times*, 25 June 1998) but who ultimately 'lack ... ambition' (*The Times*, 19 June 1996) and go into games suffering 'pre-match anxiety' as they did against England in the 1996 European Championships because they were, apparently, 'the side with more to fear' (*The Times*, 22 June). Fearfulness is, indeed, often attributed to Spanish footballers by British sports media texts. Following a World Cup match against Paraguay, *The Times* recycled this notion in the following (stereo)typical fashion, focusing first on the Spanish goalkeeper and then on the team as a whole: 'The heat in Saint-Etienne ... ensured there was sweat on the brow of Zubizarreta as the anthems played; or was it fear?' (20 June 1998). Having initially posited the concept of Spanish fear, the article goes on to reinforce it: 'In the 10th minute, Zubizarreta turned *with anxiety bordering on panic* when a corner from the right seemed to evade everyone in his goalmouth' (ibid.; our italics). Finally, throughout the game, which ended in a 0–0 draw, the article reported that 'Spanish nerves continued to be taut' (ibid.).

Paradoxically, the Spanish team's apparent strength and will-power also feature in the articles analysed. Clemente, the former national team manager, rarely missed an opportunity to outline his belief in his own team's qualities in this respect and was, by way of example, quoted in *The Times* as saying: 'I'll never let anybody say we don't play our guts out on the field' (24 June 1998). The theme inherent in this self-image does, indeed, appear throughout the British press articles studied and is, historically, a long-running one dating back at least to the 1920s. One of the earliest articles on Spanish football to appear in Great Britain would have been the match report in *Athletic News* of the first-ever international between England and Spain held in Madrid in 1929. Spain were victorious and inflicted on England their first defeat outside Britain in the professional era. The match report excused this defeat partly because it was too hot ('not football weather') and partly because of the way the Spanish team played: 'they make ground by speedy dribbling which is cruder than the [English] Corinthian style'.[23] This early example of football writing labelled Spanish strength as somewhat crude and, 70 years later, we find the same imagery used to typify Spain: 'Spanish defences are always hard' (*The Times*, 19 June 1996), Abelardo is 'violent' (ibid.), Nadal 'ferocious' (ibid., 21 June 1996), a 'hit man' (ibid., 22 June 1996), Hierro 'the personification of his team in sheer physical presence and power' (ibid., 19 June 1996), and the latter two players stand 'shoulder to shoulder in a powerful midfield buttress' (ibid., 15 June 1998). Images of the Spanish obstructing British progress might be felt to connect with events from history outside football. Predictably, there are, indeed, references in the recent data gathered to the 'Spanish armada' (*The Times*, 19 June 1996) in memory of the fleet sent against England in 1588, while phrases such as 'The Spaniards put up an almighty blockade' (*The Times*, 24 June 1996) conjure up images of more recent Anglo-Spanish disputes involving fishing rights and the sovereignty of Gibraltar. On a related note, portraying Spanish players as demonstrating the 'the cut and thrust ... found in a bull ring' (*The

Times, 24 June 1996), although clearly a cliché, is a further reminder that Spain is often perceived in Britain as a cruel country and the physical strength of its team is continually portrayed as harsh and negative: the Spanish are 'uncompromisingly tough', 'England's most difficult hurdle' at Euro 96, 'tenacious in their negative objectives' (*The Times*, 22 June), 'As powerful a nation as any in Europe, with the addition of some grit from their Basque coach' (*The Times*, 8 June 1998).

The last example demonstrates that there is an awareness, in *The Times* at least, that Spain is a state of many nations, but the analysis goes no further than to recycle familiar stereotypes about its components. For instance, Clemente was earlier referred to as the 'feisty little man from the Basque Country' (*The Times*, 22 June 1996), whose team, 'harshly organised in the uncompromising Basque tradition' (*The Times*, 10 June), contained 'tough northerners' who played with 'the fighting spirit of the British' rather than 'the individualistic flair' of other Latin countries (*The Times*, 22 June).

To sum up, the coverage examined here of foreign footballers operating in England tends to designate the foreigner as the Other. Despite their increasingly customary presence in the English game, foreigners are invariably indicated as such in press reports; they are marked out as foreigners first (the Australian, the South African, the Italian, the Frenchman) before their individuality as footballers can be evaluated. Moreover, a certain English fear of foreigners is revealed in the press which is at best ambivalent, at worst hostile towards their presence in the game, often qualified, as we have seen, as an invasion or infiltration of these islands, thereby adding to the evidence that English society, far from celebrating plurality and difference, acts in apprehension of them, particularly in the area of nationality in which prejudices and stereotypes are so frequently reinforced.[24]

Indeed, when media sports texts discuss specific nationalities the dialectic of (English) self and (foreign) Other is predicated upon a limited set of traditional characteristics, stereotypes represented linguistically, in which many negative traits appear in familiar and rarely challenged guises. Davies aptly summarises the attitude revealed when he notes that 'in football, it's OK having all these foreigners about, just so long as they take care to reinforce our prejudices that foreigners, generally speaking, are diving whingers, bent as a fish-hook and as often as not fairly bonkers with it'.[25] However, it should also be noted that the stereotypes (re)constructed do offer positive sides as well. When Italians are represented in the press, for instance, they are portrayed as skilful and artistic if liable to volcanic outbursts of temperament betraying their Latin heritage. Familiar images of German identity are also apparent in football writing in England. Here Germans are dour and unimaginative but nonetheless commendable for their strength of will and machine-like efficiency. Above all, though, English views of Germany remain dominated by that country's military history. Images of German aggression and belligerence have been circulating in many cultural arenas, such as cartoons and political satire since the late nineteenth-century representations of Bismarck as the warlike Prussian bully[26] and they still find expression in late twentieth/early twenty-first-century media discourse on football. Fair or not, those militaristic images of the pushy Germans simply will not go away. France is portrayed as a land of dazzling elegance and flair, attributes that French footballers are expected to produce every time they step on to the pitch. Negatively, doubts still remain about the strength of French players' morale, doubts that hardly seem to have been dented even by France's victory in the 1998 World Cup final. Finally, Spain is represented as a potentially strong and powerful country but also as one that is temperamental and underachieving.

Ultimately, we would contend that football writing of the type we have examined here functions ideologically in that it contributes to the preservation of the notion of a Europe of nations, with each state separated from its neighbours not only by geopolitical frontiers but also by recognisable psychological characteristics as well. Furthermore, each country's virtues and failings may be seen to contrast, sometimes sharply, not only with each other's but more specifically and especially with those of England, thereby maintaining the idea of a separate, unique English identity within Europe. It will be interesting to study in this volume how similar, or otherwise, the typical portrayals of the European countries examined in the British media are to those constructed by the 'quality' daily press in France and Spain. Do the stereotypes of England's European neighbours presented in media sports texts derive from a parochial, insular and uniquely English view of the world or are they, on the contrary, apparent across the continent as a whole and, therefore, indicative of a common European viewpoint on how we all see each other?

PART TWO:
FRANCE

La Belle France: Winning with Style

Questions of national identity are intimately linked with football in France. France's national team competes in the international arena with other countries and is seen as representative of the nation itself. Wahl notes that it was in the early days of international football, which coincided with the rise of chauvinism in Europe before the Great War, that the national team's performances and style started to be identified with the fortunes of the French people.[1] This awareness of common nationhood is further reinforced by the symbolism of French football. Before international matches, the *Marseillaise*, the national anthem, is sung. Supporters wave the national flag, the famous blue, white and red tricolour, and are able to see these national colours reflected in the kit worn by the team itself as France is unique among the nations examined here in that its strip exactly replicates the colours of the country's flag: blue shirts, white shorts, red socks. This symbolism is carried over into French sports media discourse as French national teams are often referred to linguistically as 'the Tricolours' and 'the tricolour team' (for instance, *Libération*, 12 October 1997). Finally, the French Football Association (the Fédération française de football or FFF), has as its emblem the national bird of France, the Gallic cockerel, which duly appears, crowing with some pride of late, on top of the letters FFF on the shirts of the national team. It is not our intention here, however, to discuss further these examples of what might be termed banal nationalism.[2] We are more interested in the ways in which the discourse of football writing in sections of the 'quality' daily press fashions a specific and readily identifiable portrayal of France which is grounded in the French self-image. What are the principal features of French autotypification and how are they communicated by football match reports and related articles? As we shall see, the picture painted is somewhat complex and not entirely static.

The French team is perceived as an extension of the nation[3] and, when it is successful, it becomes a source of much national pride just as, for instance, England's frequent failures on the pitch often become a source of much soul-searching and national mourning (see Chapter 1). It could be asserted, though, that the bond between the football-going public and the national team is stronger in France than in some of her European neighbours such as England (where loyalty to club sides often generates ambivalence towards the national team) and Spain (where regionalism is so strong that the 'national' team might not be felt to represent the whole of the politico-administrative unit called Spain – see Chapters 7 and 8). When France won Euro 2000, then, to crown a remarkable and unprecedented double following their World Cup triumph of two years earlier, the links between the national team and the country itself were made explicit by a delirious French press. *Sud-Ouest*, for instance, affirmed that 'The Blues ... have become our best ambassadors, the perfect example of national excellence. They are our luxury liner France, our Concorde, our Ariane rocket, our great vintage wines. They are the best and most accomplished representation of French exceptionalism, that subtle combination of tradition and innovation' (3 July 2000). If the French team's exploits are portrayed as communicating a cultural identity, the essence of 'Frenchness' itself, then it is important to examine in some detail the elements that constitute that portrayal in the 'quality' daily press.

The first one in the portrayal of France in the football pages of *Le Monde* and *Libération* concerns the way in which the national team plays. The feeling is that style is, or should be, a typical French trademark. This belief is long-standing. Wahl notes that before the Great War the magazine *Les Jeunes* had already established a parallel between the style of the national team and certain French characteristics.[4] In football, apparently, as in military history, the French typically engage in open, heroic attacks against opponents who are usually better organised and who profit when French energy fades and morale cracks. 'Frenchness' here rests on the concepts of courage, inspiration and creativity as opposed to the brute force and machine-like qualities of adversaries such as the Germans and the English. Eighty-five years later, this perception of French flair and style is alive and well in the language of football writing.

First, in this context, French players' technical abilities are often conveyed by the vocabulary of the performing arts. Christian Karembeu, for instance, was described as 'an artist' at one game during the 1996 European Championships (*Libération*, 19 June) while team members waiting for their chance to play in the tournament were described in the language of the cinema as 'extras' (*Le Monde*, 26 June) implying that the first team are the stars of the show that is French football. Similarly, the manner of the victory over Denmark in the 1998 World Cup finals was praised by *Libération* for the 'clear, rhythmic movements' of its 'choreography' and the 'arabesques traced by the team in midfield' (25 June). There is also a marked tendency to represent French flair on the football pitch by employing images of shining lights. Such images connect with the lengthy tradition of political and cultural discourses portraying France in general as a guiding light for the rest of the world, a shining beacon of excellence. The verbs *rayonner*, 'to radiate' and *briller*, 'to shine' are frequently used of France, especially by politicians making the case for its greatness and particularly, but not exclusively, in the context of cultural policy. When the top civil servant Jacques Rigaud speaks of '[his] country's vocation to radiate beyond its borders' in a treatise on French cultural exceptionalism, he speaks in a long line of public figures who have used the familiar beacon image to describe their country. The list includes, among many others, the nineteenth-century historian Jules Michelet ('French history is a trail of bright light, a veritable milky way on which the eyes of the world are always fixed'), the Communist Party leader in the post-war years Maurice Thorez ('France's destiny is to be a torch bearer'), the twentieth-century choreographer Jeanine Charrat ('France ... has always been an example for the world, a cultural beacon of light') and the contemporary far-right politician Jean-Marie Le Pen ('I shall do everything to ensure the name of France continues to shine brightly in the world').[5] The practice is also apparent in French football writing which thereby reiterates the links between media sport and culture as a whole. In one game at the 1996 European Championships, for instance, Pedros was described as 'alight' (*Libération*, 20 June) while a shot on goal by Bhogossian in a friendly against Russia was said to stand out 'like a flash of light in the darkness' (*Libération*, 26 March 1998). Similarly, in the run-up to the 1998 World Cup, *Le Monde* advocated the inclusion of David Trézéguet 'to light up a lethargic forward line' (29 May). Moreover, when a player is not available, as when Zinedine Zidane was suspended during France 98, his absence is conveyed in now familiar terms: 'the Blues will have to find their way without their guiding light' (*Le Monde*, 20 June).

Zidane, indeed, became a key figure in French football writing in the period under discussion. Media sports texts so often personalise what is, after all, especially in the case of football, a collective effort. He was, therefore, seen as the 'soul' of the team (*Le Monde*, 30 June 1998), 'the successor to Michel Platini' – the stylish artist behind the 'champagne football' of the 1980s (*Le Monde*, 9 June 1998) – and the 'creative genius' on whom 'France is counting' for victory (ibid.).

This desire for French teams to display creativity, style and flair has been noted by numerous commentators[6] and this basic need is reinforced, if not fuelled, by sports media discourse. Previewing the 1998 World Cup finals, *Le Monde* affirmed that 'It will be up to the French' rather than their opponents 'to be ... audacious' (27 February) because this is the French tradition; supporters expect it. In this respect, *Libération*, too, is revealing:

> above all, the French supporter wants to see a fine game ... the French want their football to be like an ambassador, presenting an appealing image of their country which is otherwise bogged down by practical issues that, deep down, hardly interest them (9 July).

It follows that a perceived absence of style in a French national team quickly becomes a subject of some concern and French teams are, indeed, swiftly castigated if it appears that they are playing without their supposedly typical flair: 'France flops in the last match of the year', blares out a *Le Monde* headline (14 November 1997), and yet the friendly against Scotland, which is the subject of the article that follows, actually resulted in a French victory (2–1). 'In France', explains *Libération*, 'winning is not enough. In the land of Cyrano [de Bergerac] and Platini, there must also be panache, style and openness' (4 December 1997). This is why 'narrow victories obtained with very little artistry convince no one' (ibid.) and usually end up being qualified as 'pale' or 'dull' (as in *Libération*, 31 October 1997 on a 2–1 win over South Africa). Here, an absence of style is conveyed by vocabulary describing a lack of light while creativity is communicated by just the opposite (see above). Winning in this way, for the French mind, is, then, 'slender consolation' (*Libération*, 13 October 1997). By the same token, defeat can (just about) be tolerated so long as the national team has achieved some glory by going down – not with all guns blazing, which would be the English model (see Chapter 1) – but with style, grace and elegance, which would be the only hallmarks of heroic failure in France. In this respect, the World Cup semi-final defeats at the hands of the former West Germany in 1982 and 1986 have attained the status of legend in French football circles and seem to have brought (almost) as much pleasure as the triumph of winning the 1984 European Championships sandwiched in between.[7]

Such was the context in which France's manager between 1994 and 1998, Aimé Jacquet, had to prepare his team for the 1998 World Cup finals on home soil. Because his teams at the 1996 European Championships and at the Tournoi de France in 1997 did not display the openness and style expected of the nation's footballing élite, Jacquet himself suffered tremendous criticism at the hands of the press. The sports weekly *L'Equipe magazine* caricatured him as 'Aimémé', the coach who believes it is possible to win matches without scoring goals, while its sister publication *L'Equipe*, the most widely read daily paper of any description in France, was totally merciless in its criticisms.[8] Even the more moderate 'quality' dailies under analysis here were also harsh in their evaluation of Jacquet before the World Cup because his teams have 'bored France' and 'charmed no one' (*Le Monde*, 23 June 1997); they are managed by a 'technico-tactician' (*Le Monde*, 22 April 1998) experimenting with 'test tube football' (*Le Monde*, 14 November 1997), which might well avoid defeat but which is ultimately 'mechanical' (ibid.), 'boring and disappointing' (*Le Monde*, 23 June 1997). France's performances in the 1998 World Cup finals, though, forced something of a re-evaluation of the team on the country's football press and public. In this respect, the admirable support of their manager shown by the senior players was probably crucial. Marcel Desailly explained to *Le Monde*

(11 June) that it should be quite acceptable to win World Cup games 1–0, while Laurent Blanc put the case that nobody would thank the team for entertaining if it then went on to lose (ibid.). Similarly, Jacquet's long-serving captain and now France's most capped player Didier Deschamps, who was once quoted as saying 'shutting up shop is not our style' (*Libération*, 18 June 1996), affirmed that winning must be the first priority at France 98 (*Le Monde*, 11 June).

Gradually, France's football journalists came to realise that the accent on stout defence and the avoiding of defeat was not actually incompatible with a degree of style and flair. Early in the competition, *Le Monde* asked the question, 'Has the French team the means to reconcile the need to win with the desire to put on a good show?' (ibid.), which was later answered by its homologue *Libération*: 'the country has found a team which is strong in defence, bold in attack. Aimé Jacquet has duly reconciled the need for a fine display with the taste for winning' (4/5 July). France not only won the World Cup in 1998 but did so by conceding only two goals in open play (fewer than any other team), by scoring 15 (more than any other team) and by beating the favourites, Brazil, 3–0 in the final, not without some style. Jacquet was vindicated and forgiven for reminding the French people about the virtues of discipline, team spirit and hard work.[9]

The second element in the portrayal of France in the newspapers analysed concerns the perceived psychology of the nation itself. Initially, the morale of the French is often qualified as shaky, with French footballers lacking the 'typically German' quality of self-belief (*Le Monde*, 28 June 1996). However, as the national team progressed further and further at the 1998 World Cup finals a re-evaluation of this perception also was forced upon a recalcitrant press.

During the 1996 European Championships *Le Monde*, for instance, was concerned that the French team 'does not really know how far it can go' (14 June) and later ascribed its defeat in the semi-final to its lack of mental strength and will-power (28 June). In French eyes, this 'inability to win at the highest level' (ibid.) was partly a result of fear of failure, which was itself fuelled by memories of previous defeats in crucial matches. A victory over Bulgaria at Euro 96, therefore, was heralded not only as welcome revenge over the side which had prevented France from qualifying for the 1994 World Cup in the United States but also as a victory 'over ourselves, over our own obsessions' (*Le Monde*, 20 June).

Similarly, throughout the build-up to the 1998 World Cup finals, French sports media discourse continued to develop the theme of the fragile French psyche, the low morale liable to crack at decisive moments, a nation doubting its own abilities. *Le Monde*, for example, previewing a friendly against Norway, spoke of 'doubt, this evil which so often gnaws away inside the minds of French forwards' (25 February), while *Libération* reported a friendly defeat in Russia largely in terms of 'fear'; the mistakes made in the game were, apparently, the result of 'fear of doing badly three months before the World Cup' (26 March). Again, the French team played a friendly in Finland immediately before the World Cup finals which was designed, according to *Le Monde*, not to finalise tactics and formations but rather 'to calm the nerves of [the] players' (9 June). Despite the 1–0 victory, though, the newspaper was adamant that this triumph 'does not seem to have quelled the tension existing within the squad' (ibid.).

Even after France had made, by any standards, a successful start to the 1998 World Cup finals, beating South Africa 3–0 and Saudi Arabia 4–0, the spectre of doubt continued to moan and groan, haunting the sports pages of the national press. In this respect, some of the players were as culpable as the journalists. The central defender Marcel Desailly noted during the first phase of the tournament that 'we have more reason to fear ourselves than our opponents' (*Le Monde*, 18 June). Similarly, the narrow victory over Paraguay in the first match of the knock out phase (achieved thanks to the World Cup's first ever 'golden goal', scored by Laurent Blanc) was reported in now familiar vein: '[France] are still alive. But they were afraid. Afraid of themselves, of their failure in front of goal, of their inability to break through the opponents' defence' (*Le Monde*, 30 June). *Libération*, too, asserted that it could detect in the Paraguay game 'a collective tension visible *right from the kick off*' (29 June; our italics) and bemoaned the absence of the suspended Zidane as France now had no playmaker 'to put his foot on the ball and calm the nerves' (ibid.).

By the time the French had reached and won the semi-final, however, a magical transformation seems to have taken place. 'The French team World Cup 1998 version knows nothing at all about fear', trumpeted *Le Monde* (9 July), with *Libération* echoing the sentiment: France can now 'consign to hell that fear of the final hurdle' that has led to her faltering so many times before (9 July). Similarly, after victory in the final over Brazil, *Libération*'s editorial acknowledged that '[manager] Jacquet has forged a team with a winning mentality' (13 July). *Le Monde* agreed: 'this is a great team, so confident of its own ability' (14 July). Is it possible that the press is merely reporting a sudden metamorphosis in the collective psychology of the French team which took place during the semi-final victory over Croatia? Such things are possible, of course, but is it not more likely that, consciously or unconsciously, there is a realisation among French journalists that the stereotype of the suspect French morale is just that, a stereotype based on interpretations of the past which is not necessarily always borne out by reality in the present? Consequently, if previous defeats in major tournament semi-finals (Euro 96, Mexico 86, Spain 82, Sweden 58) have, over the years, been attributed to fear and a lack of mental strength leading to a collapse in the face of a more confident opponent (see above for examples from Euro

96) rather than to a combination of failed tactics and misfortune, then passing the semi-final hurdle in 1998 has to be explained by just the opposite trait: France has now acquired self-confidence. In this respect, at least, we are tempted to agree with Dauncey and Hare when they say that 'in the process of winning, the French under the guidance of Aimé Jacquet rewrote some of the rules about ... national sporting stereotypes',[10] which itself implies that national identity can, to an extent, be renegotiated and evolve.

Remarkably, though, old stereotypes can prove very resilient and have considerable powers of survival. In the often discursively incoherent world of football writing, it is quite possible, therefore, for an old stereotype to coexist with the new. Alongside the *Libération* editorial praising France's winning mentality, the match report of the final asks what did France need to do going into the second half 2–0 up? Hold on? Attack? 'But above all, don't start to have doubts now' (13 July). Similarly, *Le Monde*, in the first paragraph of an article reviewing the final can call up a psychologist Jacques Crevoisier to explain how team spirit and confidence lead to success, while asserting, in the last paragraph of the same article, that 'France would not be France without a moment of panic' (14 July), referring to Marcel Desailly's sending off towards the end of the game. This said, however, early analyses of data from the sports media texts generated by Euro 2000 tend to confirm the 'new' image of the French as having rid themselves of their suspect morale. The triumphant French teams of 1998 and 2000 are now seen as confident in battle, as having allied 'much needed mental strength' (*Libération*, 3 July 2000) to their traditional attacking flair and technical abilities. 'Talent and morale' now go hand-in-hand, according to *L'Est Républicain*, and breed 'a culture of success, a fine habit for our footballers to adopt' (3 July 2000). *Le Monde*, too, is unequivocal: 'To the innate technique displayed by most of the players has been added formidable discipline and a winning mentality' (24 June 2000). The French now, apparently, are demonstrating quite simply that 'They are unbeatable' (*Le Parisien*, 3 July 2000).

The next element in the portrayal of France in the football pages of *Le Monde* and *Libération* derives from the country's lengthy military history. It has been argued that France was born out of military conflict in 843 when the Treaty of Verdun ended the civil war in the Empire of the Franks and established the kingdom of France as a separate, sovereign entity.[11] In the thousand or so years following Verdun, France has embroiled itself in military conflict after conflict, to the extent that militarism has to be seen as an integral part of French society. It is not without significance that part of the official celebrations of France's national day (14 July) involves a military parade and that military 'heroes' feature so prominently in the history textbooks of successive French educational systems (for instance, Vercingétorix, the leader of the Celtic resistance against the Roman occupation of Gaul, Charles Martel, the Frank whose army defeated the invading Moors in 732, Joan of Arc, Napoleon and General de Gaulle).[12]

It is not surprising, then, given this socio-historical context, that, as with England (see Ch. 1), the reporting of the French national football team should draw so heavily on military imagery. On the one hand, military metaphors are used in a general sense, in which case they are, partly at least, probably prompted by the physical and adversarial nature of the game of football itself (see the Introduction) while, on the other, culture specific military references are employed which are unique to the French context and opaque to those unfamiliar with French history.

In the first category we have the customary talk of fights, battles and troops. In the run-up to the 1998 World Cup finals, *Libération* bemoans the fact that the French team still lacked 'artillerymen' (12 October 1997), that is, decent strikers and, by the same token, takes comfort in the good form of Stéphane Guivarc'h, which augurs well for France who are 'looking for a gunner' (22 December 1997). Similarly, the French players are qualified as 'the troops', 'valiant soldiers ... called up' to participate in the World Cup (*Libération*, 6 May 1998).

In the second, vastly more interesting category, there are numerous examples of culture-specific military imagery. It must not be forgotten that France was a monarchy for almost ten centuries before the Revolution of 1789 ushered in a relatively more democratic era. The French monarchy and its military history live on in contemporary football writing. For example, previewing the 1998 World Cup final opposing France, the hosts, and Brazil, the favourites, *Le Monde* could not resist the connotations of the site of the final itself: the Stade de France at Saint-Denis. The stadium, described as a 'modern cathedral where crowds gather' on its inauguration stone, is a short distance from the cathedral of Saint-Denis, resting place of the kings of France and sacred place of the French monarchy: ' "Montjoie ... Saint-Denis!" was the battlecry of the king of France's armies. Now it has become that of French football before the final battle ... On Sunday, France awaits the consecration of its kings' (12/13 July). The French players are soldier-kings, consecrated by victory in a football match.

Similarly, the importance of the Revolution in the French mind cannot be overestimated. Suzanne Citron has ably demonstrated how it became a foundation myth for the modern French state and how it still provides ideological reference points for contemporary French society.[13] References to it in the intense atmosphere of France's progress to the final of the 1998 World Cup consequently abound in the press. When France qualified for the final by beating Croatia in the semi-final *Le Monde* announced 'the day of glory has arrived' (10 July) repeating the famous segment from the *Marseillaise*, the Revolutionary war song adopted as the national anthem in 1795. Victory in the final itself prompted a further reference to the familiar mythic events of the Revolution (which was almost obligatory given the publication date)[14] as the fall of Brazil was greeted with the same fervour as the storming of the Bastille (*Le Monde*, 14 July).

Napoleon is, of course, a tragic hero figure who looms large in French military history. The highly educated readership of the newspapers under analysis would be entirely familiar with his exploits and would, no doubt, revel in the portrayal of France's team in Napoleonic terms. When France lost away to Russia in a friendly in March 1998, *Le Monde* drew parallels between this defeat and Napoleon's retreat from Moscow in 1812. The then manager Aimé Jacquet was compared to Napoleon, surprised by the depth of the Russian winter as well as his opponents' tactics and the players were likened to the Emperor's *Grande armée* which entered Russia only to return bedraggled, in ignominious defeat (27 March).

Later, during the 1998 World Cup finals, *Le Monde* further recycled the Napoleonic myth. While preparing for the group game against South Africa, the French team stayed at Mallemort, which happened to be the same town in which Napoleon arrived in 1814 following his escape from imprisonment on Elba and from where he started to march on Paris, rallying soldiers and civilians to his cause. 'With the same desire to conquer and the same doubts' as Napoleon, we are told, Jacquet arrived at Mallemort, a town decked out in 'Come on France' banners as it once had been with those proclaiming 'Long live the Emperor'. Now, as then, the newspaper concludes, 'the country is behind ... its leader' (13 June).

On occasions, the identity of France's opponents appears to be responsible for generating culture-specific military references. At France 98 the French played Saudi Arabia, exotic, 'unknown', 'mysterious' opponents (*Libération*, 18 June), whose Arab identity combined with the prevalence of military metaphors in French football writing to produce the following warning: caution is necessary in this game, France must not prepare like 'legionnaires confident of victory' (ibid.), a reference to the military defeats inflicted on the French Foreign Legion by supposedly inferior Arab forces.

As a final example of the type of military imagery which pervades French football discourse, we note how *Le Monde* during France 98 reports the manager, Jacquet, asking the French people to have confidence in his team: 'This sounds like an appeal, which is quite appropriate because the ... next game will take place on a certain 18 June' (14/15 June). This reference, full of military and cultural resonances, is quite baffling to a reader without a detailed knowledge of French history. It was on 18 June 1940 that General de Gaulle broadcast a radio appeal from the offices of the BBC in London to the French people, urging them to carry on fighting and to resist the invading German forces. The war is not over, de Gaulle said, hope must not disappear, the flame of resistance must not and will not go out. This appeal is now part of the mythology of the French nation and is often invoked, as here in a football context, as a patriotic rallying cry, a summary of the French people's solidarity in adversity as well as their commitment to resist oppression and fight for ultimate victory.

The fourth and final element in the construction of French national identity concerns an issue fundamental to any understanding of contemporary France: ethnicity. The presence in the national team of players from France's ethnic minorities is by no means a new phenomenon, stretching back through Platini, Fernandez and Tigana of the mid 1980s, to Kopa in the 1950s and beyond.[15] In the period under review here, however, the issue took on a significance never seen before because of the inclusion in the squad not just of (white) Breton and Basque Frenchmen (such as Guivarc'h and Lizarazu) but also of so many players from France's most disaffected ethnic minority groups: black African-Caribbeans and second-generation North Africans or *beurs* (such as Desailly, Karembeu, Thuram and Zidane).

During the 1996 European Championships, for instance, the extreme right-wing politician Jean-Marie Le Pen criticised the 'racial' composition of the French team as artificial and castigated some of its 'foreign' members for not wanting, nor even knowing, how to sing the national anthem (*Le Monde*, 25 June). Christian Karembeu, one of the players implicitly attacked in this manner, inadvertently added fuel to the fire of the debate in an interview given to the Spanish press following his transfer to Real Madrid. His comments about his Kanak identity and pride in his New Caledonian origins were misinterpreted (wilfully in some quarters?) as a statement that he did not feel French at all and the player had subsequently to explain in a lengthy piece in *Le Monde* that his sentiments were not incompatible with 'wearing with pride the French national team shirt' (21 January 1998).

The tensions surrounding the loyalty to France of footballers from its ethnic minorities as reported in the 'quality' daily press connect, of course, with wider, unresolved social and political problems which go to the heart of the issues of 'race', identity and ethnicity. On balance, though, the majority of commentators (whether politicians, academics, diplomats or journalists) view the inclusion of ethnic minority players in the national team as a positive development. Bernard Stasi, for instance, affirmed that 'When one looks at the French football team, one really sees before one's eyes the whole of France in all its richness and diversity',[16] while Patrick Mignon, with remarkable prescience some months before France 98, noted that 'it would perhaps not be so bad to win the World Cup, especially with players called Zidane, Karembeu, Thuram'.[17] Daniel Bernard, the French Ambassador to the United Kingdom, duly picked up the theme after the triumphant end to the competition and was quite overflowing in his summary:

The make-up of France's World Champion team, a mosaic of players of different races and religions from a huge variety of backgrounds, some far from metropolitan France, but all wearing the same blue, white and red strip of their country, is more than just a symbol: it is a source of hope, of promise for the future. *Les Tricolores* – second-generation North Africans, Basques, Arabs, Kanaks, Africans, West Indians and natives of Normandy – perfectly illustrate the multifaceted unity of the France of today and tomorrow.[18]

Similar ideas abounded in the print media during France 98. Indeed, immediately after France's team of *blacks, blancs, beurs*[19] won the World Cup, *Le Monde* and *Libération* alike treated their readers to a deluge of largely utopian moralising on the subject. The mediation of the national team's success elevated it to the status of exemplum, a symbol dispensing invaluable instruction in the lessons to be learnt from history, morality and politics. France's footballers, therefore, incarnate 'the French concept of a nation: a country built on immigration' (*Libération*, 10 June); 'the French people are discovering, in the faces of their team, that they have become a mixed race Republic, that this works, that we can all love one another, and that we can win' (*Libération*, 10 July). Morally, this French model, 'visibly based on universality' (ibid.) is seen as superior (especially to the ethnically-based German concept of *jus sanguinis*) because this 'multicolour team [is] a mirror of the mosaic that is France' (ibid.), a personification of 'the ideal of the French melting pot' (ibid.), which, by virtue of its having 'virtually no equal anywhere in Europe' (*Libération*, 10 June), is viewed as a singularly positive defining feature of French identity. Politically, it is worth noting with Mignon[20] that it is not solely multiculturalism that is being celebrated here by sports media discourse in France but also the French Republican notion of integration. Thus the French team was represented as an 'example of the success of integration' (*Libération*, 10 July) and Zinedine Zidane, the player of North African descent so often mediated as single-handedly personifying his team's qualities (see above), became a human summary of the new, harmoniously pluralistic France and was, above all, 'an icon of integration' (ibid.).

As Coelho notes, 'It is fascinating, even though sometimes frightening, how a football team's performance gains vast and complex social signification and symbolism which overtake the simple outcome of a sporting competition'[21] and the success of France's 'Blues of all colours' (*Libération*, 10 June 1998) certainly seems to have struck a chord with the French 'quality' press. Most of the reporting of this key issue is, though, influenced by the euphoria surrounding France's first-ever World Cup final victory and tends, as we have seen, towards a stereotypical and utopian portrait of the imagined unity of an integrated Republican society. In this respect, print media discourse on football in France would seem to operate with an ideological function: to promote a consensus around a shared image of the nation based on the traditional French concept of creating unity from diversity. Mignon, taking a rather more objective stance than that adopted by the press, makes a vital point in this respect when he reminds us, though, that 'The celebrations of 12 July were indeed symbols of a call for unity because that unity is far from real.'[22] Without minimising the validity of Mignon's point at all, however, it is possible that the highly loaded symbolic success of the *blacks, blancs, beurs* played not a small part in the beginning of a change of attitude in France and further contributed to the discrediting of extreme right-wing ideas. Sonntag, writing before the 1998 World Cup, had already postulated that a French national team, the faithful reflection of its country's immigration policy and ethnic diversity, taking pride in its multicultural make-up, would place populist racism in an awkward position[23] and in January 1999, the far-right Front national split into two new political groupings, the Front national pour l'unité française (under Jean-Marie Le Pen) and the Front national-Mouvement national (under Bruno Mégret). It would be quite fanciful to suggest that the disarray of the extreme right could be attributed solely to the success of the 'multiracial' national football team since the political and personal tensions leading to the schism had been present for some time. However, it is not without significance either that the extreme right should be forced to re-evaluate its ideas and structures at a time when the potential for success of a 'multiracial' society had been ably demonstrated by football and somewhat extravagantly reported by French football writing.

We have seen, then, that football writing in France's 'quality' daily press does much more than explain the game's technicalities when covering the national team. It also feeds the national imagination in a variety of ways. The football writing studied serves to recycle myths from French military history and, thereby, further reinforces an ideological consensus around the concept of the nation defined by Renan as the memories of the (supposedly) great things we have done together.[24] Next, in its exuberant coverage of the issue of ethnicity, the French press also presents football as an idealised metaphor for French society. France's team is represented as a way for people of diverse origins to live and work harmoniously together in pursuit of a common aim. Finally, the texts analysed communicate ideas about essentialist French national identity. Style and flair are still felt to be vital and non-negotiable elements of 'Frenchness', although there is now a realisation that creativity is not incompatible with the discipline and hard work necessary for success at the highest level. Similarly, the old image of suspect French morale has given way to a portrayal of the French acquiring a 'new' confidence and mental strength. In this respect, at least, the picture of national identity painted has proved to be dynamic rather than static and, above all, demonstrates that it is possible for France to have style and win.

Une et indivisible:
Regional Diversity in a Unitary State

France is one of Europe's oldest countries. Its history as a sovereign state dates back to the ninth century when the kingdom of France was established following the division of the European empire ruled by the Franks. Over the centuries, the country's frontiers have expanded (and contracted) before reaching the present borders which encompass a territory of over 550,000 sq. km and which make France the largest state in Europe. Politically, France is defined in article 1 of its present constitution as 'une République indivisible', that is, it is a unitary state which may be contrasted with the federal or devolved structures of some of its closest European neighbours (such as Germany, Great Britain and Spain). However, because of its geopolitical dimensions and historical development, France displays considerable regional diversity within its borders. Regional diversity is not only admitted, it is increasingly positively celebrated in so far as it is not perceived as a threat to the unity of the nation. Guy Michaud (Emeritus Professor at the University of Paris X) and Alain Kimmel (Professor at the Centre international d'études pédagogiques) reflect this official viewpoint in their best-selling introductory textbook *Le Nouveau guide France*, when they describe the country as 'rich and diverse', 'a melting pot of civilisation' the 'essential characteristic of which is diversity'.[1] Indeed, in the last 50 years or so, there has been a growing awareness and recognition in France of the different regional cultures, customs, lifestyles and art which exist within the country's borders. Manifestations of these regional identities take many forms, of course, and range from the everyday use of languages other than French (such as Alsatian) and the study of regional literatures in the education system (such as Occitan at the University of Limoges), to devoted expressions of support for regional sports teams. In this context French football clubs might be felt to reflect notions of regional and local identity which are commonly held by the inhabitants of the locality in question and which serve, therefore, both to define that locality and to differentiate it from others. In particular, the language of French football writing may be seen to play a significant part in this process of fashioning and perpetuating clearly defined regional and local identities.

Duke and one of the present authors have explored the concept of a football club being regarded as a regional ambassador[2] and this model may, to an extent, be applied to France. According to this concept, a region's most successful club is seen as representative not only of the city in which it is based but also of its entire region, whether the region is defined in historical terms or in more modern, politico-administrative ones. As we shall see in more detail later, the success of Lens in winning the 1997/98 Division 1 championship (and narrowly missing a league and cup double) was regarded not just as a success for the town itself but for the whole Nord-Pas-de-Calais region. Furthermore, the notion of regional ambassador can have added pertinence in France because the evolution of top-flight football there has led to a unique situation. Most of France's principal population centres can boast a top-flight team, meaning that football, unlike rugby or basketball, is played at high levels and watched by relatively large numbers throughout the nation (over 8.25 million spectator-entries to Division 1 and 2 matches in 1998/99); however, with the exception of Paris, no French town or city currently has more than one club in the top two divisions, with the result that some French clubs are the only focus of support for an entire region. For example, Bordeaux's nearest rivals, Niort, Toulouse and Nantes are approximately 165, 215 and 275 km away, respectively, in different politico-administrative areas, which effectively confers on Bordeaux the status of representative and ambassador for the whole of the Aquitaine region. Indeed, the importance of manifesting and thereby appealing to a sense of regional identity is indicated in France by the relatively large number of professional football clubs, especially when compared with England or Spain, that include references in their full name not just to the town or city in which they are located but also to their wider geographical location. By way of example, the following might be cited: FC Nantes *Atlantique*, CS Sedan *Ardennes*, ES Troyes *Aube*, Montpellier *Hérault* SC, FC *Girondins* de Bordeaux (from the Gironde), *La Berrichonne* de Châteauroux (from Berry), AS Nancy *Lorraine* and AS Beauvais *Oise* (our italics; the list is by no means exhaustive).

Moreover, the strong sense of common identity generated between clubs and the locality in which they operate is itself further reinforced by the role played by local political authorities in French football. Football in France has a public service mission and the considerable involvement of local authorities derives naturally from this ethos. The stadiums – Auxerre's excepted – are owned by local councils and local authorities have traditionally given the clubs large sums of money in the form of subsidies. The Pasqua law of 1996 intended to end such subsidies by 1999, in line with European directives prompting some clubs to begin reducing the proportion of their income deriving from this source. Olympique Lyonnais, for example, saw local authority funding drop in the ten years from 1989 to 1999 from 21 per cent of its budget to only 3 per cent.[3] However, the Jospin administration which took office in 1997 extended the deadline for the abolition of subsidies pending the campaign led by its sports minister Marie-George Buffet to persuade the European Union that sport is not an industry like any other and that it should, therefore, still be allowed to receive support from public money. Consequently, in many cases financial support for clubs from local authorities remains considerable, typically amounting to as much as 15 per cent of a club's income. In the season under consideration, for instance, Nantes received Fr8.7 million (approximately £0.9 million) in local government aid and Paris Saint-Germain was subsidised by the City of Paris to the tune of Fr35 million (£3.7 million), that is, 10 per cent of its budgeted income (*Libération*, 14 September 1997). The traditional and substantial involvement of local authorities in football, then, has served further to strengthen the notions of place, community and locality which are significant features in the identity of a French football club[4] and, most importantly from our point of view, these features are reflected by football writing in a variety of ways.

First, such perceptions are reinforced by a simple discursive technique which, reflecting the importance placed by French football clubs on their symbolic, emotional and political links with their region of origin, describes the clubs in terms of the locality in which they are based. Thus Auxerre is frequently qualified as 'the Burgundy team' (as in *Libération*, 20 April 1998), Guingamp as 'the Bretons' (*Libération*, 13 April 1998), Metz as 'the Lorrainers' (*Libération*, 19 April 1998) or Bastia as 'the Corsicans' (*Libération*, 27 April 1998). Football teams, then, may be read as an expression of place, they symbolise a territory the real or imagined values of which they are felt to convey and, as Ravenel notes, in this sense they contribute to the reinforcement, perpetuation, even construction of local identities.[5]

The simple identification of a club with its region of origin is, however, not by any means the only mechanism at work in the print media's construction of French local identities. The vocabulary and imagery employed serve to paint pictures of cities and regions which are generally instantly recognisable and self-perpetuating in that they connect with widely held views in French culture at large. Moreover, these pictures are historically quite long-standing. Wahl has discovered that the notion of distinct regional identities was already being applied in journalists' descriptions of football at the turn of the twentieth century. He quotes an article from *Sporting*, for example, which qualified the style of play of teams from the south of France as 'quick, but a little disorganised' (22 June 1917) and states that in his studies of the archives of the early sporting press, such as *La Vie au grand air* and *Le Miroir des sports*, there are recurring images of 'the strong northern lads, the quicksilver southerners, the rugged Bretons'.[6] As we shall see, contemporary print media discourse is, indeed, founded on such rather basic appreciations of French identities, but, more interestingly, it also goes on to extend and develop them in more specific ways. Let us examine in some detail how match reports and related articles in *Le Monde* and *Libération* (re)generate the imagined identities of a selection of French cities and regions, beginning with the 1998 Division 1 title winners, Lens.

Lens is, even by French standards, a relatively small town (population 35,000) situated in the Nord-Pas-de-Calais region. Historically, the region's economy has been dominated by industry and, until the cessation of activities in 1990, by coal mining. Founded on this industrial and mining heritage, the reputation of the population of north-eastern France is that of an industrious, hard-working, down to earth people: 'Like all northerners, [they] will not admit to being beaten and are banking on their energy and their sense of solidarity to breathe new life into their region'.[7] It is interesting to see how these stereotypical traits are applied by the print media to Lens, the football club, which thereby becomes a vehicle for the transmission of the traditional imagery surrounding the Nord-Pas-de-Calais. Racing Club de Lens was founded in 1905 and admitted to the professional ranks in 1934 with the support of the Société des mines which helped to finance the building of the Félix-Bollaert Stadium between two coal seams alongside the Paris to Dunkirk railway line.[8] The historical link with the mines, which is but one aspect of the club's development, is a regular motif in football writing on RC Lens. On the eve of winning the championship in 1998, Lens featured on both the front page and in the editorial of *Libération*. The Lens region, we are told, is 'enthusiastic and proud of its mining traditions' (10 May) and its football team has 'the merit of reminding us how human values can survive ... The mining spirit, shot through with courage and solidarity ... lives on in this astonishing club' (ibid.). Similarly, Marcel Barrois, a local trade union leader, was called up to reinforce the portrait: 'the mentality of the miners still lives on in the stands ... Going to a match here is one of the ways of passing on our heritage' (ibid.). Indeed, in addition to sporting scarves and replica shirts, as do their homologues across Europe, many Lens fans highlight the distinctiveness of their heritage and identity by attending matches wearing miners' helmets.

With the decline of certain industries in the 1980s, and especially the closure of the last coal mines in 1990, the Lens region was thrown into recession with its consequences of increased poverty and unemployment. The local football club, already mediated as an extension of the region's structures and values, came to be portrayed as the symbol of a necessary rebirth, a sign that the devastated region could make a comeback. Thus when it seemed that Lens were on course for the league and cup double, *Le Monde* affirmed 'the wounds of a region are about to be soothed' (14 April 1998) and when they were on the point of winning the title, *Libération* reported that 'RC Lens carries the hopes of a region severely hit by recession ... an entire region devastated by unemployment ... is hoping for victory' (10 May 1998). By duly winning the championship, 'the standard bearer of an entire region's hopes' (*Le Monde*, 12 May 1998) enabled local people 'to forget the succession of hardships and humiliations endured for such a long time' (ibid.). The mayor of Lens André Delélis echoed the sentiments by describing this triumph in a sporting competition as 'revenge for a whole region cruelly struck down by recession and ignored by the media and the powers that be' (ibid.).

As well as images deriving from the Lens region's socio-economic past, the reputed qualities of its people are also communicated by football writing. The former RC Lens manager and native of the region Daniel Leclercq recognised in *Le Monde* that 'this team has always been labelled as hard-working and willing' (9 May 1998), in direct contrast to Marseille, where he spent part of his playing career, which is 'more geared up to song and dance than hard work' (ibid.). The theme is also picked up by *Libération* when it speaks of 'valiant RC Lens personifying the work ethic of an entire region' (10 June 1998) and in descriptions in both newspapers of the style of play of Lens. Football here, according to *Le Monde*, 'is dedicated to attack, based on commitment and willingness ... traditions that are not going to be betrayed' by manager Leclercq (28 April 1998). Similarly, *Libération* can speak of 'heady football, dedicated to all out attack to which no other team can lay claim' (27 April 1998). In focusing on the qualities of commitment, courage and hard work when covering Lens, the French press reflect the principal elements found in the self-definition of the local people: as Bromberger discovered in his empirical fieldwork, the single word used most by Lens supporters to describe their own team is, indeed, 'courageous'.[9]

If the Lens region is regarded in footballing and socio-economic terms (the two cannot be dissociated) as one of the most willing, committed and industrious in France,[10] then the feelings aroused by Corsica are usually quite different. The Mediterranean island is known to be picturesque but is also, apparently, reputed for its history of criminal activity and its population of 'tough', 'proud' people 'given to violence'.[11] These myths will, in part, be founded on the history of the island which became French in 1768. A significant percentage of the population retains separatist ambitions and latterly this has been expressed in terrorist campaigns both on the island itself and on the mainland. The suspicion and even fear with which many in mainland France view Corsica is reinforced by football writing in subtle and not so subtle ways. In particular, coverage of the island's main club, Sporting Club de Bastia, is used to recycle mainland perceptions of the imagined identity of Corsica.

According to Ravenel, Corsica is already a special case in the football world in that it has more in common with other European islands than with the rest of French football, which is largely based on urban population centres. Bastia slots into the same category, then, as Tenerife, Maritimo Funchal and Cagliari with its strongly partisan crowd, spartan stadium and facilities and poor reputation in safety and security measures.[12] Corsican difference is reflected by print media discourse on football. The words 'hot' and 'passionate' frequently pepper articles devoted to Bastia while the unwelcoming (and almost bestial?) nature of the local crowd is conveyed by the Furiani stadium being referred to as a 'den' (as in *Libération*, 16 September 1997). Similarly, Corsican football is usually represented, in the image of the island on which it is played, as aggressive, rough and ready. When Paris Saint-Germain (PSG) beat Bastia 2–0 in a league game in the season under consideration, they were said to have escaped 'the ambush' set for them by the Corsicans (*Libération*, 14 September 1997). Again, the same newspaper affirmed that, in order to beat Benfica in a UEFA Cup tie, 'the Corsicans will have to count on their roughness to bring down an opponent of this stature' (16 September 1997); in the next round against Steaua Bucarest, we learn that Bastia 'showed its usual face, bustling energy to spare and that innate sense of solidarity passed on from generation to generation' (*Libération*, 6 November 1997). In this connection, we would agree with Gritti, who notes that the stereotypical primitivism of Corsica is a pre-existing myth in circulation outside the world of sport which media discourse is all too ready to latch on to, to recycle and – supposedly – to present further evidence of.[13]

Finally, the issue of ethnicity also plays a part in the Corsican question. Constitutionally, Corsica is a region within the unitary and indivisible state of France and Corsicans cannot, therefore, be seen as a nation or a people in their own right. Indeed, the term 'Corsican people' was struck out of a proposed legislative text in 1991 by the Constitutional Council (France's supreme court) for this very reason.[14] However, more recently Prime Minister Jospin acknowledged the existence of the Corsican people on national television (TF1 4 May 1999) and in 2000 his administration put forward a proposal to reform French local government so that Corsica could benefit from a different system to the 21 other regions in that it would be governed by a single elected assembly with certain legislative powers independent of Paris. In this respect, France's politicians had finally caught up with what has certainly been prevalent in the popular imagination for some time: that there is a distinct Corsican identity. In football circles, then, it has not been unusual to hear pleas for clubs on the island to adopt a Corsican-only selection policy when recruiting players,[15] similar to the Basque-only policy followed by Athletic Bilbao (see Chapter 8). These pleas are still fuelled by nostalgic memories of the one and only time that a Corsican 'national' team played a match. In 1967, France's new coach Just Fontaine invited the football journalist Victor Sinet to select a team of

Corsicans against whom the national team could play a friendly. The match went ahead on 27 February in Marseille and a crowd of some 25,000 saw the Corsicans win 2–0. Sinet, Corsican coach for the day, apparently motivated his players before the game by telling them: 'What really matters is you all have the same blood flowing through your veins. You've been chosen because of your legendary qualities, your temperament, your ambition and your pride.'[16] Finally, it is not unusual to witness descriptions of Corsican difference in French football writing which reinforce in less than subtle ways the supposed ethnic distinctiveness highlighted by Sinet: when Giuly was transferred to Olympique Lyonnais, for instance, he was described in unflattering terms as 'the little Corsican ... Lyon's new imp' (*Le Monde*, 23 October 1997) which might be felt to border on the racist in that it draws attention in pejorative fashion to the ethnicity of a footballer with no valid reason for so doing.

To consider Lyon itself, the links between this city and its principal football club, Olympique Lyonnais (OL), founded in 1950, are often stressed in the language used by the print media. Just as Liverpool players in England are frequently qualified as Merseysiders, so, too, are Lyon's footballers described in terms of the main river running through their city, the Rhône, and are called, in French, *rhodaniens* (for instance, *Libération*, 13 April 1998). Moreover, the highly successful youth policy adopted by OL in the late 1990s[17] is reflected in print media discourse by the use of the word *gônes* to describe Lyon's young players, *gônes* being Lyon street slang for a young person or kid (as in *Le Monde*, 6 November 1997). Furthermore, images of Lyon are still informed by the history of the city itself and, in particular, by its Gallo-Roman heritage. For one writer, echoing French perceptions in general, it is 'the city with 20 centuries of history and architecture'.[18] Lyon was the capital city of Roman Gaul and the hub of its economy and transport network. Connections with Roman times are frequently made in a football context. One of Lyon's supporters' clubs, for instance, demonstrates its allegiance by displaying banners on match days bearing the name Lugdunum, the Latin name of the city when under Roman control.[19] Above all, though, links with the Roman past are kept alive in Lyon visually by OL's ground, the Stade de Gerland, and discursively by media coverage of the stadium. Designed by the architect Tony Garnier in 1926 and now classed as a historic monument, the stadium is built in the classical style and thereby replicates the columns and arches that would have been typical of public buildings in Roman times. Football writing on Lyon continues the Roman theme by, not unsurprisingly, referring to OL's ground as 'an arena' (*Libération*, 27 April 1998), as opposed to Bastia's 'den' (see above) but also extends it into a metaphor for the city itself. Like Lyon apparently, the Gerland stadium is 'stylish' (*Le Monde*, 5 June 1997) but also rather somnolent, 'a sleeping beauty of monumental architecture' (*Libération*, 27

April 1998), to be contrasted with the supposedly more passionate football hotbeds of Saint-Etienne to the west and, to the south, Marseille.

Passion is, indeed, one of the traits most associated with Olympique de Marseille (OM), one of France's oldest, most successful and best supported clubs. OM was founded in 1899, has won ten FA Cups, eight Division 1 titles and the European Champions Cup and regularly attracts more than 45,000 spectators to its Stade-Vélodrome. The football writer Alain Pecheral sides with the local tradition that attributes the 'hot-tempered character of [this] region's people' to the Mistral, the violent wind that blows from the north, while his colleague José Carlin states quite simply that Marseille is 'a city at home with every passion and every excess'.[20] It is not surprising, then, to see these received ideas re-presented in the 'quality' daily press under consideration here. 'Football, Marseille's burning passion' was the headline to one *Libération* article on the club (4 December 1997) which went on to state that 'the passion for football in Marseille flows from many sources and courses through everyone's veins', as well as to affirm that OM's fans are 'passionate and open, often to excess'. Typically, we are told, during matches at the Vélodrome, the crowd 'yell their support at the top of their voices right up to the final whistle' (*Libération*, 9 April 1998). Most importantly from our perspective, OM's fans are shown as being entirely in tune with the character of the city itself, they are 'the exact reflection of their city' (*Libération*, 4 December 1997), while the team they support is also portrayed as manifesting the same qualities in their style of play, which is traditionally reputed to be open, spectacular, explosive:[21] Strasbourg had to contend in one league game, for instance, with 'the Marseille spirit' (*Libération*, 21 November 1997), while other observers speak of 'Marseille frenzy'[22] and OM's 'brilliant, offensive style which *is* Marseille itself'.[23] Fans, team and city are bound together, then, in a discursive triangle with each side purportedly reflecting the same essentialist qualities of the other two. The qualities reported can, however, also be negative. OM's supporters are often qualified by the press as 'fickle' (for example, *Libération*, 8 August 1997) and 'unlike those of Lens, [they] have not always been totally loyal in the past' (*Libération*, 10 May 1998). This trait, too, is felt to be part of a wider Marseille identity in that the club and its fans are typically represented as 'the incarnation of a local identity' (ibid.).

The identity of Marseille in the French mind, though, is not based solely on the stereotypically passionate and volatile nature of its inhabitants. Other elements which feature derive from the city's history, economy and relationship with the rest of France in general and with the capital in particular.

It is claimed that Marseille is France's oldest city, founded as Massalia by the Phocean Greeks in the sixth century BC and these historical origins are frequently exemplified in journalese with references to Marseille as 'the Phocean city' (*Libération*, 4 December 1997) and to OM players as 'the Phoceans' (*Libération*, 21/22 February 1998). From its beginnings, Marseille has been a maritime city and its economy has, therefore, been inextricably linked with the sea. Often, then, when OM's exploits are being reported in the press we find the use of nautical imagery reflecting this feature of the city's development. When OM were beaten 2–0 away at Strasbourg, for example, a *Libération* match report described them as 'beaten, exhausted, shipwrecked, sunk by storms far from their base' (23 November 1997).

Finally, Marseille has the reputation in France of being rebellious and revolutionary and largely defines itself by its opposition to Paris, seen by Marseille as representing a distant, unsympathetic and largely unjust authority. As Pecheral notes: 'Between the southerners who feel neglected and the northerners who accuse them of being paranoid, a chasm of misunderstanding has opened up which is nowhere near to being bridged.'[24] Indeed, the bitter rivalry in the football context between certain sections of OM and Paris Saint-Germain supporters, with its manifestations of mutual hostility, both symbolic, through chants, songs and banners, and real, through acts of violence and aggression, has been well documented.[25] What is more our concern here is to explore the ways in which this rivalry is reflected if not fuelled by sports media discourse and, in this respect, the match reports of the two OM-PSG fixtures of 1997/98 are most revealing. Reporting on OM's 2–1 victory in Paris in the first half of the season, *Le Monde* spoke of 'the *overheated* atmosphere' of the game taking place at the Parc des Princes which was 'full of noise and *anger*' and where '600 Marseille fans *gave as good as they got* from the 43,000 Paris fans whom they made *nervous* by their very presence'. The match itself was '*tense*' and, even though 'time moves on and players come and go', 'the *tradition* of OM-PSG games was respected' in that they '*always* lead to conflictual encounters on the park' (*Le Monde*, 11 November 1997; our italics). The language of the reports of the return fixture in April 1998 is depressingly similar and, therefore, serves further to (re)construct the image of the inimical relationship between Marseille and Paris. PSG are OM's 'execrated opponents' (*Le Monde*, 10 April), while the game itself was described as a 'recurrent duel', a 'confrontation', 'an arm wrestling match' played by '22 men who were fearful but nonetheless ready to slug it out' (*Libération*, 9 April). It is almost as if there is a pre-existing template labelled 'OM vs. PSG equals mutual hostility' which the match reports have to be made to fit to satisfy expectations. What is certain is that the football writing studied does nothing to challenge or even moderate the widely held assumptions about the unfriendly rivalry between France's two biggest cities.

To turn to Paris itself, several facets of the perceived identity of the

nation's capital are explored and effectively regenerated by the print media
coverage of its principal football club Paris Saint-Germain. First, the status
of Paris as France's political capital cannot, of course, be ignored and PSG
are, therefore, frequently referred to as 'the capital's club' (*Le Monde*, 5 May
1998) and its team as 'the players from the capital' (*Libération*, 19 October
1997), which serves as a simple discursive reminder of the predominance of
Paris in French politics. Secondly, for centuries, of course, Paris has been
adorned with prestigious and grandiose monuments reflecting successive
rulers' desires to create a bright, shining, impressive capital to symbolise the
power of the French state (such as the Renaissance royal palace of the
Louvre, Emperor Louis-Napoleon III's *grands boulevards* and President
François Mitterrand's Grande Arche de la Défense) and, more prosaically,
generations of tourists have learnt that Paris is known as the 'City of Light'.
It is interesting to see in football writing this particular imagery of the
shining example of greatness used to communicate PSG's exploits. PSG's
youth team had a good season in 1997/98, for instance, and *Le Monde*
consequently reported that 'Paris's colours are shining bright this year' with
the club as a whole being described as 'a beacon of light in the Paris region'
(3/4 May 1998). Again with this example, we may note the concept of
regional ambassador at work once more. Paris Saint-Germain, we are told,
'flies the flag for a great sporting region (the Ile-de-France)' (*Le Monde*,
26/27 October 1997).

Next, the city of Paris has been likened to a 'sort of theatre, where
everyone acts as if they are on stage and knows that they are being
watched'.[26] The cliché of the (overly) dramatic Parisian will be founded,
partly at least, on the social and cultural importance of the theatre to this city.
Le Monde has repeated the often-made assertion that Paris has more theatres
per inhabitant than any other city in the world (8 May 1996) and, with over
80 major theatres, there are, indeed, probably more theatregoers there than
football spectators. It is fascinating to note how this element of the identity
of Paris resurfaces in print media discourse on 'the capital's club', PSG. At
the start of the season under consideration, for instance, the introduction of
the PSG team to the supporters was described as 'a pleasing curtain raiser to
the season' (*Libération*, 1 August 1997) and PSG's stadium, the Parc des
Princes, as a 'theatre where the unlikeliest dénouements unfold' (*Libération*,
29 August 1997). Similarly, PSG's qualification for the European
Champions League at the expense of Steaua Bucarest in a two-legged
preliminary round was qualified by *Le Monde* as 'tragi-comic' (24 October
1997): PSG were defeated heavily in the first leg away – tragedy – and had,
therefore, to win by at least five goals in the return leg, which they duly did
5–0 – comedy. PSG then went into the Champions League proper and an
encounter with Bayern Munich, believing that they would have 'top billing'
(ibid.), but another heavy defeat (1–5) followed by a narrow victory over

Gothenburg (1–0) provided further proof that 1997/98 would be, in true Parisian style apparently, another 'tragi-comic season' (*Le Monde*, 28 November 1997). By the turn of the year, though, even the references to comedy had disappeared as four consecutive league defeats prompted the headline: 'Football – Paris, what a tragedy', followed by the statement that the latest defeat at the hands of Nantes 'has effectively plunged the capital's club into yet another crisis' (*Libération*, 16 February 1998). The same theme was picked up the following day by *Le Monde* which noted: 'Every winter, PSG plunge into a psychodrama' (17 February 1998). Furthermore, the necessity for Paris to put on a good show was noted by the PSG President Charles Biétry when he explained the reasons for bringing in a new manager Alain Giresse, which had, on the surface at least, little to do with technical considerations and more to do with the image of the club: Giresse would, it was hoped, encourage 'a more spectacular game to charm the supporters' (*Libération*, 5 May; *Le Monde*, 6 May 1998). The myth of the theatrical, dramatic, showy Parisians is, then, recycled as, once again in a French context, a football club is mediated in terms of the salient features of the imagined identity of the city in which it is based.

The pre-eminence of Paris in national life has long been a feature of French society. Clovis, king of the Franks, made Paris his capital city (replacing Lyon) in AD 508 and successive governments, whether led by monarchs, emperors or presidents, have consolidated the city's position by concentrating France's most powerful political, economic and cultural institutions there. As well as dominating politics, the Paris region is today also home to 25 per cent of all of France's industrial workers, 60 per cent of its car workers, 28 per cent of its service sector workers, 60 per cent of its researchers and 30 per cent of its students, all concentrated in a region occupying no more than 2 per cent of the surface area of the country as a whole. According to one observer, for these reasons 'Paris owes it to itself to be exceptional'.[27] Paris Saint-Germain football club, as a representative of the capital and its region, becomes imbued with exceptional qualities in that it is expected to be dominant, to do well and to be, as Paris is to France, a focal point, the centre of the French universe. The former PSG President Michel Denisot recognised these expectations when reviewing the season under consideration: 'PSG is unlike any other club. Everything here is always under scrutiny' (*Le Monde*, 7 April 1998). In similar vein, when the former international Alain Giresse was appointed coach, *Libération* commented that he had left 'the shadows of Toulouse to find himself full in the spotlight at the most overexposed club in France' (5 May 1998). *Le Monde* agreed that this would be 'a Parisian adventure' for Giresse and, despite the fact that he had previously achieved promotion into Division 1 with Toulouse, his job at Paris would, apparently, be in stark contrast to 'the comfort of [his] peaceful life at Toulouse FC' (ibid.). Long-held views of

Paris being a hive of activity, a magnet for the ambitious and the centre of
attention while the provinces are virtually somnolent are, then, reconstructed
in French football writing. Indeed, representations of Paris as the glorious,
progressive centre of civilisation, the *capitale du monde*, were
commonplace in the early nineteenth century and art, literature and, latterly,
film have all since ascribed specific values of magnificence and power to the
French capital. As Fell and Tinker point out, there exists in France a series
of resilient discourses around Paris 'the power and durability of [which] ...
have played pivotal roles in cultural explorations of French identity'.[28] From
our point of view, it has been interesting to observe how these notions also
resonate in sports writing about the world of Parisian football.

However, when Paris Saint-Germain fail to live up to the hyperbole
generated around them, they are castigated in the sports pages of the
newspapers usually on the grounds of arrogance and dilettantism,
highlighting the dark side of the force that is the image of Paris in France:
PSG is 'a club with an oversized ego' (*Libération*, 16 March 1998).
Criticisms such as this reflect the views of many rival supporters whose
hostility towards the Paris club is largely based on the fact that it is too rich,
too proud, just too Parisian.[29] Following successive defeats which sent PSG
crashing to the depths of fifth place in the league, *Libération* was
particularly scathing: the 'annual crises' and 'convulsions' have now led to:

> the feeling that PSG is still not a football club. Born of the (political)
> will that the capital needs a big club (why?), the team renting the Parc
> des Princes has been from the beginning just a shop window, first for
> Chirac then for Canal Plus.[30] PSG has never been able to rally support
> from the public ... Its spectators are, to generalise a little, from show-
> biz, neonazis, journalists and schoolchildren. You can swirl this
> mixture around any which way and there will still be no spirit, no soul,
> no heart. And with no soul, unlike Metz, Lens or Marseille, there is no
> real club ... The whole shop needs reinventing (16 February 1998).

The tenor of the criticism is clear. Paris Saint-Germain, reflecting French
perceptions of Paris itself as 'capricious', 'carefree' and 'frivolous',[31] is
artificial, superficial, arriviste, a group of dilettantes not yet worthy of the
name football club.

To sum up, football clubs in France are mediated by football writing in
the 'quality' daily press under review as emanations of place. They are
(re)presented as an extension of a given territory and, as such, reflect
commonly held perceptions about the qualities, values and identity of a
town, city or even an entire region. Many of the elements of the imagined
identities portrayed are clichés, pre-existing stereotypes which are virtually
substantiated by the 'evidence' provided by the exploits of France's top-

flight football teams or, more precisely, by the narration of those exploits in the sports pages. Ultimately, a vision is communicated of a France rich in its regional diversity, of a nation portrayed as a colourful mosaic ranging from the industrious, renascent Lens to the flamboyance of the ancient city of Marseille, from stylish, classical Lyon to the fiery island of Corsica and, lastly, to the theatrical temperament of the nation's capital, Paris, with its complex and not altogether harmonious relationship with the rest of the country. Discursively, then, the sample of French football writing studied here serves to recycle the world view of the educated élite in which France is celebrated as one nation but 'complex and rich in its diversity'.[32] Just as the national team is mediated as a symbol of the success of France's immigration policies, a metaphor of integration (see Chapter 4), so domestic football is used as a vehicle for portraying the perceived richness and variety of France's geographical and historical heritage.

Ils sont fous ces Romains!
The Other in French Football Writing

'They're crazy these Romans!' Such is the exasperated cry of France's best-known cartoon character Asterix the Gaul, when confronted with the strange, uncivilised and, quite simply, un-Gallic behaviour of the Roman invaders of his country. Asterix first appeared in 1959 in issue number 1 of the weekly magazine *Pilote* before starring in his own albums, published by Dargaud. From 1967 he has been the principal character in numerous full-length, animated films and, in 1989, a theme park devoted to his adventures was opened at Plailly. The social and cultural significance of Asterix and of his bemused attitude to foreigners is great in France, as Larousse indicates: 'The adventures of this little Gallic warrior ... put on full view the French national stereotype.'[1] Bemusement and exasperation, tinged with pity and fascination, when faced with the uncivilised comportment of the significant foreign Other (who has the misfortune of not being French) may, indeed, be felt to be part of this stereotype.[2] It will be interesting in the present chapter, then, to explore the ways in which football writing in *Le Monde* and *Libération*, representatives of the 'quality' daily press, constructs the identities of two of France's closest and most important foreign neighbours, England and Germany, neighbours with whom she has had, to say the least, somewhat problematic diplomatic and political relationships.

Alterity does not concern only the foreigner, of course. In a patriarchy the representation of women is such that they, too, are constructed as the significant Other to the dominant male. Despite making great strides in equal rights and related legislation in the latter part of the twentieth century (right to vote, 1944; equality of the sexes before the law, 1965; legalisation of contraception, 1967; equal pay act, 1972; legalisation of abortion, 1975; sex discrimination in the workplace act, 1983), and despite constituting almost half of the contemporary workforce, women in France have still not been able to break down the barriers and pierce the glass ceiling which prevent the realisation of true equality between the sexes. Women are still grossly underrepresented in senior management posts, in the army and the police force, in politics, in engineering jobs, in science and technology and, of course, in certain historically male-dominated sports such as football. Furthermore, the role of women continues to be represented in a variety of areas, from fiction to journalism, as primarily passive and domestic, caring and nurturing, maternal and sexual. We shall also examine here, then, the mechanisms at work in our sample of French football writing in what might well be seen as the (re)construction and perpetuation of traditional representations of women through football, which is still perceived in France as, in the depressingly predictable words of one television commentator, 'a man's game'.[3]

The image of England represented by the French press articles and match reports analysed is similar in some respects to that observed in England itself (see Chapter 1), especially regarding English players' physical attributes and commitment. The apparent lack of technique in English football is frequently criticised in France, though. For instance, Daniel Jeandupeux, general manager of Caen, regards it as 'incredible' from a French perspective that 'In England ... the crowd get excited by tackles and cheer long, high clearances into the stand ... compared with a French crowd who appreciate technique above all else, a nutmeg, a back heel, a neat one-two.'[4] Similarly, the major biweekly magazine *France Football* recently lamented: 'this lack of individual talent derives from the evolution of the English game, the style of which is now obsolete, and explains why, from Sunderland to Portsmouth, a crunching tackle is almost always preferred to a stylish one-two' (27 June 2000). Images of the English in particular and of the British in general as being somewhat unsophisticated and rudimentary already circulate widely in Europe as a whole. The TMO/INRA survey of Europeans' perceptions of their neighbours introduced above (see Chapter 3) ranked Great Britain only twelfth out of 14 in the category of *attractive people*, thirteenth in those of *likeable/cheerful people* and *quality of life* and bottom in that of *gastronomy*. Clearly such notions are also transmitted by, in this case, French sports media texts reflecting on the plodding English approach to football. However, due acknowledgement is also usually given to the positive side of the English stereotype: apparently England win (sometimes) because of their considerable physical strength, passion and courage, traits which we have already seen lauded by the press in England itself. A victory over Holland during the 1996 European Championships, for instance, came about because 'the Dutch collapsed in the face of English energy' (*Libération*, 20 June). For the French, it is, indeed, English and German teams which personify the virtues of physical and mental strength, energy and sheer power. The Euro 96 semi-final between England and Germany, therefore, was too good an opportunity to miss for the re-presentation of such stereotypes: this was another in a long line of 'Anglo-German football wars' (*Le Monde*, 29 June) in which the Germans resisted 'the searing offensive' and 'brave charges' of their opponents who were full of 'English zeal' (ibid.). The myth of English power is clearly kept intact by such discourse.

Similarly, the reports of England's 0–0 draw with Italy in October 1997 which secured qualification for the following year's World Cup finals also focuses on the physical aspects of the English game. The English defence, led by 'the colossus Campbell', was 'sturdy ... with no grace but made of marble' (*Libération*, 13 October) and, although the English had proved that they could play a tactical game and outwit their shrewd Italian opponents, they did so 'without losing their *traditional* qualities of heart and commitment' (*Le Monde*, 14 October; our italics). At the World Cup itself, these now familiar attributes were frequently foregrounded. Despite being 'as combative as ever' (*Le Monde*, 24 June 1998), England lost a group game against Romania, which the newspaper in question interestingly qualified as 'a victory for technique over physique' (ibid.). Needing to win the following game against Colombia to be sure of progressing to the next phase, England took their opponents 'by the throat' (*Le Monde*, 28/29 June), 'lay siege' to their goal (*Libération*, 27/28 June) and 'opened fire on them' (ibid.). Again, following England's 2–0 victory, *Le Monde* made a comment that says as much about French expectations of what a football match should be as it does about perceptions of the pedestrian but practical English: 'By nature, the English are not poets. This was no fancy work of art here in the Bollaert stadium, but it worked' (28/29 June).

Finally in this respect, as with the coverage in England, it was the France 98 game against Argentina which allowed French journalists fully to develop the myths surrounding English courage and bravery. The English forwards, with their 'natural power' (*Le Monde*, 2 July), 'threw themselves into a frenzied assault on Roa's goal' while the whole team, especially after being reduced to ten following *that* sending off, displayed the 'fighting spirit which inhabits the English' (ibid.). England were, of course, eliminated on penalties but, for the French, this defeat merely served to enhance the image:

> England are out. Long live English football, with its incredible energy, its limitless courage and its apparently indestructible enthusiasm ... they would love to shake off this image of being magnificent losers but it suits them so well ... in the country which invented football and good manners, any setback which may be put down to fate can always be excused, even celebrated (ibid.).

In summary, 'Yes, of course, they were heroic, the English, they always are when they have to fight against adversity and destiny' (*Le Monde*, 7 July).

'English fighting spirit' is praised in France when applied to a sporting contest, but it is also seen as generating a negative and much feared characteristic of many of the England football team's followers. The violent incidents occurring in the crowd at the Italy–England game in 1997 were used as a springboard by the French press to raise once again the spectre of the stereotypical England supporter. *Le Monde*'s match report immediately equated violence with English football by its headline, 'The hooligans have qualified for the 1998 World Cup' (14 October) and by the very first sentence of the report itself: 'There was sweat, blood and tears which, no doubt, Winston Churchill would have appreciated, but there was also beer, litres and litres of beer downed under a burning sun' (ibid.). It is further significant that more space in the report is devoted to the crowd disturbances (six columns) than to the events on the pitch themselves (one and a half columns). The print media discourse employed not only constructs the English as inherently fear-inspiring and aggressive but also represents France as a gentle oasis of civilisation about to be invaded (again) by barbaric neighbours: 'the hooligans must already be thinking about the sun, the beer and the charms of sweet France' (ibid.). It is true that the violent incidents which occurred during the 1998 World Cup finals in which English followers were involved (notably in Marseille) did nothing to counter the image already set up by the French press the previous autumn but it also has to be recognised that, in focusing on the activities of an atypical and unrepresentative minority of English people, the French press itself is partially responsible for the perpetuation of the stereotypical image of the English abroad as brave but aggressive, combative but dangerous, essentially threatening to French civilisation which is, of course, how generations of schoolchildren in France will have seen England portrayed in history text books covering diplomatic relations between the two countries from the Hundred Years War (1337–1453) to Napoleonic times and beyond. It could be argued, then, that the media contribute to the amplification of 'hooliganism'. By exaggerating the import of any disorder, as *Le Monde* does here, a climate of apprehension is generated that might actually intensify the problem the reporting has presumably set out to criticise.[5]

The second element in the portrayal of the English in French football writing derives from the United Kingdom's political status as a monarchy. Frequently the England team is referred to in the French media as 'Her Majesty's players' (*Libération*, 10 June 1996) and English supporters are often described as 'the monarch's subjects' (*Le Monde*, 20 June 1996). Even English 'hooligans' – who, as we have seen, tend to haunt the French mind – get the royal treatment: at the France 98 game against Argentina, we are told, the security forces had to 'eject three rows of Her Majesty's imbeciles' (*Libération*, 1 July). Again, the qualities of English footballers are often conveyed in this vein. The Liverpool striker Michael Owen's emergence as a world-class player at France 98 did not go unnoticed by the French press which promptly dubbed him 'the joy of the Crown' (*Libération*, 15 June)[6] and 'the Kingdom's white knight' (*Libération*, 1 July). Clearly much of this is tongue-in-cheek punning but it does nonetheless demonstrate both the belief in France that England and the English are completely identifiable with 'their' monarchy and, indeed, that the French themselves, despite their recent history, have still not rid themselves of their own fascination for royalty which can now be indulged vicariously by reading about that of other nations. It is interesting to note, though, that, despite the obvious fact that the monarchy is a British institution rather than a solely English phenomenon, royal motifs of the sort which pepper football writing about England are rarely if ever associated by French media discourse with the other three constituent countries of the kingdom. In a sense, this is quite galling for many British observers, given that it sets England apart from the rest of the United Kingdom when actually focusing on one aspect which all four British nations have in common. Furthermore, in other respects, the French regularly prove that they are totally incapable of grasping the simple but real differences between England and Britain and consequently, even in a sporting context, erroneously use the terms 'English' and 'British' as if they were interchangeable. The following extract from *Le Monde*'s preview of the France 98 game against Argentina aptly illustrates the point:

> This is the fourth time the two countries have met in the World Cup with the advantage at present lying with *the British*. In 1962, *the English* knocked the Argentinians out. The 1966 match in *Great Britain* is etched in the memory ... *the British* crowd hurled insults at the Argentinian players. Twenty years later, though, the Argentinians got their revenge over *the English* with the infamous hand of God goal. (30 June; our italics).

Finally, we note in French football writing another set of characteristics which might be considered part of a wider English identity as perceived by the French: psychological inhibition. England is a land of tradition, afraid to step into the modern world, to break with the past, and the England football team personifies this refusal to acknowledge progress given that 'football here is a nostalgia business' (*Le Monde*, 25 June 1996). England is 'tied to its memories' (ibid.) constantly reliving its past glories. This country, apparently, is too bound to tradition to modernise successfully: 'The years and the tournaments come and go, nothing changes in the home of football' (*Le Monde*, 11 June 1996). The English 'put all their heart into respecting traditions which have no more to commend them than does that of high tea' (ibid.). To focus the stereotype even more sharply, the same article contrasts England with Holland, their main group rivals at Euro 96. The Dutch, open-minded, experimental, inventive modernisers, represent 'the continental antithesis of British obsessions' (ibid.). Ironically, England beat Holland 4–1 with a performance prompting the statement that 'the English have got rid of their inhibitions' (*Le Monde*, 20 June). However, the very next sentence in the report qualifies this somewhat adventurous remark with 'Or rather they have clothed their traditions with one or two last minute novelties.' This example illustrates one of the mechanisms prevalent in stereotypification. When the evidence suggests that the old stereotype is currently inaccurate (as here when England played with supposedly un-English style), the evidence itself is manipulated by sports media discourse to fit the preconceived image, even at the risk of setting up contradictions, inconsistencies, or discursive incoherence (here the flair England displayed to beat the Dutch is merely an afterthought, an additional element to the traditional virtues of stout defence and energetic work rate).

By the end of the 1997/98 season, though, there seemed to be an awareness in the French press that England, 'the homeland of football' (*Le Monde*, 17/18 May), was undergoing something of a change. England's reputation in French football circles has tended to be one of arrogance born of insularity and a snobbish refusal to accept innovation, especially from abroad.[7] However, *Le Monde*, at least, saw in the Arsenal side which won the Premiership in 1998 a sign that 'the chauvinistic little world of English football' (ibid.) was evolving. Ignoring the charms of the infamous Arsenal defence (Winterburn, Adams, Bould, Keown, Dixon), and putting the focus more on the midfield and attack which, at times, might contain up to three Frenchmen and two Dutch players, *Le Monde* claimed that Arsenal, led by a French manager, Arsène Wenger – the point could not be lost – were now favouring a type of football which was 'more fluid, more individualistic, more pleasing to watch' than the previous 'rigid, labouring ... physical' system (ibid.). Linking football to broader social and political developments, the newspaper then went on to affirm that 'fashionable' Arsenal, operating in 'the chic London world of today ... symbolise perfectly *Cool Britannia*, the new modernist England, open to the world and dear to the resident of 10 Downing Street' (ibid.).

For all this, old images of England as a land of eccentric tradition persist in the French sports media. During the 1998 World Cup finals, after England's mediocre start (one win, one defeat), *Libération* commented that manager Glenn Hoddle's plans for the next game were 'as clear as a cup of tea clouded by a dollop of milk' (26 June). The bizarre tradition of spoiling perfectly good tea by adding milk to it acts, for the bemused French, as a metaphor for the unfathomable eccentricity of their neighbours to the north.

Turning to those to the east, French perceptions of German identity reflected in football writing are unequivocal and replicate almost exactly, element for element, the stereotype of the German already encountered in the British press (see Chapters 1 and 3). First, the Germans are a strong, powerful but aggressive people. At Euro 96, for instance, they displayed 'tonnes of muscle and determination' (*Le Monde*, 18 June) and a characteristically 'hard-hitting style' (*Libération*, 10 June). It was in the group game against the Czech Republic that these particular traits were brought out by the French press: here the Germans 'flexed their muscles' and caught the 'physically inferior' Czechs in a deadly 'German pincer grip' (ibid.). With the same two teams about to meet again in the final of the tournament, *Le Monde* would go further in reconstructing the stereotype of the warlike German. In its preview of the match it described the German manager as the personification of his team and, by extension, of his nation: 'It is difficult to find anyone more German than Berti Vogts [who] is the incarnation of German football's strength and success' (*Le Monde*, 30 June). Furthermore, the piece from which this extract is taken appears immediately alongside an article on the history of German–Czech diplomatic relations which ostensibly seems out of place on the sports pages. However, by recalling memories of the German invasion of Czechoslovakia in 1939 as well as raising the spectre of German economic imperialism there in the 1990s and by juxtaposing these to a preview of a football match, the article implies that, not only is football an extension of society, an arena into which nations' political and diplomatic relationships are transported but also that the role of the Germans is always to be the aggressor. Having portrayed the Germans as aggressors in the preview, the same newspaper's report of their victory in the final employed familiar imagery to complete the stereotype: 'nothing stopped their march ... when the time came to make the kill, they did not hesitate, relishing their role as assassins' (*Le Monde*, 2 July).

Two years later, the 1998 World Cup finals provided further opportunities for France's football journalists to recycle the image of the belligerent Germans, typically through the use of implicit and explicit military metaphors. Germany's 2–0 victory over the United States, for example, was described in the following terms: 'the Americans *fell*, *victims* of a German team true to itself, formidable by tradition' (*Libération*, 16 June; our italics). Similarly, the defeat of Mexico was attributed to the 'morale' of Germany's 'old warriors' who came back from a goal down like 'an armoured division on the move' (*Le Monde*, 1 July). The German 'tactics' were 'simple and consisted, above all, in imposing their physical strength' on their opponents 'to intimidate' them because, after all, 'the German footballer thinks physically' (*Libération*, 1 July). Apparently, Franz Beckenbauer was the only exception to the rule that German players are tough, physical and aggressive, and it is significant that his 'sophisticated style of play' is qualified as typically 'Latin' (ibid.); in other words, sophistication and refinement cannot be truly German characteristics because, even when displayed by a German, they are Latin qualities. Moreover, the way to beat a German team, apparently (such things are possible) is to confront them with the very qualities they do not possess: imagination, creativity and intelligence. This was why, according to *Libération*, France need not fear meeting Germany in the semi-final of France 98 as France's 'brilliance' (ibid.) in these respects would see them through.

That the media in France should feel the need to reassure French supporters in this way ahead of a projected semi-final meeting with

Germany is highly significant, of course, and has resonances which connect with the recent history of Franco-German relations both on and off the football pitch. The military metaphors and references to the belligerence of the Germans which are so prevalent in many countries' football writing[8] take on a special significance for the French in that they will both derive from and recall the successive German invasions of France in 1870, 1914 and 1940. In 1870, during the Franco-Prussian War, German troops inflicted a speedy and crushing defeat on France after breaking through the front lines at Sedan (and capturing the head of state, the Emperor Louis-Napoléon III). In many respects, the trauma felt by France was translated into the sporting context, as Holt notes in his study of sport and militarism at the turn of the twentieth century:

> National self-image ... may be crucially determined through the perception of the ethnic qualities of rivals; and here the French, despite their geographical size, revealed their inferiority complex in relation to the victors of Sedan whose ever-increasing demographic and economic superiority was the source of profound national anxiety.[9]

The German incursion of 1914, of course, led to four more years of war in which over 1.5 million French people lost their lives and then, in 1940, for the third time in less than 70 years, German troops again invaded France breaking through, as in 1870, at Sedan on the way to a full-scale occupation of the country. It is easy to imagine how these events can colour French perceptions of Germany. It is also interesting from our perspective to witness how such events are transported into the language of sports media discourse which is, therefore, both informed and shaped by them. President Mitterrand and Chancellor Kohl of Germany might well have shaken hands in 1984 on the battlefield of Verdun in northern France, thereby symbolically placing the finishing touches to the process begun in the 1950s to end centuries of enmity between France and Germany, but residual images of the historical Franco-German relationship still linger in French football writing. Newspaper articles about German football teams will, then, as we have seen, be based typically upon a series of premises: the Germans will be physical, intimidating and aggressive; they will inspire fear and will be almost impossible to beat. The 'analysis' is all the more pertinent for the French in that they believe they have direct experience of its validity. In both 1982 and 1986 France was beaten by West Germany in World Cup semi-finals. In the 1982 encounter the German goalkeeper Schumacher's literally bone-crunching challenge on Patrick Battiston has tended to be seen in France not as an isolated aberration but as a metaphor for Germany's aggressive and bullying approach to its more refined, sophisticated French neighbours,[10] while the comprehensive defeat of 1986 merely served, as

Dauncey and Hare note, to strengthen 'the French psychological block over their inability to beat their neighbours and old enemies across the Rhine'.[11] It is this almost pathological obsession with the German Other which both prompted *Libération* to try to allay French fears ahead of the expected semi-final meeting ('don't panic, they're big but we're brilliant; we can win') and which explains the reaction to the fact that the meeting would not take place after all following Germany's elimination in the quarter-finals by Croatia.

On the one hand, the reaction was one of unbridled joy that 'the German giant' had been 'struck down' (*Le Monde*, 7 July) by the Croats (does everyone outside Germany enjoy seeing Germans lose?). On the other, though, there was genuine disappointment that now France had been deprived of its 'destiny', its 'secret mission ... to eliminate Germany' (*Libération*, 6 July). Knocking out the Germans in the semi-final would have been a reward for previous generations of French players and managers who had all tried and failed to beat German teams in the past. Above all, it would have been the opportunity 'to settle some old scores' (*Le Monde*, 7 July), to exact 'revenge' (*Libération*, 6 July) for the defeats of 1982 and 1986. Revenge is a powerful motif in French history, particularly when applied to the Germans. The ideological discourses of politics and militarism in the 1880s and the 1890s were replete with references to the concept of gaining revenge over Germany for the Franco-Prussian War, following which Alsace and Lorraine were annexed by the German Empire.[12] Subsequently, the Great War of 1914–18 was portrayed in France as a mission to put right what once went wrong[13] and retrieve the lost provinces by defeating the old enemy, while the events of 1940 and the succeeding occupation continue to haunt the French mind. These events are rarely referred to explicitly in the French football writing studied (in contrast to the overt Second World War references in the British press, see Ch. 1 and 3); perhaps they are still too close in time or too painful psychologically to be reflected upon in sports writing. However, when *Le Monde* states that, in addition to settling 'some old scores dating back to the bitter defeats of 1982 in Spain and 1986 in Mexico, there were also some complexes to be banished from the mind' (7 July 1998), it might be read as referring to something more than just a football game, summarising as it does the almost desperate desire of the French to prove that they can now match the Germans whom they 'no longer hate ... but ... aren't fond of' either.[14]

Next, confidence and self-assurance are also presented as typical German characteristics by the French match reports and articles analysed. Belief in ultimate victory is, it would seem, something which is 'rooted deeply in the German players' (*Le Monde*, 28 June 1996). Even when playing England, the committed host nation of Euro 96, 'Nothing could shake the German team's confidence ... Not once did a German player tremble' (ibid.). Again, during France 98, the former Olympique de Marseille coach Roland Gransart expounded similar views:

> German teams always display the same characteristics: an unshakeable
> strength of character, discipline, and a belief in their own ability to win
> ... their attitude, never give up, derives from the deep-seated belief that
> they cannot possibly lose. German players follow orders to the letter
> and always work as a team ... the German game is very simple, if a little
> inflexible; it's based on constant movement, determination and
> confidence. (*Libération*, 29 June)

This theme of self-assurance ran throughout France 98 right up to
Germany's defeat in the quarter-finals. 'Eleven Germans never admit to
being beaten on the pitch', trumpeted *Libération* after the Mexico game (30
June); thanks to 'German perseverance, mental strength [and] lack of self-
doubt, they never give up' (*Libération*, 1 July). How, then, could the
elimination as early as the quarter-final be explained? Not by a lack of self-
belief or mental discipline, to be sure, as these have frequently been posited
as immutable German characteristics. No, according to *Le Monde*, the
Germans still believed in themselves, it was simply that being an 'old' team,
their legs could no longer carry them to victory (had they won, of course,
age would have been portrayed as experience and been seen as beneficial).
An explanation was found for the defeat of the invincible Germans, then,
which still allowed the essentialist myth of German self-belief to be
preserved.

Finally, to complete the depiction of Germany in French football writing,
we note the same representation of technical efficiency as was found in
British sports media texts. Previewing the 1996 European Championships
match against Italy, *Libération* (19 June) remarked on the 'rigour' and
'practicality' of the German team which is 'never spectacular but
maddeningly efficient and disciplined' and described one of its number,
Eilts, in mechanical terms as the 'pressure regulator' moving up or down the
field as required to adjust the team's overall balance. To French eyes
conditioned by media representations of flair and style as necessary
accompaniments to sporting endeavour,[15] this 'fine Germanic order' (*Le
Monde*, 21 June 1996) is not all that pleasing æsthetically. Indeed, *Le Monde*
affirmed that in a tournament which was by and large 'dull', the Germans,
being dull themselves, were 'the most appropriate winners' of Euro 96 (2
July). Once again it is worth pointing out that the perception of Germans
held by other nations, in this case the French, is an echo of notions already
contained in the German self-image (see Chapters 1 and 3 for further
examples). Gebauer, for instance, has noted that the dominant values in
Germany, since the late 1970s at least, have been technical efficiency, hard
work and success above all else. In this respect, despite a healthy cynicism
towards it from some sections of the public, the national football team is
often used by politicians and the press as a vector for communicating these

notions. A certain pride is expressed in regarding the German team as yet another celebrated German brand or marque, rather like Mercedes or Porsche, that advertises to the world Germany's capacity for high quality technical achievements.[16]

In terms of imagery in the French press, the metaphors most frequently used to convey German efficiency and reliability are, indeed, mechanical and automotive ones. Germany is often referred to as a 'machine' (as in *Libération*, 29 June, 1 July 1998) which is 'on track', 'running on diesel' (*Libération*, 26 June 1998); when substitutions are made, as against Yugoslavia in a 1998 World Cup game, it is 'to get the machine back on course' (*Libération*, 29 June) the substitutes themselves being implicitly compared, therefore, to spare parts pressed into service to increase efficiency. Similarly, before the quarter-finals, we are informed that 'as predicted, the powerful cars are still in the race. Among the leaders, the German saloon is advancing towards the chequered flag with its usual reliability after having negotiated ... Mexico corner' (*Libération*, 1 July). Lastly, the French press also delighted in the use of another mechanical image which speaks volumes about their perceptions of German identity: Germany is 'a sort of steamroller combining physical power with dogged determination' (ibid.). It is perhaps worth noting, though (because it contrasts with other countries' views, see Chapter 9) that for all their aggressive, dour reputation, the Germans are still regarded as 'a model nation' (*Libération*, 21 June 1996) whose 'discipline ... is to be envied by many' (*Le Monde*, 21/22 June 1998).

Preliminary analysis of the French sports media texts generated by Euro 2000 tends to suggest, however, that the awe in which Germany has traditionally been held in France is on the wane, undoubtedly partly because, having won the World Cup, the French had rid themselves of the tag of poor relations and partly precisely because the German team itself was no longer as successful as it had been in the past. An article in *Libération*, for instance, is worth quoting at some length in this respect:

> Germany won Euro 96 with its usual weapons, force, power and mental strength ... The typical German player at Euro 2000 is big, strong, willing [but] this image also explains the feeling of heaviness and the lack of agility that weighs down the Germans' boots. Cultivating only nerves of steel and muscles of iron ... seems to have reached its natural limits. The way neighbouring countries play football, the Latin teams especially ... gives them the edge in technique, creativity and speed. (20 June 2000)

The article concludes that the German accent on physical strength leaves its teams lacking. Athleticism is no longer enough and only an awareness of the need to develop creativity and flair will allow Germany to become great again. The giant has been knocked off its pedestal and has, therefore, lost some of the respect (and fear?) in which it was traditionally held in France.

Thus far, we have examined the portrayal of two foreign nations in French football writing. Women do not obviously constitute a nation in the conventional sense of the word. It has been noted, however, that given the nature of political institutions and social structures in patriarchies, women might be considered 'a submerged nation within a state'[17] in that they may be perceived as a community with a shared sense of common identity, sentiments and descent, and certainly the study of the representation of women is one of the most pressing of the post-modern era with its accent on questions of gender and identity. How, then, are women portrayed in relation to football in France? As we shall see, the representational strategies used by the French media tend to be traditionalist and do not necessarily reflect accurately the increasingly positive role played by women in this sport as players, administrators and especially as fans.

The number of women officially registered with the French Football Association as players has increased from 2,170 in the 1970/71 season to over 26,000, playing in some 900 clubs in 1997/98.[18] A nationwide league was set up in 1974 and, of course, a French national team competes in friendlies and in international competitions organised by FIFA.[19] Paralleling this growth in the number of females playing football, there has also been an increase in the number of women fans and television viewers, to the extent that women may constitute up to 14 per cent of a typical French league crowd[20] and it is estimated that women accounted for at least 20 per cent of the crowds attending the latter stages of the 1998 World Cup.[21] Similarly, some 40 per cent of television audiences in the host country for France 98 matches were women, with the figure rising to 50 per cent for games such as France–Italy and the France–Brazil final.[22] Moreover, evidence that the interest in football shown by French women is not waning is provided by an IFOP-Télé-Star poll suggesting that 60 per cent of women have watched football on television since the 1998 World Cup.[23]

It is to be noted, however, that women's involvement with football in France is not translated into positive portrayals in French sports media discourse. The women's game is given scant coverage. On occasions, specialist publications such as the monthly *Onze Mondial* sporadically carry features, particularly on major tournaments such as the World Cup, but usually coverage is limited to the bald reporting of results which, in specialist magazines and in 'quality' daily newspapers alike, appear alongside or even after the results from children's leagues. When the national team beat Holland away in April 1999, for instance, the event passed unnoticed by the mainstream press and even *France Football*, the self-styled 'Bible of football', saw fit to record only the result without any report or analysis whatsoever.[24] One of the reasons why the time and space devoted to women in football are minimal is, of course, because there are so few women working in the French media covering the sport. For example, even during France 98 there were no female presenters to be seen on terrestrial or satellite television in France other than on the specially created, temporary satellite channel Superfoot 98.[25] Similarly, as *The Times* reporter Lynne Truss discovered on a visit to the Stade de France where journalists were given a press pack including a range of men's toiletries only, women are simply not expected to be football journalists and are, therefore, not catered for as such.[26]

The marginalisation of women in football continues when their role as fans is reported by the press. Speaking, for example, of the faithful Lens supporters who made the 1,000-mile round trip to support their team in a game at Monaco, *Libération* notes that 'some of them took their wives and children' (9 March 1998): men are fans, women are wives, appendages to be taken by men on a journey to a match. Similarly, during the 1998 World Cup, *Libération* carried a cartoon which says much about male attitudes to women in football. The cartoon shows two men watching a game on television. One, referring to events on the pitch, says, 'So, they're going down like flies now'. His friend, misinterpreting the comment to supposedly comic effect, replies, 'Tell me about it. My wife left after Chile–Cameroon, my daughter gave up during Spain–Bulgaria and my mother's threatening to leave me before the knock-out phase' (29 June 1998). The implication is clear: women's interest in football can be only superficial and ephemeral; it is men who have the desire and conviction to watch football over long periods and who sustain that commitment and interest in what is essentially a male domain. Even when it became clear that women were actually watching the World Cup in large numbers, both on television and at the grounds themselves, print media reporting still insisted on portraying them in stereotypical fashion. Women were, apparently, 'converted' by France 98 and are now football's 'new recruits' who are discovering the pleasures the sport has to offer. What are these pleasures? The sight of the French goalkeeper Fabien Barthez's muscular thighs or a glimpse of David Trézéguet's firm abdomen! Indeed, according to our report, football can 'answer all women's desires [from] the protective arms of Zidane [to] the childlike little Lizarazu'. Women look at players such as Thierry Henry with 'maternal eyes that disapprove when he is tackled from behind' (*Libération*, 10 July 1998). Again, French women watching and attending the final 'did not understand all the subtleties of the game but were able to grasp enough of the basic rules to be able to watch'; they looked admiringly at Zinedine Zidane and Lilian Thuram and played their part in 'keeping up the morale of the troops' (*Libération*, 14 July 1998). Many gender stereotypes are recycled here in a football context. Women watch football not for its own sake nor because of an attachment to a particular team but because they are sexually attracted by the players; the players are not viewed by women as athletes but either as childlike characters who arouse maternal feelings in them or as superior male guardians who will protect them; women are incapable of understanding the game's technicalities because to do so, presumably, requires a reasoning, logical (male) mind; women's role, as in wartime, is to nurture and to support the (male) 'troops' who are fighting on their behalf.

Women, then, cannot be admitted in French media discourse on football on the same terms as men and are consequently firmly contained within a highly conservative view of the role of women in society where they are seen primarily and traditionally as wives, mothers and carers. Nor will such portrayals change so long as outdated attitudes persist which regard football as a solely male preserve. Even as eminent and articulate a figure in the French game as the former national team manager Gérard Houllier, now at Liverpool FC, can unconsciously fall into the trap of presenting women as outsiders, the Others who are 'suddenly' taking an 'interest in *our* sport'.[27]

To conclude, French football writing may be analysed as a site on which discourses of national identity and gender are constructed around the concept of alterity. In French culture the English and the Germans are highly significant Others, at once admired and feared for their reputed qualities. For all their apparent eccentricity and attachment to tradition, the English are portrayed in French sports media discourse as commendable for their courage, commitment and fighting spirit. The last attribute, however, plagues the French mind, all too aware of the occasions both inside and outside the football context on which the aggressive English giant has presented a threat to French civilisation. Similarly, the traditionally perceived qualities of German discipline and efficiency are well regarded in France, but French football writing continually purports to find evidence of German belligerence and aggression and to report these in such a way (largely through military metaphors) that traditional images are recycled and perpetuated of the bullying German ogre, images deriving from French interpretations of politico-diplomatic history. Finally, we have noted examples of the structuring role of sports media discourse in (re)generating positions for men and women in French society. The media's coverage of football is framed in highly gendered terms and, in this respect, stereotypes are simply not transcended by football writing, which continues to imagine a conservative and traditionalist identity for women. Women are portrayed through their involvement with football as passive (their activities as players and administrators are hardly ever mentioned in the French press), as objects/possessions (to be taken to matches by men), as flighty (unable to watch a tournament from start to finish), as unintelligent (incapable of understanding the technicalities of the game), as fulfilling submissive sexual and maternal roles and ultimately as outsiders in 'our' man's game.

PART THREE:
SPAIN

La Furia española:
The Pride and the Passion of Spanish Football

The debates in Spain over the rapidly evolving nature of 'Spanishness' are as vibrant today as they have been at any time during the post-Franco period, and Spanish football writing in the 'quality' daily press reflects some of these complexities. While the following chapter will focus on the ways in which different nations and regions within Spain are portrayed, this chapter explores the key features of notions of Spanish identity as mediated (and, we would argue, constructed) by football writing. The way in which the football press copes with defining and constructing such a nation, particularly during European Championships and World Cup tournaments, offers a perceptive insight into the Spanish psyche which can be fully appreciated only when taking into consideration developments in Spain's recent political history. To what extent is the reality of Spain as a single, indivisible unit acknowledged?

The bloody Civil War (1936–39), which divided the country into the defeated Republicans and victorious Nationalists, left a legacy of a divided state with bitter resentment in most quarters. This was followed by the Franco period (1939–75) in which extreme centralist policies outlawed any demonstrations of (local) nationalism or regionalism. The non-Castilian languages such as Basque, Catalan and Galician were banned in public places. Nations were repressed and suppressed. So the 1978 Constitution, which marked officially the beginning of the transition to democracy and established the creation of 17 regions called *Comunidades Autónomas*, each with negotiable degrees of self-rule, was a huge U-turn, to say the least, in political policy. The historical roots of the conflicts and the cultural legacy of these recent political upheavals have left deeply-engrained effects on the Spanish mentality, especially in terms of the debate over the existence of a 'Spanish' identity.[1]

It is not only recent developments that help explain the portrayal of identities in Spanish football writing. Historically, the notion of a single Spanish identity simply did not exist. Before Isabel of Castile married Fernando of Aragón in 1469, Spain had never been a single, unified kingdom. The alliance between Castile and Aragón was a strong one and gradually the *reyes católicos* (Catholic monarchs), as they were known, conquered the rest of Spain. When the former kingdoms united in the fifteenth and the sixteenth century the rapid success of the unification of

Spain at least partly lay in the high degree of autonomy granted to the regions, although Castile played a dominant role. Although attempts were made in the seventeenth century to enforce a more effective centralisation policy, Philip IV refused to act upon the counsel of his adviser the Conde-Duque de Olivares, who advocated political, administrative and legislative unification.[2] As a result, many local institutions remained intact, especially in the *nacionalidades históricas* (Catalonia, the Basque Country and Galicia). A feeling of 'Spanishness' never really took root. Each former kingdom retained a high sense of collective identity.

Within contemporary football writing there is recognition that Spain lacks simple definition. These complexities are exaggerated still further by the political leanings of the newspapers under examination. Nevertheless, in the two main national newspapers we look at, *ABC* and *El País*, it is agreed that Spain as a whole lacks any clear characteristics which could define its inhabitants as belonging to one nation. Spain needs a more concrete identity, both in terms of its people or 'race' and also in its style of football. The two are, indeed, carefully linked. The stereotypes so often held outside Spain (flamenco dancers, passion, vibrancy and colour) are associated with southern Spain, especially Andalusia, but not with the north. Within Spain a more varied range of stereotypes does exist but they are associated with individual regions rather than with Spain as a nation (see Chapter 8). In footballing terms, it appears that Spain is currently caught between two movements or styles: being typically Spanish (and relying on *la furia,* that is, passion and commitment, physical prowess and courage) and 'progressing' to become more 'European' (more advanced technically). Our evidence illustrates how the press portrays Spain as striving for the latter, and then resorting to the former when all else fails. The extent to which this goal of 'Europeanness' mirrors the aspirations and realities of Spanish society will be discussed later. Several other aspects of Spanish autotypification which recur throughout the data involve inherent contradictions of self-belief and optimism versus self-doubt and pessimism, as well as constant references to *fatalismo* (fatalism, the doctrine that all events are subject to fate and happen by unavoidable necessity), *victimismo* (the notion that Spaniards are always cast as victims and are subject to suffering) and to simple 'bad luck'. Such complex notions of Spanishness are complemented by familiar stereotypes, reinforced by images which pervade football writing – of a Spain that is warm, vibrant and colourful; of images of bullfighting and religion; of military terminology specifically linked with Spanishness. There is, therefore, a certain 'national' image of Spain reflected in the football press and a certain notion of Spanishness mediated. However, these concepts are not static, nor are they simple constructions.

Although we find evidence in the data of the portrayal of Spain as a single nation with a single, albeit complex, national identity, we are not allowed to forget that Spain as a state consists of several nations and regions. The ways in which the press deals with this reality are fascinating. According to León Solís,[3] *El País* displays a *discurso diferencial,* which highlights the differences between nations/regions within Spain, while at the same time acknowledging the status of Spain as a single politico-administrative unit. *ABC*, on the other hand, traditionally favouring more centralist policies, exemplifies the *discurso unitario* which promotes the notion of a single national identity. There is little evidence in the national press of the third category referred to by León Solís, *the discurso disjunctivo*, in which differences between regions are not only acknowledged but there is also a less conciliatory and more potentially divisive assertion that Spain consists of different countries. Evidence of this third style of discourse is more frequent in the regional press. There are many examples of these styles beyond the sports pages of the newspapers analysed here. Similar biases are apparent in the coverage of other 'national' matters such as the language issue, for instance.[4]

Within the context of discussions of the national team, the sports pages of *El País* and *ABC* avoid overtly entering any debate on distinguishing between nations and regions, and this is easy to do given the deliberately neutral status of the term *Comunidades Autónomas* (Autonomous Communities) to describe the units created by the 1978 Constitution, drawn up just three years after Franco's death. But while there is a general reluctance in the sports pages to enter into political debate over the separatist aspirations of certain *Comunidades Autónomas*, there are other, equally absorbing examples of how the press plays a role in the (re)construction of a national identity through the use of different discourse styles.

Within Spanish football writing we see a movement between an *inclusive discourse* (in which the reader is encouraged to feel part of the *Selección* – Spain's national team) and an *exclusive discourse* (in which the writer distances himself – and all the writers in the data are male – from events surrounding the *Selección*). This interplay between discourse styles is perhaps less politically loaded than those styles outlined by León Solís, but it is equally significant in terms of its impact on the readership.

The idea that the inhabitants of any country might all share the notion of a single 'national' identity is highly contentious. In Spain's case, where the politico-administrative entity is clearly made up of several constituent nations, this notion becomes even more abstract. Significantly (and perhaps unsurprisingly), it is recognised in our data that Spain suffers through a *lack* of collective identity. Parallels can be drawn between the Spanish national side and the country it is supposed to represent: 'this national side, traditionally erratic and unpredictable, doesn't even have a defining style or characteristics of its own to pass down over generations' (*El País*, 8 June

1998); 'We are always criticising Spain for not possessing a recognisable and well-defined style of play' (*El País*, 19 June 1998). Javier Clemente, manager of the *Selección* between 1993 and 1998, and renowned for his controversial assertions regarding the national squad and the fickle nature of its fan base, confessed, 'I don't think the national side has ever had a very strong sense of identity as a national team' (*El País Semanal*, 2 June 1996). As football writers search for a successful stereotype they can be proud of, this lack of defining qualities is often quoted as being a shortcoming which has adverse consequences for the Spanish style of play: 'Spain must define its identity ... It needs to know whether it is the bullfighter or the bull' (*ABC*, 12 October 1997); and later, during the 1998 World Cup, Clemente is berated for his alleged preoccupation with the opposition: 'Clemente usually approaches games with the opposition in mind' (*ABC*, 24 June 1998). There is a feeling that he should concentrate his attention on building a much needed Spanish identity rather than becoming 'obsessed with the opponents' (*El País*, 15 June 1998).

Most countries have many symbols of nationhood (such as a national flag), of which football is just one, but Spain has until recently had little truly national culture, therefore the role of football in the creation of a national identity is key. This feature of sport, and of football in particular, is recognised in one article which is worth quoting extensively:

> One of the most effective liturgies which prop up weakening nationalisms is the ritual of football as a spectacle, especially if it is played out as it is today on the high altar of the *global village*, in a cosmopolitan display in which national teams are exhibited and paraded in all their trappings. And on the stage everyone becomes infected with the same patriotic rivalry, which filters through universal screens until it contaminates every household, where the familiar illusion of a mythical national identity is reproduced. This even happens in Spain: the only European state which, for various reasons, failed in its attempts to construct a national identity. Other societies have a whole repertoire of emotive symbols (the flag, the national anthem and other emblems of nationhood), conferred with sacred moral authority, which make them feel proud of their national identity. And for those other societies, football, embodied by their national team, is just one element among others, within the varied panoply of their patriotic culture.
>
> So, as Spain lacks any national culture, the national football team constitutes practically the only symbol (along with other Olympic teams) capable of expressing a common collective identity, filling the inhabitants with emotion by making them feel members of the same collectivity. For this reason football is so important in Spain, since,

without faith in or love for the homeland, only faith in football and love for the national team can bring a feeling of pride in being Spanish. (*El País*, 13 June 1998)

The writer, Enrique Gil Calvo, claims that football in Spain has a special status since Spaniards, unlike other Europeans, have no other symbol of nationhood. In an era of increasing globalisation and media coverage, it is significant that nationalistic displays take on such importance. So, given the significant role of football in Spain as the medium of construction of a national identity, the way in which it is reported and commented upon takes on increased significance. Football is unavoidably political and the discursive practices employed to discuss it should be examined carefully.

There exists a further belief, again alluded to in the above quotation, that the lack of passionate support for the *Selección* is due to the fact that it represents no real community, imagined or otherwise.[5] 'The truth is that we have never been able to get excited about the Spanish national team, despite the efforts of commentators who are hoarse with telling us that we should do' (*El País*, 8 June 1998). The role of the media is astutely recognised here where it is claimed that 'the affirmation of a nationalist tradition depends less on the goals than it does on the commentators who tell us about them' (ibid.). Elsewhere in the same edition of *El País*, readers are reminded that, as 'Vázquez Montalbán point[ed] out, the Spanish League was the key factor in the national cohesion in the Spain of the Autonomies (post-1978). It seems a contradiction that it isn't the national team that unites everyone but the competition in which everyone has to face everyone else which maintains unity' (*El País*, 6 June 1998). During the early phase of the transition to democracy the Spanish Football League allowed players and supporters to be Basque, for example, and proud of it. In contrast to the earlier Franco period, a certain degree of regionalism, or nationalism on the part of the *nacionalidades históricas*, became tolerated and socially acceptable. Again, the lack of unifying power of the *Selección* is assumed and warrants comment. We are constantly reminded in the football press of the fact that the *Selección* represents a country of different nations who do not all live side by side comfortably: 'the *Selección* has never been the main priority in our football, which has an overtly tribal character to it. While in Brazil, Italy, Germany or Argentina the national teams are their number one clubs, this has never been the case in Spain' (*El País*, 13 June 1998). Indeed, it would be very strange if such unity were to exist at the level of the Spanish state in a country which has lived uncomfortably during most of its history as a political unit.

Club football is at the heart of Spaniards' passion for the game. In club football, 'old enemies' confront one another on the football stage. When Real Madrid clash with FC Barcelona it is not just about football: two opposing and conflicting political ideologies meet (see Chapter 8). But when the *Selección* plays 'it is not an epic, there is no drama, it lacks the fundamental element of football, the ingredient that turns it into something more like theatre than like sport in general' (*El País*, 8 June 1998). Spain has no real enemies, hence it is dull and passionless. Some writers go as far as to blame Spain's historical failure to achieve good results in international competitions[6] on the players' lack of interest in the national team: 'There was a lack of conviction in the Spanish team' (*El País*, 21 June 1998), while some claim that footballers are too preoccupied with football at club level, and, more recently, with their own personal situation (ibid.).[7]

Interestingly, it is also mentioned that one of the reasons why Spain fails to capture a passionate audience is simply because of this lack of success of the *Selección* on the field. This notion that Spanish fans support and identify with a team while it is winning but lose interest and even become hostile when that team begins to lose its way becomes a theme that is recurrent in various guises throughout the data. Spanish national identity, then, seems to be portrayed as an artificial construct which is responsible somehow both for the lack of passion and of loyalty among Spanish fans and for the poor results on the pitch. A vicious circle is created.

Some football writing does display, however, a clear attempt to create or define a sense of 'Spanishness', a feeling of common suffering and of mutual support. There is also evidence that the journalists' tools consist at least partially of commonly shared sentiments, a vital ingredient in the construction of a national identity. The discourse surrounding the *Selección* at the start of both the 1996 European Championships and the 1998 World Cup promotes this feeling of unity with a simple yet extremely effective linguistic technique – the employment of the first person plural ('we') when referring to the national team: '*We* can beat Nigeria' (*El País*, 12 June 1998); '*Our* Spanish team is great!' (*El País*, 13 June 1998); '*Our* players need to play well' (*ABC*, 13 June 1998); '*We* will not fail' (*ABC*, 9 June 1996) (our italics). We can term this style of writing *inclusive discourse* since the writer deliberately involves the readership, including them as part of the national set-up. It speaks explicitly as though the team and the readers are united as one.

However, this particular linguistic tool creates images of togetherness which are often superficial and writers commonly revert to an *exclusive discourse* when it suits. As the European Championships and World Cup tournaments progress into the second phases and Spain's performances on the pitch continue to disappoint, the press distances itself from the *Selección*; it no longer employs verbs in the first person plural when making reference to the *Selección*. This is a particularly salient feature of football writing in our data during France 98 in which relations between the press and Clemente soured acutely shortly after the start of the competition, never to recover: '*Clemente's* side played badly' (*El País*, 21 June); 'Spain thought *it* could win this World Cup' (*El País*, 22 June; our italics throughout). This discourse is employed during the latter stages of the international competitions and serves to create semantic space or distance between the readership and the *Selección*. The two are no longer one. The readers become spectators, onlookers and no longer participate in the event. The inclusive discourse of just a few weeks earlier has disappeared.

This does not, however, mean that other methods are not employed which serve to mediate notions of a Spanish identity. Despite the persistent assertions that Spain is a country consisting of diverse nations, and despite the claims that the *Selección* lacks passion and has weak support, there are nonetheless several strong themes which recur throughout the data and suggest that the idea of a Spanish identity is not as alien to the press as they might have us believe on occasion. Indeed, Spanish football writing relies as heavily on concepts of national identity as do the British and the French press. Equally, it assumes a set of shared notions of identity. The single most important concept is that of *la furia española* (literally, Spanish fury). *La furia* is defined as 'anger; courage; fury; rage; violence with which one attacks or fights; name given by the Romans to their goddesses of revenge, corresponding to the Greek Erinias',[8] and the concept of *la furia española* is one with which Spaniards themselves are highly familiar, as well as one which is associated closely today with football. This is a useful shorthand for journalists, who are able to evoke complex emotions and appeal to a large proportion of the population of Spain while alienating few people. The concept is perhaps the nearest the Spanish come to a sense of Spanishness. While associations are historically closest with northern Spain, in particular the Basque Country, recognising the physical prowess and courage of early Basque teams, more Latinate southerners can also identify with the term and do not reject the connotations of passion and commitment. Although arguably Catalans do not relate strongly to the concept, even though its origins are closely identified with Basqueness rather than with Castilian centralism, even they do not object to its connotations.[9]

The style of play of the national team is a crucial ingredient in the self-definition of a nation state and is particularly interesting in the Spanish case. In order for Spain to be judged positively, the *Selección* must possess certain characteristics relating to *la furia*. It must prove its passion and commitment. The ideal national team is summed up in one preview to France 98: Spain's 'dream team has, a priori, an aggressive, attacking and quick style of play. Professional. A combination of muscle and skill. A dream team ... A team that can win anything' (*ABC*, 13 June). Ideally, the *Selección* should combine *furia and* skill: 'It is a team with high aspirations. It has strength. It has skill. It has quality and speed' (ibid.). What Spaniards seem to want, and what the press yearns for, is a *Selección* capable of playing skilful football, with flair and originality, but also with whole-hearted effort, determination and team spirit. During the early pre-match phase, when expectations were being built up by the press, one of the sources of such high optimism clearly lay in the style of football Spain was expected to display: 'It is a totally attacking side ... each player with his own different concept of football ... This is a side with strong possibilities of triumph. Of ultimate triumph' (ibid.).

However, there is nothing worse in the eyes of the media than a Spanish team that fails to display evidence of *la furia*. Before Spain's first game at France 98 the press already berates the national side for not demonstrating the levels of technical ability to which they aspire, but more critically for not displaying the *furia*: 'A new stereotype is being created to substitute that of *la furia*: Spain, it can be said, doesn't have a winning mentality, it's a team that works hard but has no sparkle' (*El País*, 12 June).

References, direct or indirect, to *la furia española* are constantly applied to the *Selección*. Although such references are frequent throughout the data, it is during the later stages of international tournaments when they appear most consistently, in fact, in most articles in one form or another. In the 1998 World Cup Spain's chances of progression to the second phase hung in the balance following an unexpected (according to the Spanish press) defeat by Nigeria and a disappointing draw against Paraguay. At this point, all talk of tactics, team selection and formation was abandoned. Beneath the headline 'The *Selección* appeals to its physical strength' one article stated: 'Spain's players must forget tactics and restore more ancient values such as race, physical strength and courage. The *Selección* wants revenge and nothing is better according to the players than releasing all the rage from within them' (*El País*, 23 June). Spain needed to 'get rid of its impotence and the rage the players are carrying within them' (*ABC*, 19 June). When the going gets tough, Spain resorts to *la furia española*: 'The best tactic is the heart; the Spanish team reclaims the concept of *la furia*' (*El País*, 23 June). There is a general appeal to '*casta*, physical strength, speed, and a will to win' (ibid.). Several of the players themselves, such as Alkorta quoted below, verbalised the same sentiments by advocating the abandonment of the style of play appraised by the Spanish as being 'European' and returning to old Spanish ways: 'Tactics are no use: it's the players who win the game by getting stuck in' (ibid.). When all else fails, therefore, the essential quality defining the Spanish style of play is *la furia*: 'As the tactics have failed, we must rely on passion' (*ABC*, 20 June).

Paradoxically, perhaps, exclusive reliance on *la furia* is not always done with pride. Articles such as those quoted quite clearly herald the Spanish *furia* as epitomising 'Spanishness' by appealing to the amalgam of emotions of pride, passion, courage, fury and even revenge. However, there is an underlying, and occasionally more overt, disappointment that Spain is not able to compete at international level by playing 'the European way'. Spain is conscious that its national team has never enjoyed any real success, and it is also aware that major European triumphs at club level have relied heavily on either foreign players or on players (usually South American) who have been 'nationalised' as Spaniards. It is a continual disappointment to Spaniards that they seem unable to produce skilful footballers with high levels of technical ability.

Following all the appeals to *la furia*, Spain's 6–1 victory over Bulgaria was met with mixed feelings (not least because other results failed to go in Spain's favour; thus Spain was still eliminated from the competition): 'As Spain's goals rained down in the second half, the fury – or was it incompetence? – overcame everyone' (*ABC*, 26 June). Spain's ideal 'dream team' remains the combination of *furia* and more subtle qualities of skill and technique. Relying on *la furia* is seen as reflecting the failure of Spain's progress as a nation. The ideal combination, to blend the (supposedly) traditional Spanish ingredients with more 'European' reliance on skill and technical *savoir-faire*, fails to succeed. Commentators are all too quick to criticise Spain's role as European partners and to underplay its achievements and progress since Spain's integration into the European Union (then the European Economic Community) in 1986. Within a generation, Spain developed rapidly from being a politically ostracised 'outsider' in Europe under Franco to becoming a key European player demonstrating its organisational and economic capabilities by hosting the 1992 Olympics in Barcelona and the Expo 92 exhibition in Seville. During the same period Spain revolutionised the infrastructure of its major cities and its transport networks and became one of the fastest growing economies in Europe.[10] Yet the Spanish press remains reluctant to give credit for such progress. Major international events such as the ones mentioned, rather than provide catalysts for unity and the promotion of a sense of national pride, have been surrounded by controversy in the media over nationalist/regionalist issues such as which flag should fly in the most prominent place and which language(s) should be used for official purposes. So although some successes are recognised, and involvement as a member of the European Union is acknowledged, this has not come accompanied by any truly increased sense of pride in a Spanish identity. However, evidence of a single national identity is still present.

As though a microcosm of Spanish society, the role of the football world strikes a similar chord. Players such as Raúl, and Akorta – representing a generation of determined yet supposedly skilful players – had raised Spanish hopes like never before of being able to produce a team the country could be truly proud of, one which combined the grit and determination expected of a Spanish player with the skill yearned for by so many. Little wonder the bitter disappointment when it all went sadly wrong.

While *la furia española* is probably the single most overtly unifying concept in the football writing in our data, there are other indications that a process is taking place which recognises and either constructs or re-constructs elements of a national identity. This is done via the recurrence of various semantic and linguistic features. There is plenty of evidence that repetition of lexical items within print media texts conveys specific connotations and creates expectations of a 'national' character. This process ensures that the readership shares common ideas concerning the Spanish as a people. There are indeed many features which involve the complex interplay of seemingly contradictory characteristics: the high optimism in the early stages of tournaments versus the fatalistic negativity when things begin to go wrong on the field; the apparent self-belief versus the inevitable and predictable disappointment; the pride in a forward-thinking nation which looks to Europe for its role models versus an inferiority complex which borders on a paranoia that it might be considered backward by outsiders.

Even before Euro 96 began it seems that Spain was preparing for the worst and making excuses for the poor performances expected to follow. The talk was of 'the long season' the players had endured, of their 'physical and mental tiredness' and of their 'fatigue' (*ABC*, 8 June). As a tense nervousness overshadows the pre-match build-up, Clemente refers to his players as 'burnt out' (*ABC*, 9 June). Hardly an inspirational comment from a national manager during the build-up to an important tournament. Clemente, widely quoted by the newspapers, refused to let Spanish hopes of victory build. Reports are littered with talk of 'nerves', 'reservations' and 'fears'. Yet simultaneously, those same newspapers elsewhere seemingly display a staggering level of confidence. Spain are 'the favourites' (ibid.) and the opposition, Bulgaria, is 'a difficult side, but within Spain's reach' (ibid.). Hence we read a curious and simultaneous mixture of pessimism and optimism. The balance between optimism and underlying fatalism is a recurrent feature of football writing throughout international tournaments. It is implicit throughout the data that inevitable failure will be the result of the Spanish efforts, and the up-beat tone of sports media texts produced during the early stages of the tournament serves to try to divert the fatalism.

Many Spaniards acknowledge *fatalismo* as being a national characteristic which has its roots in the Disaster of 1898 when Spain lost the remnants of its empire after almost four years of colonial wars. The effects of this collapse of the Spanish Empire cannot be understated. The political climate in Spain was transformed as criticism of the state of the nation was fired from all quarters. Many questioned the validity of the single nation state as the country's severe decline became a national polemic. Balfour explains how 'the effect of the wars, and to a greater extent of modernisation encouraged the growth of a plurality of identities in more developed parts of

Spain'.[11] Furthermore, a literary movement in the early twentieth century, known as the Generation of 98, played on the failure of the nation to maintain the unity of the colonies. Spain suffered a severe and long-lasting crisis of confidence which, perhaps ironically, was to become part of the *national* psyche.

Hence it is claimed that it has become part of the Spanish mentality to believe in ultimate defeat and this characteristic features strongly in football writing. 'Few teams have such a fatalistic attitude towards the World Cup as Spain' (*El País*, 6 June 1998). It is commented in this same article that, in order for Spain to attain its aspirations, it must change its mentality from its 'traditional pessimism' to a 'culture of winning' (ibid.). A belief in bad luck plays a huge part in this pessimism. The Spanish press portrays and perpetuates the myth (or reality?) of a Spanish *Selección* that suffers from frequent bad luck. 'Spain has suffered serial bad luck which has prevented it from achieving its aims in the World Cup' (ibid.). The article goes on to list every missed scoring opportunity, every injured player, every disallowed goal which resulted in elimination from the tournament. In both the 1996 European Championships and the 1998 World Cup Spain's defeats are put down, in part, to 'bad luck' (*El País*, 14 June and 21 June 1998; *ABC*, 21 June 1998). Even errors are described as 'unlucky' (*El País*, 14 June 1998).

This fatalistic attitude causes the Spanish to suffer a certain inferiority complex which might be further traced as a legacy of Franco times when Spain was used to being excluded from and denigrated by the rest of Europe as a backward country on the periphery of the continent. In the sports pages we see frequent references to 'inferiority complexes' (as in *El País*, 13 June and 22 June 1998). In the football writing during France 98 a similar combination of optimism and fatalism is present, but this time the balance has reversed somewhat. In contrast to the initial fatalism tinged with optimism with which the 1996 European Championships were reported, the France 98 previews were brimming with apparent optimism while only hinting at nerves among the team camp. As soon as Spain qualify for the World Cup finals we read assurances that this time 'Spain will not fail' (*El País*, 22 September 1997), and already attempts commence to build up self-belief and rid the nation of its self-doubters: 'The *Selección* is ready to approach the World Cup without any of Spain's old complexes' (*El País*, 12 October 1997). Interestingly, the article does not explain what the complexes are. The writer seems to expect the readership to know. In this sense, it could be argued that the readers share common experiences, one sign of the existence of a national identity.[12] Similarly, 'Clemente has got rid of the *Selección*'s inferiority complex and belief in bad omens and even the scepticism. No one is even saying "I'll believe it when I see it" any more' (*El País*, 22 September 1997). While apparently claiming that Spain is losing this particularly negative feature of its 'national' character, the fact the comments are made, drawing on a notion of identity implicitly shared by the readers, actually serves to reinforce the stereotype and keep it in the mind of the readership. Denying a characteristic is but one way of reinforcing the belief in its inherent nature. Predictably, later reports prove that the concept has not been exorcised from the Spanish self-definition. Far from it.

Immediately before the 1998 World Cup, then, there is frequent press talk of how the *Selección* is 'good enough to beat anyone' and 'has nothing to fear' (*ABC*, 10 June). Persistent repetition of vocabulary such as 'triumph', 'victory' and 'optimism' conveys a sense of self-confidence. Such is the emphasis on conveying this exaggeratedly strong message that the reader is almost left to wonder whether the optimistic outer voices are hiding the less convinced inner doubts. Whom were the newspapers trying to convince?

Even here amid the optimistic hype, as the first match approaches, the nerves customarily associated with the national team begin to surface. Clemente banned journalists from the team camp and training sessions. This is reported by a disgruntled press as a sign of nerves and weakness under pressure. Following Spain's first game and beyond, there then follow abrupt changes in writing style, the changes, perhaps predictably, largely coinciding with matches involving Spain, but also relating to the relationship between the press and the Spanish training camp. There are two key aspects of reporting during the first phase of the 1998 World Cup. First, there is disillusion with the team's performances which leads to a dissipation of the initial optimism. Secondly, the focus of press discontent centres increasingly on the manager as the pressures on him increased daily. These are, then, gradual processes and are realised again via linguistic techniques and careful choice of lexical items.

After just one match (the defeat by Nigeria), an early setback in the tournament, there is, on the one hand, 'a sadness which we know deep down is fatalistic. Yet we refuse to resign ourselves to something which, time and time again, seems inevitable' (*El País*, 14 June); 'an absurd melancholy' as Spain seems to enjoy wallowing in its defeat (*El País*, 18 June). On the other, there is an attempt to maintain some of the initial optimism. One headline reads: 'The *Selección* reasserts its optimism' (*El País*, 15 June) and 'the players all still believe they are the best' (ibid.). Kiko, for example, is quoted as claiming 'we are highly focused and very optimistic about achieving something important' (ibid.). The defeat is played down as being 'a setback and nothing more' (ibid.). Furthermore, the editor senses that 'there is a feeling that Spain will overcome Paraguay and Bulgaria and will qualify for the quarter finals ...What happened against Nigeria was just a fluke' (ibid.). So despite the huge setback to Spain's chances of progressing to the quarter final of the World Cup, there is still a level of optimism maintained. But the reader is left to feel that it is almost an unfounded optimism – all historical precedents suggest Spain will not recover, and the press remind us of this constantly. At the same time as this shift occurs, the focus of press attention falls increasingly on the manager. The *Selección* is not 'ours' any more, it is Clemente's. Headlines focus on his apparent shortcomings (rather than that of the team even): 'Clemente refuses to admit his mistakes' (*ABC*, 15 June). It is clear on every page that it is Clemente's responsibility to extricate Spain from this difficult situation. Pressures on him increase during the build-up to the second game, against Paraguay, and the words associated with him are loaded: 'Clemente is overwhelmed by the World Cup' (*El País*, 12 June); 'Clemente's methods have created chaos ... and confusion' (*El País*, 13 June); and 'Clemente is getting nervous' (*ABC*, 19 June). Furthermore, there is talk of a 'tense atmosphere that surrounds the Spanish training camp' (a somewhat astute observation given the existent press ban at that time!), the build-up to 'the crucial match', 'this dramatic match', 'this decisive encounter' which 'Spain must win' was fraught with 'anxiety', at this time of 'crisis' (*El País*, 19 June). As the 'huge expectations' become a heavy burden for Spain's manager, it becomes increasingly obvious that this sector of the press has little faith in his abilities and that they are preparing to exploit him as a scapegoat.[13] There are several reasons why the press chose to take advantage of the situation to attack Clemente – some of the possible interpretations will be discussed in the following chapter – but what is significant here is the use of a simple yet subtle linguistic tool that succeeds in distancing the reader from the *Selección*.

Thus the data are a rich source of material in which journalists play with (often already pre-existing) ideas of 'Spanishness'. They reflect the mood swings between blind optimism and pessimistic fatalism, acknowledge the important role of *la furia española*, allude to Spain's inferiority complexes when faced with other powerful nations and portray the team as one which aspires to 'Europeanness' just like the country as a whole. This complex, intricate jigsaw of Spanishness created by careful journalism and the piece-by-piece construction of the several elements of national identity are complemented by a more simple yet equally illuminating (re)construction of symbols of national identity via the depiction of the elements (stereo)typically associated with Spanishness. The transmission of clichés, sometimes stereotypes, by sports media texts is revealing. A detailed textual analysis of the hundreds of press articles in our data confirms that football writing, and match reports in particular, use this mechanism which then becomes a key factor in the establishment of a national identity. What may at first glance appear to be innocent, even lazy, journalism in fact provides us with an important insight into Spanish cultural assumptions and hence into a Spanish imagined identity.

The ways in which such images and metaphors have been developed have been the subject of previous studies,[14] but it is nevertheless relevant here to draw on some of the findings of this earlier work. Although many of the examples of imagery, metaphor and stereotypes in football writing have parallels in other European countries (see Chapters 1 to 6), there are several which recur with sufficient frequency to warrant special attention, or deal with seemingly common themes in a highly culture-specific way. As in the case studies of England and France, extracting the recurring themes from the data is most interesting when we bear in mind the culture-specific nature of the references. Thus seemingly banal images and metaphors transform into highly illuminating insights into Spanish culture. Let us look at a few examples, namely the use of religious imagery, military terminology, references to the weather and bullfighting.

Despite recent trends suggesting that the *practising* of religion no longer plays as important a role in the lives of Spaniards as it did a generation ago, Spain remains a stubbornly Catholic country in which almost 87 per cent of the population *profess* to be Catholic. Just two per cent follow other religions.[15] Spain became a nation as a result of the process of religious segregation, and 'if being a Spaniard means being a Christian, in Spain being a Christian means being a Catholic'.[16] The Spanish Inquisition meant that by 1970 there were no Protestants left in Spain, and for most of Spain's history religious freedom has been notional rather than real. Franco, while not banning other forms of worship, outlawed their external manifestation. It was not until the 1978 Constitution that Spaniards won the unambiguous right to worship as they pleased. The theme of religion in football writing may, therefore, be culturally loaded. Players are 'idolised' or 'worshipped' in most countries. Fans 'congregate' in 'temples' in Spain just as they do throughout Europe. Fans and players alike 'pray' for success on the pitch. Many of the religious terms are little more than unimaginative clichés, the religious origins of which have often been forgotten. Yet in the Spanish case, the religious angle can be extended and often concerns the reflection of the Christian and especially Catholic doctrine with reference to 'saints', 'candles' or 'purgatory' featuring strongly. Outstandingly good players are 'sanctified' (*El País*, 2 October 1995). Managers stand and watch from their 'pulpits' (*El País*, 6 November 1995). After their disappointing performance against Nigeria at France 98, the Spanish players were described as they emerged from the dressing room as a 'rosary of men with their heads down, and sad, sombre expressions ... The apparition of Zubizarreta was the most awaited' (*ABC*, 14 June). Later on in the tournament, at the time when most reports were desperately appealing to *la furia española* to help Spain to qualify for the next round, the number of religious references also increases, epitomised by the headline in *ABC*: 'The time has come for Spain to win ... and pray' (24 June). The article that follows makes several references to 'having faith', 'needing to trust' and 'not giving up hope' (ibid.). *El País*'s build-up to the game relied equally on appealing to faith: 'Whatever happens, whatever we say, we must keep faith and maintain hope' (23 June).

Similarly, after a Croatian team (consisting of six footballers who play regularly in the Spanish league) beat Germany 3–0, one headline read: 'The Spanish League sends Germany to hell' (*ABC*, 5 July); and the French defender Thuram is described as 'the forbidden apple' of Real Madrid's *presidente* Sanz (*ABC*, 9 July); while 'Chile said goodbye to France 98 with pride. They wore their red cassocks with passion' (*ABC*, 22 July). Occasionally, the religious imagery is taken beyond the cliché and developed into more interesting, original text. After Espanyol failed to score in four consecutive home games, the writer takes the religious theme to its ultimate conclusion: 'The older fans maintained the blind faith of the enlightened ... the crowd unafraid, in communion with their team. Then the goal arrived, and with it ecstasy [the state of the soul when in mystical communion with God]' (*El País*, 2 October 1995).

Many other references carry more specifically Catholic overtones. 'The eighteenth league fixture saw Atlético de Madrid return to the top of the table and two innocent victims sent to purgatory' (*El País*, 27 November 1995). The 'innocent victims' were not sent to hell, as it was only November and there was an opportunity for them to redeem themselves before the end of the season. But in the meantime they would have to suffer in purgatory. The image of a burning candle, a strong tradition of the Catholic church, is unexpectedly frequent: 'Sevilla's mission was to run and run ... with their cross on their back ... They lit a candle for [goalkeeper] Unzúe who kept it burning' (*El País*, 16 September 1995). In a similar vein, Mendieta, of Valencia, was described as being 'in a state of grace' following a series of outstanding performances for the club (*ABC*, 23 February 1998). A level of basic understanding of certain aspects of Catholicism is assumed. For many Spaniards the linguistic metaphors might be perceived as little more than clichés. It is only when these items are extracted from the cultural context of a still strongly Catholic country that their heavy cultural baggage becomes evident. Arguably the deep fatalism already discussed could be said also to have its roots in religious belief. Although religious imagery and metaphors abound in our data elsewhere, the frequency of references relating more closely to Catholicism, such as 'purgatory' and 'lighting candles' to remember great players of the past, is found only in the Spanish data. It is, therefore, the heavily Catholic overtones of religious imagery in the Spanish database that make it so distinctive.

As with the example of religious imagery, much of the military terminology which pervades the sports pages of the Spanish press mirrors that found elsewhere in Europe.[17] There is the customary talk of 'battles' and 'fights', of 'defending' and 'attacking', vocabulary that has already been appropriated as football's own lexicon rather than that borrowed from another field. In Spain such clichés abound: Real Sociedad's stadium is described as 'the fort of Anoeta' (*El País*, 10 November 1997) and the sections where their supporters gather as 'their territory' (ibid.); similarly, 'Oviedo used all their ammunition' (*El País*, 27 November 1995); 'Atlético de Madrid have the spirit of a warrior' (*El País*, 2 October 1995); at France 98, 'The Scots began to lose control of the central midfield, the zone the Norwegians were invading gradually. On three occasions, Norway even crossed into [Scotland goalkeeper] Leighton's territory' (*ABC*, 17 June); 'the battle of Saint Etienne' (*ABC*, 2 July) between England and Argentina is later described as 'a crude fight' (*ABC*, 5 July); and 'Denmark, the enemy ... destroyed Nigeria, first with cannon fire, when the Africans were still alive; later with stab wounds, when they tried to revive themselves' (*ABC*, 29 June). Occasionally, more imaginative usage of military terminology is introduced. Following a match in which six players were booked, it was reported that 'Sevilla and Atlético de Madrid decided to fight in unoccupied territory [midfield] and the match ended without a victor. The result was a battle with many injured [booked] and surprisingly no fatalities [sendings off]' (*El País*, 2 October 1995).

However, again as with religious imagery, military metaphors may also be distinctive and differ radically in content from those employed in other countries. Indeed, without some awareness of recent Spanish history some of the references would be baffling to a foreign reader. In contrast to British and French football writing, where well-organised, disciplined teams are likely to be described in military terms, the Spanish press is more likely to resort to military metaphor when referring to teams who are *lacking in* shape, direction, strategy, leadership or organisation. Such perceptions of 'an army' are present in the following extract:

> The manager opted to simulate a revolution ... he made many changes and ended up with a disorganised army with no intelligence service and with too many troops. The battle was a formality ... In two aerial attacks, Mérida conquered Real Sociedad. (*El País*, 16 October 1995)

This might at first seem surprising given the strong associations between the armed forces and notions of strong discipline and organisation. It says a lot, however, about Spanish perceptions of their armed forces, 60 per cent of whom are youths carrying out their compulsory military service.[18] For many Spaniards such descriptions also conjure images of the poorly organised, demotivated forces of the Spanish Civil War. Both sides, the victorious Nationalists and the defeated Republicans, consisted of volunteers with little or no military experience, and readers from outside are reminded of the 1995 film *Land and Freedom* directed by Ken Loach (in which one inexperienced trooper manages to shoot himself as he practises loading a faulty weapon) or of George Orwell's novel *Homage to Catalonia*.[19] Little wonder, then, that Spanish football writing paints a different picture of warfare from that of other countries. War is not glorified to the same extent as in football writing in England, for example. It is difficult to glorify a bitter, bloody war which took place on home soil in view of the whole population. The Spanish press presents a more stark reality, a reality shared by Spaniards.

A further interesting aspect of the Spanish press involves the use of a single word: 'reconquest'. The high frequency of this is unique in our data. It is not unusual to come across almost clichéd 'conquests' in football writing throughout Europe, but a salient feature of Spanish writing is that references to *re*conquests outnumber those to conquests by six to one. The reconquest of Spanish territory by the Christians from the Moors in the fifteenth century is, of course, one of the most important aspects of Spanish history and the unity of Spain as a political and administrative entity dates back to this period. All schoolchildren in Spain must study this period, which features strongly in school curricula as well as in many local customs and traditions, and are thus extremely familiar with this period of history. It is not surprising, therefore, in a forum which seems to reflect national identities and to wallow in any element of national pride that we should encounter images and metaphors which remind us of that period. It is almost the norm in football writing to refer to a team coming from behind as a 'reconquest' (for instance, *El País*, 1 and 14 December 1997; 4 January 1998); 'Valladolid's reconquest was complete' (*ABC*, 8 December 1997). Perhaps what is being mediated here through the pages of the reports is another element of a shared, national experience.

As well as these examples, where the choice of vocabulary proves to be highly illuminating, there are other themes which recur throughout the data. Although the Spanish press does not over-indulge the foreign reader with too many reproduced clichés of Spain, we do see a startling number of references to both the weather and bullfighting.

The stereotypical view of Spain renowned for its hot, dry climate is conveyed in its football writing, despite the fact that some parts of the country, in the north in particular experience rainfall and temperatures not dissimilar from those in parts of England. Reports may be peppered with references to the hot Spanish climate, helping to perpetuate a mythical Spain. Teams playing in a lethargic manner are customarily accused of having a *siesta*. On one stiflingly hot day, the atmosphere in one stadium is described as 'Too hot. Too sunny. It was a good siesta. Sevilla and Atlético de Madrid made a toast to the sun during the second half' (*El País*, 9 October 1995). This seemingly national obsession with the need for sun also pervades football writing during the 1996 European Championships held in England. The constant references to the hot weather and the advantages it would bring to the Spanish *Selección*, so accustomed to playing in heat and not capable of performing their best unless doing so (as in *El País*, 8 June, 14 June and 16 June), serve to reinforce the stereotype shared by so many outside Spain that it is a country which enjoys a year-round warm climate. Of course, this is not the case for large areas, which suffer long, cold winters, precisely during the football season. Notably, however, it is the Spanish press that is perpetuating this myth, even though in writing on domestic football the meteorological metaphors are more imaginative, and the weather becomes more of an issue when it contradicts the stereotype. When Athletic de Bilbao played host to Atlético de Madrid the poor weather conditions at the time were blamed for the low standard of football: 'Perhaps this was why the match had such stormy periods, with the wind changing direction and no one managing to get the better of the weather' (*El País*, 14 September 1997). Similarly, it was the excuse for Sevilla's defeat by Leganés: '[Sevilla] lacked their great star, Tsartas. Or perhaps they no longer believe in themselves. Or, more likely, they lost because it was raining' *(El País*, 3 November 1997). The 'inclement' weather in Galicia inspired one report which carried a metaphor for rain throughout and 'the Riazor pitch [home of Deportivo La Coruña] withstood the downpour with dignity' (*El País*, 10 September 1997). Surprisingly (for the journalist), a good match was played under adverse conditions.

Finally, there is a surprising amount of vocabulary in Spanish football texts familiar to those with an interest in the sport that remains the symbol of Spain for many outsiders: bullfighting. The borrowing of images and metaphors involves primarily, although not exclusively, the transference of terminology from the field of bullfighting into that of football. The match is commonly referred to as *la corrida* (the bullfight), and in one example the scorching heat made the players so lethargic that 'In fact there was no bull' (*El País*, 9 October 1995), that is, there was no match at all. A player who scores a winning goal is *el matador* (the one who eventually kills the bull) and one who produces an outstanding performance is *un torero* (a bullfighter). Indeed, it is not unusual for football fans to chant '*torero*' in appreciation of a player who has demonstrated exceptional skills, as they would a bullfighter who has pulled off a particularly impressive move. Similarly, they might wave white handkerchiefs to express deep emotion, another custom originally associated with bullfighting rather than football. Those players who are less artful, such as the English in the example below, are not the bullfighters but rather the bulls: 'Anderton and Sheringham, with their limited resources, like to go at defenders like bulls' (*ABC*, 18 June 1998).

Just a brief outline, therefore, of some of the key themes which recur in football writing can provide an insight into a culture and provide us with a glimpse of the legacy of Spain's past as well as some current trends. While some of the language employed mirrors European print media discourse elsewhere, other aspects are deeply rooted in Spanishness. Perhaps the notion of a Spanish identity is not as alien to the Spanish football readership as some would have us believe. There are clearly elements of a shared experience and other aspects which hint at the construction of an imagined identity in progress. In this respect, and for all the complexities of the regionalist/nationalist issues unfolding in Spain (which will be explored in the following chapter), *El País* and *ABC* would seem to be playing a part in the construction of a national unity by engaging in what Rowe *et al.* have termed the 'symbolic process of nation-making through sport' via 'the key mythologising role of the media'.[20]

Viva la diferencia: Spain's Nationalities and Regions in its Football Writing

Piecing together the intricate jigsaw of relationships between football clubs and notions of national and regional identity in Spain is mind-boggling. This chapter, nevertheless, attempts to analyse some of these complexities and to shed light on some of the factors which lie behind the discursive practices employed in the sports pages of the newspapers under consideration by the examination of certain relevant historical and cultural factors. It will briefly outline the background to the current *estado de las autonomías* (the Spain of Autonomous Communities) and introduce some of the complexities of nationalist/regionalist issues in Spain.[1] The role of Real Madrid as a symbol of national unity will then be explored, and press coverage in the data of football clubs from the *nacionalidades históricas* (in particular Catalonia and the Basque Country) will be analysed. As in the previous chapter, we can see how images and metaphors employed in the press continue to work to perpetuate existing stereotypes, this time of the characteristics of the 'nations within the state' and sometimes of other regions, too.[2]

The complex notions of regionalism and nationalism in Spain involve rapidly evolving concepts. The political situation has changed enormously within a relatively short period. Interest in the nationalist/regionalist issue grew towards the end of the nineteenth-century.[3] Carlism (support for Carlos, second son of Charles IV, and his sons as legitimate heirs to the throne, to the exclusion of Ferdinand VII's daughter and her heirs) dominated the political history of nineteenth-century Spain and was strongest in the *nacionalidades históricas*, marking them out politically on the key question of the Spanish succession. By the turn of the twentieth century such domestic antagonisms were sharpened by the emergence of political and social movements based on regional and class exclusiveness as well as by a reaction to Spain's retreat from empire. As Balfour notes:

> Spain's precarious unity between its different regions had been constructed around a common endeavour to extend its dominion and its religion to the empire and to extract the wealth contained therein. With the loss of the last colonies [1898], the already fragile ideological ties binding the regions to the centre from which that empire had been run were put under even greater strain.[4]

Nationalism developed in Catalonia and the Basque Country for various reasons, then, but it also expressed pride in the only areas of Spain that were beginning to develop a modern industrial economy.[5] This rise in nationalist expression was happening at a time when football was emerging as a popular sport all over Spain, but particularly in Catalonia, the Basque Country and Andalusia. Football clubs, therefore, became important symbols of identity, although not in the same way all over Spain.

Within the Basque Country (known as *Euskadi* in the Basque language) no one club represented 'Basqueness', unlike in Catalonia where FC Barcelona was an established Catalan institution well before the Spanish Civil War (1936–39). There was no equivalent in the Basque Country. Athletic de Bilbao, and to a lesser extent Real Sociedad, have both been seen as symbols of Basqueness from outside the Basque Country, and acted as such within, but neither club provides a unifying effect on a politically, socially and economically divided Basque Country. In recent times there has been a fear that football would encourage intra-Basque rivalries and divisions, especially between the provinces of Guipúzcoa and Vizcaya, Athletic de Bilbao representing the latter and Real Sociedad, in San Sebastián, standing for the former. So, the great rivalry between Athletic de Bilbao and Real Sociedad 'can be considered as a reflection of the historical differences Basque nationalism has encountered in arousing a single Basque conscience'.[6]

There was, however, talk throughout the twentieth century of the establishment of a single Basque 'national' football team. As early as 1908 there is evidence of discussions surrounding the foundation of a Basque team to participate in the *Campionato de España*. During the Civil War football did become, for a time, via the *Selección de Euskadi* (Basque national team), a sign of shared identification.[7] Also, since the start of the transition to democracy in Spain in the late 1970s, a *Euskadi* team has participated in around a dozen 'friendly' matches, the first in San Mamés against Ireland on 16 August 1979. A similar team was founded in Catalonia, although the need to create a new team to represent the 'nation' was not imperative there given the status of FC Barcelona as a symbol of a *unified* Catalonia, which it had already become by the 1920s.[8] Contrary to popular belief, and to opinions held by some writers,[9] the complex Catalan, European and international dimensions of FC Barcelona are characteristics which were established before the Franco period and actually date to its establishment at the turn of the twentieth century. Recently, though, there has been a strong movement in favour of allowing Catalan, Basque and, for that matter, Galician teams to play in international competitions. In June 1998 the Basque Parliament in Vitoria passed a law which allowed Basque representation internationally. The case is currently being tested for its Spanish constitutionality (*El País*, 18 August 1998) and, naturally, such a proposal led to huge debates across Spain. The Bulgarian (and FC

Barcelona) player Hristo Stoichkov, for instance, renowned for his controversial comments, added fuel to the fire by predicting that Spain would not do well in the 1998 World Cup tournament, claiming provocatively that he was going to wear a shirt with Catalan colours beneath his own national team shirt in order to make a political statement in support of the Partido Independentista de Catalunya – namely, that Catalonia should have its own national team which could compete in international competitions. Indeed, Bulgaria were the opponents of a Catalan 'national' team who played a friendly match in the Olympic Stadium, Barcelona, earlier that year. However, the European and world governing bodies in football, UEFA and FIFA, are unlikely to allow any Basque or Catalan 'national' side to compete in official tournaments.[10]

It is the legacy of autonomy of the several regions of Spain (known now as the *Comunidades Autónomas* or Autonomous Communities) which pervades Spanish society today. Moreover, following the 36-year dictatorship in which General Franco centralised power and prohibited the regions from displaying any signs of autonomy, the 1978 Spanish Constitution represented a huge turnabout in policy. Article 2 states that 'The Constitution is based on the indissoluble unity of the Spanish Nation, indivisible homeland to all Spaniards, and it recognises and guarantees the right to autonomy for those nationalities and regions who belong to it with solidarity between them all.'[11] So, although affirming the unity of the Spanish state, far from outlawing any acts of nationalism or regionalism, the present Constitution recognises the existence of other nationalities within the single state. Not only that, but Article 3 confirms a belief in linguistic plurality and states that the languages of Spain other than Castilian 'will also be official in their respective *Comunidades Autónomas* in accordance with their statutes' and that 'The richness of Spain's different linguistic varieties is a cultural heritage which will be the object of special protection and respect.'[12] Although the possible interpretations of this clause have been the subject of much debate,[13] what cannot be disputed is the fact that the Constitution acknowledges the existence of other nations and claims to help to protect their key symbol, language.

Thus the 1978 Constitution granted degrees of autonomy to the 17 *Comunidades Autónomas* and the extent of regional autonomy reflects fairly accurately the degree of enthusiasm for home rule as well as historical, cultural and linguistic singularity. The *nacionalidades históricas* hold most power internally. The Basques and the Catalans enjoy a high degree of autonomy, including, for example, their own police forces, followed by the Galicians and the Andalusians. All have control of their own health services, dictate to a large extent their own educational systems and have their own television and radio channels as well as their own press. Indeed, local media there often prove more popular than the national media.[14]

Some of the themes present in football today, and reflected in the national press analysed here, actually predate Spain's major twentieth-century political upheavals of the Civil War, the subsequent period of Franco dictatorship (1939–75) and the transition to and establishment of democracy (1975 onwards).[15] Since football emerged as a major sport at the start of the twentieth century, the changing structures and organisation of the sport's institutions as well as its coverage in the media have mirrored the social and political systems at any given time. Thus, under Franco, the notion of a single Spanish identity and the promotion of its image were encouraged via football and this sport's role as the vehicle for frustrated nationalisms was contained,[16] while from the 1970s onwards football has been allowed to become an open symbol of nationhood or local pride within the *Comunidades Autónomas*. This is not to say that football could not act as a symbol for nationalist sentiment before the 1970s. Far from it. At a time when any expression of regionalist/nationalist autonomy was severely punished, football fans were still allowed to wave their *senyeras* or *ikurriñas* (the Catalan and the Basque flag, respectively) in football grounds, and they were allowed to sing in their own languages. Football was used as an 'escape valve for regionalist feelings'.[17] This level of tolerance that was apparently acceptable within the football context was exploited by anyone who wanted a vehicle to voice opinions against anti-centralist policies. Hence, some clubs assumed a special status and became the catalysts within the regions for those with nationalist/regionalist aspirations. For this reason, clashes between clubs who represent the *nacionalidades históricas* and Real Madrid, the staunch symbol of centralism, became tense and politically loaded, with FC Barcelona (whose name was temporarily Castilianised to Club de Fútbol de Barcelona until 1973), Athletic Bilbao (forced to become known as Atlético de Bilbao for a period after 1940) and, to a lesser extent, Real Sociedad standing as strong symbols against Madrid-based centralism.[18] It is against this historical backdrop that we need to consider football writing in the press today.

However, at the same time, it must be acknowledged that the Spain of today is radically different from that of the last century. While some in Catalonia continue to struggle for independence, as do, more radically of course, some in the Basque Country, many are content with the autonomy they have and the official recognition provided by the Constitution that they exist as a nation in their own right. According to one study carried out by the Centro de Investigaciones Sociológicas in Catalonia, only 15 per cent of Catalans say that they do not feel Spanish, and just 35 per cent feel more Catalan than Spanish.[19] Nationalism, therefore, seems to be more moderate than is often assumed by outsiders. It can no longer be assumed that all Basque and Catalan fans are nationalist hard-liners who seek independence from Spain. Some Basques and Catalans feel that they have achieved what they wanted (helped, perhaps, by the fact that for many years the left-wing PSOE government [Partido Socialista Obrero Español], in power between 1982 and 1996, relied on the support of the Catalans to remain in office and hence Catalonia was seen to be favoured by many).

There is even support for the *Selección* (the Spanish national team) in Catalonia and the Basque Country. Javier Clemente, manager of the national team from 1992 to 1998, commented upon how many Catalans waved the national flag in the Nou Camp (home of FC Barcelona) when Spain played Malta there in 1994 (*Cambio 16*, 20 June 1994), and during the 1992 Olympics the crowd in Barcelona were certainly not anti-Spanish.[20] The fact that the *Selección* had a Basque manager for much of the 1990s (and the fact that he chose many Basque players to represent Spain) helped to drum up support for the national team in the Basque Country, too. So, in the football context as well as the social and political one, Spain has entered a very different era from any before and it will, therefore, be important to see how far this is reflected in football writing. Indeed, Spanish researchers, just as their British and French counterparts, have recognised the importance of the bidirectional relationship between football and the media and the case studies presented in this chapter constitute a further exploration of the way in which football is reported by the Spanish press.[21]

We saw in the previous chapter how representations of a single Spanish national identity are constructed by print media discourse on sport, and now we turn to football at club level and how notions of other national/regional identities are represented and (re-)created.

Again, we must bear in mind the readership of the writing that constitutes our data. The fact that the data are drawn exclusively from national newspapers is important. Much of the local bias allowed in the regional press is supposedly absent from national reporting and commentary. Also, for reasons explained earlier (see the Introduction), we are analysing football writing within the national newspapers *El País* and *ABC* and not in publications dedicated exclusively to sport. Nevertheless, it must be borne in mind that, historically, the role of the press coverage of sport in Spain, and in particular of football, is crucial to the understanding of the importance of the manner and the tone of reporting. Given Spain's recent past, much is still read into the way in which events are reported. National newspapers are well aware of this and are usually careful in their expression. However, typical characteristics and familiar stereotypes (imagined identities) are reinforced through football writing in our data. Despite recent political changes, old historical rivalries are maintained with football clubs being key social institutions. We shall examine case studies relating to Real Madrid (representing Spain) as well as to Catalonia and the Basque Country. We shall then look briefly at other examples involving Andalusia and Valencia.

The Spanish press is not neutral in the depiction of Madrid-based teams, in particular of Real Madrid. Real Madrid has generally been seen as representing the regime in power. The club enjoyed the support of monarchs and dictators throughout the twentieth century (such as Alfonso XIII, General Franco and Juan Carlos), a feature resented by many, especially Catalans and Basques. Indeed, in the Franco period, to an extent and for specific reasons, Real Madrid became identified not just as *el equipo del régimen* (the team of the Regime) but also as the representative of Spain itself. As the national team was ostracised by the rest of the world, Real Madrid, the dominant team in European competitions during the 1950s, were hailed as representing Franco's Spain and the triumph of its centralist policies.[22] Even now, in more democratic times, the links that bind Real Madrid with the power and authority of the central state (and its monarchy) are still strong and, most importantly, these links are communicated discursively by the print media under examination in the present study. Superlatives are used to describe Real Madrid's football more than that of any other team. They are almost invariably 'ingenious', 'superb', 'brilliant', 'spectacular' or 'outstanding'. The neutral reader cannot help but find it odd that even reports on apparently mediocre performances by Real Madrid are peppered with flattering terminology. They played 'tremendously' during a 0–0 draw against Zaragoza, for instance, and their football is often 'brilliant', even following defeats. Of course, it is possible to play well and for the performance not to be reflected in the result, but this cannot explain the numerous occasions when the opening paragraph of a report begins with flattery, only to tell the truth later on or at least hint that Real Madrid's quality of football was poor (for instance, *El País*, 2 November, 14 September and 1 December 1997). On occasions, this trait within Spanish football writing appears even more odd. For example, when Real Madrid 'could have played really well but didn't feel like it' (*El País*, 18 September 1997), or when they 'played poorly ... without any conviction ... and looked uninterested'; apparently 'it was a poor game because that's how Madrid wanted it to be' (*El País*, 6 November 1997). In this last example, Real Madrid played badly, failed to achieve the desired result and yet are still reported as being 'in control'. Similarly, in reporting Real Madrid's defeat by FC Barcelona, one journalist wrote: 'Madrid deserved to win at times, because they kept trying and had a certain greatness in their play that Barcelona never had' (*El País*, 5 November 1997). This style of journalism contributes to perpetuating the myth of Madrid superiority – and, of course, is highly irritating for fans of other clubs, especially FC Barcelona. Indeed, the enmity between Real Madrid and FC Barcelona is perhaps the best documented rivalry in European football. The fierce hostility of the relationship has been widely attested.[23] Matches between the two clubs still carry enormous historical baggage. When the press report, therefore, on the superiority of Real Madrid (the club from the capital of the Spanish state) over FC Barcelona (the club from the capital of the Catalan nation) and when they assert that 'No one disputes the fact Real Madrid and FC Barcelona are in permanent conflict' (*El País*, 3 November 1997), it might be felt that the reporting connects with the wider issues, still hotly debated in Spain, of centralism versus autonomy.

Furthermore, Real Madrid also enjoys the role of focal point of the Spanish monarchy. Its club crest is topped with a crown symbolically reflecting its royal name granted by Alfonso XIII in 1920. The club finds itself, then, at the centre of a cluster of royal motifs in the press, reinforcing connotations of power, authority and control over the rest of Spain, with headlines such as 'Raúl's great goal crowns a regal performance' (*El País*, 13 September 1997). Similarly, Hierro 'plays majestically' (*El País*, 15 September 1997) and even Real Madrid's stadium, the Santiago Bernebéu, is 'majestically grandiose' (clearly a myth to anyone who has visited the rather decrepit areas of the ground in recent years). Again, players are frequently described as 'regal', 'magnificent' or 'majestic' and journalists tend to play on the word 'Real' (Royal) in the title of the club far more than they do with other clubs such as Real Betis, Real Sociedad and Real Murcia. Real Madrid give a 'royal' performance whereas other teams do not, no matter how well they play. They are expected to dominate on the pitch, too, as José Camacho acknowledged when he took over as manager in June 1998: 'The most important thing is that Real Madrid control the play and dominate on the pitch' (*ABC*, 18 June 1998). This is not the only hint, then, that it is more important for Real Madrid's style of play to be fittingly supreme than it is for the team to win. Only on rare occasions are readers shown a glimpse of a contrasting portrayal of Real Madrid players:

> On Monday they smile at the cameras, on Tuesday they have an appointment with their tailors, on Wednesday they get their hair done, on Thursday they go off clubbing, on Friday they remember the match on Saturday. Apparently, they are so handsome that they have won both the League and the Champions' League before the end of November. (*El País*, 9 November 1997)

Oddly, this came just a few days after the defeat by FC Barcelona when the same newspaper described them as 'deserving to win' and playing with 'greatness'.

Images of Basques and Catalans in the texts studied share certain characteristics. This is unsurprising given that these regions have similar socio-economic profiles and share a history of opposition to Madrid's centralism, the implications of which meant that policies that would have favoured these regions were often rejected by centralist governments. Both also emerged as strong industrialised economies around the turn of the twentieth century, and stood out as such in a Spain which was otherwise predominantly agricultural. This has also meant that both experienced huge waves of immigration throughout the twentieth century. Thus social and political factors distinguished the north-eastern areas of Spain from the rest of the country and there developed a notion, which has become a stereotype, that Basques and Catalans are industrious, hard-working, hard-headed businesspeople. Both are certainly portrayed as such in our data. Let us look first at some of the key ways in which Catalans are depicted.

The most frequent image of Catalonia is precisely one which reinforces the traditional idea that Catalans are hard-working. It is no coincidence that the style of football played by FC Barcelona is frequently described as 'industrious' or 'diligent', as 'a machine which keeps going' (*El País*, 4 November 1997). An association is also frequently made between the Catalan club and money-making institutions. This is only a slight extension of the stereotypical view held of Catalans as money-orientated businesspeople. This is usually done through one-off comments or words. FC Barcelona is described as a 'business' and 'the claret and blues [who] play *industrious* football' (*El País*, 16 February 1998; our italics) while the team is run 'with the efficiency of a smoothly-run business' (*ABC*, 23 February 1998). 'Barça reaped their profits' runs one headline (*El País*, 10 January 1998). After FC Barcelona experienced the highs and lows of football within one week, though, one writer takes the notion of football as a mirror of the stock market much further into a somewhat bizarre extended metaphor:

> It's as though football were looking in the mirror of the Stock Market ... euphoria and depression. It is clear that the so-called butterfly effect, which afflicts stock markets so much, has an exact equivalent in the football world ... when a big fly buzzes in the Ramblas [in Barcelona] an owl hovers over Cibeles [in Madrid]. From then on the consequences are unpredictable: football fans have nervous breakdowns, political negotiations suffer, the price of fuel increases. (*El País*, 3 November 1997)

There is an additional defining feature of FC Barcelona's style of play which refines the Catalan identity further. It refers to their collective mentality, an attitude of working together as a team rather than playing as individuals. References to the 'collective efforts' of the team are frequent (for instance, *El País*, 10 November 1997; 23 February 1998) and even the former manager Van Gaal recognises the Catalan mentality when he claims that 'Here, football is a team game not a sport for individuals' (*El País*, 14 September 1997). It is frequently said that '[FC Barcelona] play a good team game' (*El País*, 14 March 1998) and that 'their football is all about a team playing together' (*El País*, 14 September 1997).

The virtual absence of *violent* nationalism in Catalonia has meant that its inhabitants have not been subjected to the same oppression as the people of the Basque Country. Furthermore, Catalans do not claim to be a different 'race' from the rest of Spain as Basques do (see below). This, and the fact that the Catalan language is relatively easy for a Castilian Spanish speaker to learn, has made the acceptance of immigrants much easier in Catalonia than in the Basque Country. It is estimated that over half the population of Catalonia (and significantly more in the capital Barcelona) are of immigrant stock. Although ghetto-like *barrios* (neighbourhoods) do exist, it is possible for immigrants, who originate predominantly from the eastern and the southern coast of Spain, to integrate into Catalan society. Learning the Catalan language and supporting FC Barcelona are two key ways in which this acceptance as a Catalan can be achieved. This social and political role of FC Barcelona[24] is recognised by the press. For example, Van Gaal, when manager of the club, 'looked just like a politician. Not surprising really, given the fact that he represents Catalonia and its position with regard to the rest of Spain' (*El País*, 14 September 1997).

The Basque case study shares some features in common with the Catalan case. Like the Catalans, Basques are 'industrious' and 'disciplined': 'We expect the Basques to be a hard-working and disciplined side' remarks *El País* (10 November 1997) while Real Sociedad 'went to the Bernabéu [Real Madrid's stadium] to play attacking, *disciplined* football' (*El País*, 13 September 1997; our italics).

The fact that Basques consider themselves to be a different 'race' from the Spanish and that they have fought for their independent nationalist stance violently for large periods in recent times (as well as historically) makes their case singular, though. Although modern ethnologists do not consider the Basques a distinctive race, they do possess certain marked cultural and physical traits. The Basque language is unique in Europe, a language isolate, in fact, that is having no known structural or historical relationship with any other; recent research here is concentrating on trying to find links between Basque and other pre-Indo-European languages. Moreover, peculiarities in the blood, the shape of the skull and general size and strength (greater, on average, than their neighbours in Spain and France) have led many to believe that the Basques are the last surviving representatives of Europe's aboriginal population, possibly linked to the now-extinct ancient Iberians.[25] Perhaps this perception of unusual size and strength contributed initially to the notion of *la furia* in Basque football which continues to this day. Certainly, the links between the development and the importance of sport and traditional Basque society are a distinctive trait acknowledged by the rest of Spain.[26]

It is expected, therefore, that Basques will be physically strong: 'Athletic [de Bilbao] wanted a traditionally physical game' (*El País*, 14 September

1997); 'Athletic combine physical power with skill' (*El País*, 17 September 1997); 'Espanyol were defeated in Anoeta [Real Sociedad's ground]. Their efforts were eclipsed by Real Sociedad's discourse on discipline and effort ... and by the strength of their physical challenge' (*El País*, 10 November 1997).

Perhaps ironically, the Basque Country is, as we have seen, considered to be the home of *la furia española*. Football really became popular in the Basque Country before it took off elsewhere in Spain. The English influence was heavy (Athletic de Bilbao was founded in 1890 by English miners) so English football's traditional qualities of commitment and hard work (see Chapter 1) were valued assets in a team and the added passion and typical strength of the Basques were estimable. Sociologists working on the role of football and identity have claimed that:

> One characteristic of Basque football, especially at Athletic, is its genuinely English flavour ... Its style shares similarities with the English game (play down the wing, speed, strong defence, one-touch), values team spirit in which the group is more important than the individual and makes it difficult to find leaders, only team players.[27]

Similarly, Santiago Segurola refers to Athletic as playing what he calls 'Britishised' football and claims that the fans accept this style as a 'dogma of faith'.[28] He explains that since Athletic's foundation by the British there has always been an obsession with 'playing the English way, fast football, long balls, crosses from the wings for a big centre-forward to head, and little football in midfield', and he points out that every time Athletic de Bilbao pass through a difficult period they sign an English manager (a good example being the signing of Howard Kendall from Everton when Athletic were struggling). That way, the Basque style of football is restored, with all its *furia*.

The notion of a Basque identity in football including *la furia* continues today and is seen in many match reports: 'Athletic wanted a passionate contest' (*El País*, 14 September 1997) implies that it is somehow in the interest of the Basques to rely on passion. According to the press, this passion for football is an extension of the passion of the Basques: 'In San Mamés [Athletic de Bilbao's stadium] Athletic and Atlético de Madrid have played some memorable games ... They are usually tough, physical matches played at a high pace in front of a passionate crowd' (*El País*, 13 September 1997). The newspaper even adds that 'Athletic are always a strong side in passionate matches' (ibid.). In the same edition, but in an article written by a different journalist, Athletic is described as a team of 'disciplined workers' who 'were playing for the prize of productivity'(ibid.), a clear reference this time to the work ethic of the Basques. Again, the apparent strength of the

Basques as hard workers, and indeed as disciplined administrators, filters through the football writing: 'Athletic presented their documentation absolutely in order before the UEFA Cup tie' (*El País*, 17 September 1997); 'Athletic's papers were all in order' (*ABC*, 12 March 1998). Even when the Spanish national side is managed by Basque Javier Clemente, it is expected that Spain 'with a Basque in the dugout should play physically and have a strong defence'(*El País*, 13 June 1998), reinforcing the notion that Basque teams are physically strong.

Furthermore, it is evident that in club football Athletic de Bilbao stands as the symbol of Basque nationhood for the rest of Spain. The club applies a strict Basque-only policy in its recruitment of players. This institutionalised stance – never actually formalised in the club's statutes – dates back to 1919 and means that no foreigners can play for the club, and this excludes Spaniards from outside the Basque Country and (less rigorously) footballers from outside Spain. Despite the fact that the debate over whether or not to open the doors to players from outside the Basque Country recurs every couple of years, the policy enjoys the support of the vast majority of the club's fans. The roots of the adoption of such a policy owe much to the political ideology which lies behind Basque nationalism, in particular to the xenophobic beliefs of its founder Sabino de Arana y Goira. At the core of Arana's doctrine lay an undisguised hatred of immigrants, and his quest for 'Basque purity' was reflected in the community centres (or *batzokis*) he established to spread the nationalist faith. In these centres members were divided into categories according to the number of Basque grandparents and executive positions could be held only by those whose four grandparents had Basque surnames. It was this search for purity of Basqueness which lay behind the policy of Basque clubs to employ Basque-only footballers. Real Sociedad also shared a similar policy for much of the twentieth century, although the club was far less rigid in its definition of Basqueness. Thus the role of the football club in the Basque Country became highly symbolic. According to Unzueta:

> The fundamental characteristic of identity in Athletic [de Bilbao], and by extension in Basque football, is that all its players are Basque, a concept based on the assumption that there exists a Basque race which forms the basis of Basque nationalism and in which football is one of the emblematic elements.[29]

Therefore, it is not surprising that in most reports in our data this role as symbol of Basqueness is conveyed by persistent references to those features identified as characterising Basque identity. The essence of Basqueness filters through in reports such as the following, which recognises both the English origins of the sport and the Basque influence:

It is not easy to guess the future of the Athletic [de Bilbao] side whose style is so undeniably their own, but we know that the uncultured factory churns out concrete football, so simple and rough at the edges but at the same time so aggressive and direct. In order to find such a strong armour elsewhere we would have to turn to English football, rummage though Arsenal's reserves, seek through Liverpool's boot room or search behind the counter at Spurs. (*El País*, 8 September 1997)

Furthermore, it seems that this notion of 'Basqueness' is so strong that it is a transferable concept: 'Valencia played like a Basque side ... Strong in defence but unattractive ... as they beat Real Madrid 2–1 away from home' (*El País*, 3 February 1998).

Finally, we note the portrayal of another prominent Basque trait: resistance to attack, which might be interpreted culturally as a reference to the resistance to the invasion and colonisation of the Basque Country demonstrated by its population since Roman times. When Athletic de Bilbao went a goal up in one match, for instance, 'the Bilbao anticyclone became a symbol of resistance and concentration, a physical extravaganza which ended up inciting the crowd ... Athletic played the passionate football which they will surely display in European competitions' (*El País*, 14 September 1997). Here Basque football resists attack, like its people who have invoked their 'spirit of struggle and resistance'[30] to resist external cultural and political domination of the homeland for centuries. This notion is not uncommon in commentary on Athletic de Bilbao as they frequently display their 'bravery' or 'stubborn resistance' (*ABC*, 16 September 1997; *El País*, 24 March 1998). Occasionally this characteristic appears in reports on other Basque clubs, as well, such as Real Sociedad (for instance, *ABC*, 13 October 1997) with one local derby between Real Sociedad and Athletic de Bilbao being summarised as 'a battle between order and determination ... the rest was a question of resistance' (*El País*, 8 February 1998).

It is evident from these typical examples that there is a very clear picture in Spanish football writing of how Basqueness is perceived and, indeed, of the essentialist qualities that Basque football should display. It is a football that is direct, physical and, most importantly, passionate. There is even a certain pride in the English origins of Basque football. When the (Basque) manager Javier Clemente attempted to produce a Spanish national side which played the Basque way, even populating it with Basques, he himself described Spain proudly as 'more English than the English' (*El País*, 23 June 1996), and following the defeat by England in the 1996 European Championships, he said that Spain was 'the best English team on the pitch' (ibid.). Indeed, Basque stereotypes of physical strength and courage pervade many references to the Spanish style of play as we saw in the previous chapter.

It is not unusual for the press to look for a scapegoat when things go wrong at the national level, though (remember the assaults of the tabloid press on the England manager Graham Taylor following the failure to qualify for the 1994 World Cup finals). It is not necessarily of interest for the purposes of the current study that Spain's manager also suffered huge pressures from the press during and, especially, immediately after France 98. What is pertinent, however, is the nature of the accusations against Clemente and their possible interpretation. It is possible that the way in which the press deals with the Clemente case offers an important insight into the way in which a Spanish identity is being modelled. The preferred mould is not one which features those characteristics closely associated with Clemente, and, as we shall see, it is precisely those characteristics associated with his Basqueness that are often rejected.

Clemente himself believes that the press campaign against him was due in part to the fact that he is Basque. He believes that his Basque nationality is the principal reason why he was not accepted nor fully supported by the media as manager of the national side. He claims, clearly tongue-in-cheek, 'I make many mistakes, hundreds. Many of them because I am Basque' (*El País*, 21 June 1998). It is possible that he has a point. What is clear from the data is that there are frequent references either to his Basqueness or (more frequently) to features of his character which are (stereo)typically associated with Basqueness. For example, Clemente is heavily criticised for several aspects of his managerial style. His brusque and taciturn manner of dealing with people was not appreciated: ' "Hello" was the only word to pass his lips in the direction of the awaiting media' complained *ABC*, for instance (15 June 1998). Similarly, before a decisive match for Spain in the 1998 World Cup, 'the manager was asked to express the best message he could give to the fans, given the situation the team found itself in: "Hope" he answered. Blunt and to the point' (*ABC*, 24 June 1998). His stubborn character was also frequently signalled: 'Clemente doesn't admit he made any mistakes against Nigeria' (*ABC*, 15 June 1998); 'Always sticking by his guns and reflecting his personal characteristics' (*ABC*, 21 June 1998). The way in which Clemente takes total control of all aspects of the team is 'unhealthy for the side and creates an imbalance in the power structures in the camp' (*El País*, 12 June 1998), which is attributed to his monopoly of 'absorbing all the pressures' (ibid.) and his defensive manner. Finally, his policy of banning the media from training sessions and from the team hotel did little to endear him to the hearts of the press who aired their bitterness in their papers: 'Spain, with more security than Iran, preparing to resist attack: Clemente must be very nervous' (*El País*, 19 June 1998). It is precisely those characteristics associated with Basqueness, then, which are the subject of derision and criticism: his taciturn, reticent manner, along with his defensive and stubborn ways. These same traits could have easily been portrayed positively had the media chosen to do so. But these are not ones that the media want to see closely associated with the Spanish identity, so they are spurned, under the guise of rejecting Clemente's failure. One writer goes as far as to verbalise the feelings which underlie many other commentaries: 'Clemente's main problems haven't really been to do with football. It is his character that has done him most harm. His aggressive, sometimes bad-tempered manner, has created many enemies for him' (*ABC*, 26 June 1998). Although the writer here does not go as far as to make any connection between Clemente's character and his ethnic origins, this is done elsewhere, albeit often implicitly: 'The *Basque* manager has never allowed his arm to be twisted' (*ABC*, 25 June 1998; our italics); 'The *Bilbaon* stated that "how hard the team work on the field is ... important" ' (*ABC*, 24 June 1998; our italics). How much of this type of coverage is resentment from a disgruntled media and how much is down to covert racism is difficult to discern. What is clear, however, is that the press, when they attack the Spanish manager, do not let the readers forget that Clemente is Basque. Clemente himself is conscious of a certain type of racism: 'At least 80 per cent of the time I'm referred to as Basque is when I'm being criticised. If I select Basque players no one discusses how good they are, they just comment on the fact that they are Basque' (*El País*, 2 June 1996).

Furthermore, the fact that it is perceived to be the reflection of Clemente's character that is mirrored in the performances of the *Selección* further alienates those Spaniards referred to earlier who want to see a forward-looking Spain. Those who are anxious to witness dazzling, skilful football, reflecting a more modern, progressive nation, are disappointed in the defensive security accompanied by a reliance on *furia* which characterises Clemente's sides. Even when he does, arguably, perform a U-turn of sorts and introduces new players with considerable flair into his squad, he continues to be criticised either for not playing them often enough or for not bringing out the best in them. Furthermore, the press claim that it is media pressure which resulted in Clemente's selection of such players in the first place:

> Javier Clemente had ended up accepting players such as Alfonso, Kiko, Raúl, Guerrero, the injured Guardiola ... who for some reason or other failed to convince him fully. The mixture of his players, the like of Abelardo, Alkorta, Nadal, Luis Enrique, Hierro, Sergi ... with those previously cited seemed attractive and most of us like the idea, both those who blindly defended the manager and those who criticised his management. Just as he gathers together the best national team of recent decades, he fails in this World Cup (*ABC*, 25 June 1998).

Clemente, then, even when he does respond to popular demand (when he is not being stubborn, that is), fails to move Spain forward and Spain remains a country that relies on its *furia* as a source of pride. The coveted combination of *furia* and skill referred to earlier (see Chapter 7) does not materialise in success on the field.

Reports on no other *Comunidad Autónoma* display such strong notions of its identity as those on the Basque Country and Catalonia, then. However, reports on Andalusia and Valencia occasionally provide some evidence of distinctiveness. Let us turn briefly to see how this is done by football writers.

The most striking image of Andalusia held by the rest of Spain is one of a vibrant, colourful, lively region, home of the flamenco (an image that many outsiders extrapolate to portray 'sunny' Spain as a whole). It is not unusual for such images and metaphors to emerge in the press. For example, reports on Sevilla refer to 'flowery football' (*ABC*, 24 November 1997) and 'lively, tuneful play' (*El País*, 16 October 1995), while Real Betis are said to play with 'inspiration, courage and Andalusian perseverance' (*El País*, 2 November 1997). Increasingly, clubs such as Real Betis are being seen in terms of the *Comunidad Autónoma* they represent. It is not without significance that Betis play in green and white stripes, the colours of the flag of the *Comunidad* of Andalusia. Indeed, football clubs play a significant role in the self-definition of a *Comunidad* and have a part to play in linking political definitions of a region with the local population's sentiments in ways that are not dissimilar to the processes taking place in France (see Chapter 5 for the involvement of local politicians in the coverage of RC Lens). This link between politics and football in Andalusia is made explicit at times: 'The best thing that could happen is that Betis get into a European competition and triumph. It would bring pride to our football and to Andalusia', claims the politician Antonio Ortega, General Secretary of the Andalusian Party. In the same article we note: 'Andalusians accuse Manuel Ruiz de Lopera [president of Real Betis] of exploiting Betis for his own political and financial gain' (*El País*, 20 September 1997). Indeed, the fans probably have a point. Lopera, a politician in the Partido Popular (Spain's main right-wing party), is not above appealing to *beticismo* (affection for Betis) to try to ban the opposition leader Chares from Betis's stadium; his reason for doing so being that Chares opposed a proposal for a new ground for Betis. Apparently, football and politics make uncomfortable bed partners in Andalusia.[31]

Finally, Valencia is also assuming an image as a regionalist club and is often defined by its relationship with Catalonia and Madrid. The press emphasises that, although it might share linguistic features with Catalonia, Valencia's preferred allegiance is actually with Madrid. Before one encounter against FC Barcelona, Valencia's then president, Roig, incited the crowd 'by resorting to resurrecting the old anti-Catalan ghosts which still reside in certain sectors of Valencian society' (*El País*, 8 September 1997).

Indeed, his comments succeeded in encouraging the pro-Castilian Valencia fans to chant 'Madrid! Madrid!' at the travelling Catalan contingent, thereby adding further complexity to the intricate web of historical, political and social enmities in which the different components of the Spanish state are locked and which have formed a constant theme throughout this chapter.

We have seen, then, that the complexity and fluidity of Spain's recent political and administrative history is, to a considerable extent, reflected in football writing in the national daily press. Despite the transition to democracy and the provisions for decentralisation outlined by the 1978 Constitution, Spanish sports media texts continue to portray Madrid as the seat of power and authority, occupying a superior position with regard to the rest of Spain and setting it (and Castile of which it is the capital) in opposition to other regions and, especially, to the *nacionalidades históricas* of Catalonia and the Basque Country, a conflict that predates the Franco era but which was, undoubtedly, reinforced by it. Many in the *nacionalidades históricas* and the *Comunidades Autónomas* in general, though, might now be content with the degree of autonomy and recognition they have in twenty-first century Spain (which dilutes any case for greater independence or separatism), and it cannot be denied that there is, even in the national press, considerable focus on the distinctive identities of Spain's different regions/nations, especially Catalonia, the Basque Country and Andalusia. It could, of course, be argued that the accent on autonomy and tolerance of difference that are features of contemporary Spain has given a boost to the further promotion of such distinctive imagined identities and represents a certain proof (lingering images of Castilian superiority notwithstanding) that Spain has, after decades of dictatorship and attempted centralisation under several monarchs in previous centuries, finally become a more modern and progressively more open society.

La Liga de las estrellas:
Spain and the International Brigade

The portrayal of foreigners in Spanish football and, in particular, the representation of Spain's foreign neighbours in its 'quality' daily press will shed important light on the nature of heterotypification, the characterisation of the Other in discourse. These issues take on an added pertinence in Spain. Spain is frequently regarded (by many Spaniards and non-Spaniards alike) as an isolated country, geographically on the edge of Europe, cut-off from France by the physical and psychological barrier of the Pyrenees and sharing much in common with its close north African neighbours. Indeed, the legacy of the Moors, Muslim invaders from north-west Africa, who dominated most of the southern and central parts of Spain from the eighth to the fifteenth century, resides not only architecturally in their grand, stronghold palace in Granada (the Alhambra) but also culturally in the Arabic influences on the development of Spanish society. Needless to say, the years of the Franco dictatorship (1939–75) and the consequent politico-diplomatic ostracism of Spain by the rest of Europe merely served further to reinforce the image of Spain's being a country apart. In some respects, if for different reasons, it might be felt that Spain shares much in common with the United Kingdom in terms of its historically and psychologically isolated outlook on the rest of Europe. Are these features present, then, in Spanish football writing? Let us examine first the representation of foreign footballers playing in the Spanish league before moving on to consider the portrayal in the press of Europe's other dominant football nations, England, France, Germany and Italy.

Despite recent trends in the post-*Bosman* era which have affected most countries in the European Union either as exporters or as importers of footballers, and despite the fact that Spain, like England, has seen a huge influx of foreign talent entering its professional sport, the cultural impact of such a foreign presence in football is not always identical from country to country.

At the start of the 1998/99 season only nine out of the 20 managers in the Primera Liga were Spanish and there were 175 foreign players in Spain, including 35 from Argentina, 21 Brazilians, 20 Yugoslavs, 15 from neighbouring Portugal and 11 from African countries (*El País*, 26 August 1998). Indeed, foreigners represented about 40 per cent of players in the Primera Liga, with an even higher percentage at some clubs. Some 55 per cent of the playing staff at FC Barcelona were non-Spaniards, and 61 per cent at the Galician clubs Celta de Vigo and Deportivo la Coruña.[1] Moreover, the rising quality as well as increasing presence of foreigners in the Spanish first division has earned it the nickname of *la liga de las estrellas* (the League of Superstars). The influx of foreign players into the Primera Liga during the 1990s has, however, been the subject of great debate in the media, paralleling a similar debate in England. Concerns centre largely round a lack of opportunity for young Spanish players to gain experience in the professional game.[2] There are also fears that a large proportion of foreigners in the Primera Liga might dilute any local rivalries and reduce the feelings of identity that fans have with their local clubs which, as we saw in the previous chapter, remain strong.

Although Spain is experiencing much the same phenomenon as England, the Spanish case differs from the English in one significant way: Spanish football has always been the recipient of footballers from abroad. It has since its origins relied on foreign players to produce football at the highest level. Many clubs were established by foreigners, especially the English. The foreigner debate has, however, always been the source of some tension in Spanish football. FC Barcelona, established in 1899, relied heavily on foreign players while neighbouring RCD Espanyol was founded as Sociedad Española de Football in 1900 by a group of university students, proud of their no-foreigner policy which, significantly, made them different from most football clubs in that period. Indeed, the original source of hostilities between Espanyol and FC Barcelona was this ideological clash.[3] Moreover, the foreigner debate takes on a new angle and new questions of definition arise with Athletic de Bilbao and Real Sociedad in the Basque Country, as we have seen, where non-Basque Spaniards are often regarded as foreign.

In a similar vein, it has always been a latent source of frustration that Spain's greatest successes in football have relied on foreign players, albeit often naturalised Latin Americans. The great Real Madrid side of the 1950s benefited from the inclusion of foreigners such as Puskas, Di Stefano, Kopa and Santamaria (Hungarian, Argentine, French and Uruguayan, respectively). Also the Spanish *Selección* who played in the 1962 World Cup finals in Chile was known colloquially as the United Nations because it included players of so many different origins.

So the inclusion of non-Spanish players in Spanish football is nothing new. Despite a recent rise in the proportion of those foreign players, though, attitudes are rarely hostile towards them as individuals. On the contrary, their influence is often welcomed (we have seen in Chapter 7 how the press react to relying exclusively on Spanish qualities of *la furia española*). This is reflected in the press analysed where we seldom find unduly pejorative reporting.

We do, however, find examples of stereotyping, and Latin Americans are usually the victims. It is worth commenting briefly on the ways in which Latin Americans are portrayed, given the huge involvement of Latin American footballers in Spanish football throughout the twentieth century. Compared with another sub-group which features heavily, namely eastern Europeans, the stereotyping of Latin Americans is loaded. Given the historical links between Spain and Latin America, it is perhaps unsurprising that there has been such a steady flow of players from that continent into Spain.[4] Despite such close interaction, the stereotypical image of Latin Americans is not dissimilar to that found in other European countries: flair, individuality, laid-back attitude, temperamental. Not all Latin Americans share the same image or stereotype, however. Brazilians and Argentines, for example, although sharing some features which may be summarised as 'the Latin American temperament', also have distinct identities of their own.

Brazilians playing in the *Liga* provide examples of how an essentialist identity is perpetuated. Football 'comes naturally' to Brazilians: 'Ronaldo's goal was down to his natural ability, part of his character' (*ABC*, 17 June 1998). There are many examples of Brazilian footballers being referred to as 'skilful' and displaying 'technical excellence': Sinval is 'an exquisite footballer ... he has good control and first touch, is fast and effective' (*El País*, 16 February 1998). When referring to Brazilians, talk is of 'individual skill' rather than teamwork: 'It was the Brazilians who set the stadium alight ... with their Brazilian fantasy' (*El País*, 20 February 1998). This is mirrored in reports on the Brazilian side at the 1998 World Cup where individual genius was said to win Brazil games: 'Brazil had their genie in the lamp' (*ABC*, 4 July); 'Brazil saved themselves from defeat thanks again to certain individual performances' (ibid.). Even when Brazil's style of football defies the stereotype, as it did with some labouring performances at France 98, it is still assumed that 'In Brazil they value dribbling and skilful football' (*ABC*, 11 June) thereby perpetuating the familiar image. Similarly, prompted no doubt by images of the samba from Brazilian popular culture, references to 'rhythm' and 'dance' are also frequent – even when saying that players have 'lost their rhythm', and sometimes, when Brazilians are not producing dazzling performances, this is equally expected since their 'laid-back attitude' is part of their character: 'Juninho was relaxed ... as though he wanted to save his energy' (*ABC*, 17 March 1998). Again, when the same player was injured it was bemoaned in *El País* that 'he won't be able to enjoy his football carnival' (8 February 1998). This somewhat light-hearted approach to football is supposedly typical of Brazilians whose 'play is as hot as a tropical beach ... whimsical ... laid-back' (*ABC*, 24 June 1998) and can be 'undisciplined and frivolous' (*El País*, 22 February 1998).

Argentines, however, endure a very different image from the Brazilians. They enjoy some of the flair and individuality awarded to most Latin American players and references to 'rhythm' and 'dance' are still present (for example, 'D'Alessandro's discourse was more like a bolero than a tango ... The Argentine manager imposed a rhythm on the match' [*El País*, 16 February 1998]). Argentines, though, can also be 'tough' and 'defensive' with military terminology abounding in references to them: 'The Argentines have shells as hard as steel, hardened by a thousand battles' (*ABC*, 15 June 1998). So, images of individual players in the Spanish *Liga* recycle national identities found in comments on the Argentine national side who play 'tough', 'unattractive', 'vulgar' football and relish participating in a 'a crude battle' (*ABC*, 5 July 1998).

Despite a huge rise in the 1990s in the number of footballers in the Primera Liga originating from eastern Europe, there is rarely strong evidence of such recycling of identities of this particular group. Whereas Latin Americans are invariably referred to within match reports by their nationality (such as 'Rivaldo, the Brazilian') eastern Europeans rarely are, but when they are it is usually to introduce a characteristic considered as representing part of their national character. A detailed analysis of the data can reveal a few trends in the ways in which eastern Europeans are depicted. They are often 'tough' (especially after experiences of civil war and poverty in their homeland such as the 'brave and committed Yugoslav' described in *El País*, 1 December 1997), 'wise' ('the wisdom of Djukic', *El País*, 23 February 1998), 'neat and orderly' (such as Penev, the Bulgarian playing for Compostela [*ABC*, 2 February 1998]), 'physically slight but technically correct footballers' (*El País*, 9 February 1998), but ultimately rather lacking in strong individualistic characteristics which makes them like Illie, 'the anonymous Romanian' (*El País*, 3 February 1998).

Why are the identities of east Europeans not as strong as those of Latin Americans? Are the former Soviet bloc countries a relatively unknown part of the world for Spaniards, being still socially and politically distant? Perhaps the fact that the Latin Americans are a long-established presence in Spanish football as well as the physical embodiment of the Iberian peninsula's historical links with its former colonies is an influential factor leading to a greater familiarity between the communities in question and, therefore, to stronger stereotyping.

It is clear that there are two types of portrayal of the 'Other' in Spanish football writing. The first, already outlined, deals with those foreigners who are playing within the Spanish Liga. They are clearly marked out as different but they are, nonetheless, historically, for the most part, a long-standing feature of the Spanish system and are not, therefore, perceived as adversaries. The second group, other nations on the international stage, involve potential opposition to Spanish football and tend, as we shall see, to a much more extensive use of stereotyping that includes the emphasising of the supposedly negative traits of the nations in question.

Spanish football writing on England, for instance, is characterised by the recurrence of several themes most of which (unsurprisingly) reflect the stereotypes the Spanish often have of the English. First, we see the contrasting and conflicting images of the English as both 'gentlemen' and 'hooligans'. We shall also see permeating the football pages of Spanish newspapers notions that England (both the country and its football) is somewhat anachronistic as well as references to a rather arrogant reliance on a glorious past.

English fans are frequently described in Spanish football writing as 'thugs' or 'trouble-makers', with the word 'hooligan' being practically synonymous with 'English fan'. There are considerably more articles on so-called English 'hooligans' in the Spanish press than there are on any other group of supporters, or even on any team. There is as much coverage of England fans' behaviour during the build-up to a match as there is of the match itself. Unsurprisingly, these articles are riddled with references to military terminology and nationalist symbols. Even when the article explains how there was no violence at a match, so frequent are references to 'violence', 'aggression', 'thugs', 'hooligans', 'policing' and 'invasions' that the reader is left decidedly perturbed by events which did not actually take place (as in *El País*, 23 June 1998, following England's match in Toulouse during the 1998 World Cup finals; see Chapter 6 for other examples of the press amplifying 'hooliganism'). Although comments are made about how the behaviour of English fans has changed over the last decade or so, these references are brief and occur only in more in-depth articles devoted to football fandom in general (for instance, *ABC*, 8 June 1996; *El País*, 9 June 1996).

In a similar vein, when the Spanish press eventually come round to reporting on the exploits of the England team itself, the accent is placed firmly on the reputed English qualities of aggression and tenacity. A common feature of the print media discourse studied in this respect is the use of military images and metaphors. This style of writing attains its full realisation in the coverage of the England–Argentina game at the 1998 World Cup finals when one report goes as far as claiming explicitly that the match will replay the Falklands/Malvinas War, as England and Argentina are 'arch enemies' about to undertake 'a war on the pitch' in the 'revenge match' as 'Argentines have not forgotten the war' (*ABC*, 1 July). Journalists reporting on this game in both *ABC* and *El País* cannot resist the military metaphor as 'there was no cease-fire' between the teams, players got 'caught in the crossfire', there were 'bombardments', 'aerial attacks', and 'sudden raids' and neither side 'surrendered' (1 July). Once again, then, this time in the Spanish press, two nations' historical, diplomatic and military relationships are evoked in reporting on football which is thereby mediated as an extension of those relationships.

Next, there would seem to be a tripartite relationship between English culture, the (actual or potential) behaviour of English fans and the style of play of the England team which has been observed in England itself. The football writer Dave Hill, for instance, remarks on being 'struck by the similarities between our shirtless boys off the pitch and those in white shirts on it. Both examples of English manhood are predictable, artless and basically inadequate.'[5] The connection is not overlooked by the Spanish press and, indeed, appears as a given, as the following examples surrounding the English players Paul Gascoigne, Michael Owen and Paul Ince demonstrate.

The Spanish newspapers under consideration portray Gascoigne – a key figure in the 1996 European Championships – as typifying the aggressive English hooligan image, the 'Gazza phenomenon' being very much a product of its epoch in English social history:

> The Gascoigne phenomenon helps us understand the heart of the England team. Paul Gascoigne cannot be understood outside his English context. His professional and personal lives personify those characteristics that the English admire as a symbol ... He is 'one of us' or 'one of them' according to whether you attended a private or a state school. (*El País*, 8 June 1998)

There is, then, a rather oversimplified view of England presented through the medium of the coverage of Gascoigne as well as that of English fans, as a society divided neatly into images of the traditional English gentleman 'heralding fair play and privately educated' (*ABC*, 22 June 1998), versus those of the lager lout, 'state educated' (ibid.), of course.

Finally, Gascoigne is 'fiercely patriotic with a competitive streak that borders on aggression at times, a type of English bulldog ... who offers the perspective of a re-established national pride' (ibid.), a description reminiscent of the Brimsons' accounts of England fans abroad,[6] or of Ward's illustration of England followers during France 98,[7] and one which Perryman depicted succinctly as 'Number one crop, tattoos, chanting enthusiastically, can of beer in one hand, St. George's flag in the other'.[8] Gascoigne is, then, also portrayed as a virulent reaction against foreign influences in English football and represents the reassertion of English pride.

Interestingly, the performances of Ince in the 1998 World Cup finals, lauded so unanimously by the English press, were heavily criticised by Spanish writers. The Spanish try to analyse the reasons why Ince was popular in England and ultimately decide that his wholehearted approach is the trait that is valued highly among the English: 'The English will tell you that Ince has character, that this influences his colleagues, that he's a good tackler. Rubbish. The truth is that he can't play football ... He can't organise a team' (ibid.). In other words, Ince is seen as being a player with limited talent and no technical ability at all: he is all *furia* and no skill – which, as we have already noted (see Chapter 7), is not sufficient for a player of international standard in Spain, but it is apparently what the English want.

Even when the English team includes a player who does not seem to fit the stereotype of English footballers typified by Ince, such as Owen, the Liverpool striker, he is still described within the framework of this assumed English norm: 'Michael Owen is the antithesis of the English forward. He is more skilful than physical' (*ABC*, 2 July 1998). Just as the British media find it difficult to accept that an Italian striker can be big and physical (see the coverage of Christian Vieri in Chapter 3), so, too, do the Spanish press display a reluctance to qualify Owen's skill and technique as anything other than not English.

Overall, then, as far as the Spanish press is concerned, England customarily lack talent. 'England played little creative football' is *ABC*'s summary of the World Cup campaign (23 June 1998), relying instead on 'the industrious sector' and 'British tenacity' (ibid.). The image of the English being tough, something of a combination of the hooligan and the hard-working journeyman, is frequent. Even the English referee at France 98, Paul Durkin, was described as 'allowing the Austrians to be tough in defence, *as you would expect from an Englishman*' (ibid.; our italics).

When it is acknowledged that the English team has produced a commendable performance on the pitch, such as against Columbia, whom they beat 2–0 at France 98, the compliments paid refer to qualities the English would recognise as positive themselves as well as to those associated closely with English football in Spain: '[England] played more dynamic, more aggressive and, above all, more resolute football' (*ABC*, 27 June); similarly, following England's narrow defeat on penalties to Argentina, *ABC* offers almost the simple stereotype of English football itself: '[England] played long, deep, penetrative balls, quick and simple football' (1 July). This was 'a match that was more physical than skilful. More passionate than tactical' (ibid.). Among the many interesting images used to communicate English tenacity, we find: 'England didn't give up ... They kept their hopes alive right to the end. These English have the hearts of lions. They sought victory with the ardour so typical of them ... so brave' (ibid.). Thus all of the clichés of the battling and heroic English, including the lion heart metaphor, that have already been encountered in the British and the French press (see Chapters 1 and 6) are recycled here in Spain where, it is noted, the English were said to have lost 'with honour' (*ABC*, 2 July).

The combination of the reputation of English 'hooligans' and the image the English have of being passionate about their football not only puts the Spanish in awe of the England team but also apparently makes them fearful of the atmosphere within English football grounds. In a preview to Athletic de Bilbao's European match against Aston Villa, one journalist wrote that 'To win a tie anywhere on English soil is always difficult', and he referred in particular to the expected 'frightening and intimidating atmosphere' at Villa Park (*El País*, 4 November 1997). The following day, after Athletic were knocked out of the competition, it was claimed that 'The damage was done. Tradition did the rest' (*El País*, 5 November). Nothing more was said about what the supposed 'tradition' might be. Perhaps the fact that Aston Villa had beaten Athletic de Bilbao some 19 years earlier? Perhaps England's long-established footballing tradition? Or, perhaps the passionate atmosphere referred to the previous day? This would be ironic, though, given the fact that Aston Villa were playing Athletic de Bilbao, who, as we have seen, are the club presented as being the most passionate in the Spanish league (see Chapter 8).

On the other hand, images are also presented in the Spanish press whereby English fans are not frenzied beasts at all but rather 'Gentlemen who watch the match from their bars back home in London' (*ABC*, 27 June 1996). When England beat Holland resoundingly in the 1996 European Championships, the English are described as 'resuscitated from their usual lethargic state' (ibid.) while the image of the English as being boring, tucked up in their beds by 11 o'clock (*ABC*, 14 June 1996) is one which recurs in the data as frequently as references to 'fish and chips' and 'cricket'. Even the England national team is qualified as 'boring', with 'no real characters' and 'no real style to its play' (*El País*, 11 June 1998). These two contradictory and conflicting images of the English are both portrayed in one newspaper headline which reads: 'As the hooligans wreck London after the English lose to Germany, the England team win the fair-play award yet again' (*ABC*, 27 June 1996). This contradiction is also recognised astutely in an article by Jorge Valdano: 'The English are caught in two minds: they are trying to change their style of football to make it "more continental" and at the same time they want to be English and follow their genes' (*El País*, 1 July 1998). He suspects, however, mirroring the viewpoint gaining ground in England itself, that the English would appreciate a more technically aware, passing game since they value highly the successful Liverpool side of the 1970s.

Further traits portrayed through football which might be felt to be part of a wider English identity, according to the Spanish press, are grounded in the image of England being anachronistic and aloof bordering on arrogant. Its people continue to wallow in the successes of former colonial supremacy and its style of football remains unchanged while the rest of Europe has developed new techniques: 'It remains anchored in its past' (*El País*, 6 June 1996). One headline following England's World Cup defeat by Romania sums up the portrayal of the English as living in a glorious but long dead past: 'Jurassic England' (*El País*, 23 June 1998). The article continues,

'England wanted to change with the times, but they couldn't' (ibid.). The assumed English arrogance is often close to the surface in Spanish football writing: 'The English have a great opinion of themselves in all aspects of life and football is no exception' trumpets *El País* (9 June 1998). Furthermore, the English are also often seen as outsiders and portrayed as such. Football reporting reflects the popular view held by some Spaniards of the English being politically and psychologically isolated from the rest of Europe, a view seemingly supported by successive British governments' reluctance to enter wholeheartedly into European political and economic union. The English are excluded from the rest of Europe: '[They] are used to less hysterical refereeing than Europeans' states *El País* (13 June 1996), implying that the English are not Europeans at all, while another writer refers to England trying to adopt a European style of play, the assumption being that England do not already contribute to defining the European identity.

As for France, even before the 1998 World Cup victory, the Spanish press displayed great respect for French football which is reputed overwhelmingly for its teamwork and its style of play. The open and flowing style is seen as part of the French character as perceived by the Spanish and, therefore, revolves around concepts of flair similar to those encountered in the British and the French press: 'The French model works' according to *El País*, 'mainly because it remains faithful to its origins, a sort of genetic code which equates its footballers with good football, æsthetically pleasing football. It's a country which has maintained its identity' (6 June 1996). Indeed, when the Czech Republic tried to prevent the French from playing with their usual flair at Euro 96, the Czechs were referred to as 'anti-football' (*ABC*, 27 June).

Keen to reinforce the point that style and flair are required and expected in France, the Spanish press asserts that French football fans 'aspire not only to results but also to the footballing art of the era of Platini, Giresse, Tigana and co.' (*El País*, 8 June 1998) thereby situating the French team of the late 1990s within the tradition of 'champagne football' exemplified by the European Championship winning side of 1984. The expectations are that winning is not enough, France has to win in style because of the 'yearning for that creative, attacking style of play' (ibid.) that is quintessentially French. Most significantly in the context of the present study, the same newspaper then goes on to affirm that French fans 'demand fantasy and æsthetics in their football *as in everything else*' (ibid.; our italics). In other words, football is once again mediated as an extension of society. Here, French football fans' aspirations in a sporting context mirror their country's widely-held reputation for creativity and quality of life.[9]

Interestingly, as we have seen, there was a fear in France itself that the national team preparing for the 1998 World Cup finals was not worthy of the stylish tradition in which it was supposed to be operating (see Chapter 4) and this theme was picked up at some length in the Spanish 'quality' daily press, too. According to *El País*, even on the eve of the World Cup, France was still 'In search of the collective magic' (ibid.). The manager Aimé Jacquet had, apparently, 'built a strong team but he hasn't managed yet to awaken the genius and collective magic' that is expected to flow from a French side (ibid.). Mirroring French journalists' criticisms, the Spanish print media discourse examined castigates Jacquet as being 'too obsessed with results, and not caring about playing attractive, attacking football' (*El País*, 14 June). Despite the fact that, by early 1998, the French had lost only three of the first 40 games played under Jacquet, they were perceived as failing to display enough flair in their play to be truly French. Similarly, France's fans would have liked 'an exciting manager who risks all not a conservative type ... who puts a dampener on the French fantasy' (*El País*, 18 June). In short, Jacquet is accused of not letting the French be French and for 'not recognising *the needs* of his players who want to be more creative' (*ABC*, 9 July; our italics). Even when France successfully qualify for the semi-final of the World Cup, readers are informed that 'winning is not enough' (*ABC*, 7 July), apparently, as there is no worse crime for a French manager than not allowing his team to play 'in style' (*ABC*, 9 July). It is interesting to note, in passing, though, that, although the Spanish press agree that Jacquet's style of play is not exciting enough for the French, they would nonetheless like their own manager to be like him in some respects because he gets results (*El País*, 18 June).

The association is so close between the French and fine style that even when performances are clearly contradicting the stereotype, as we have seen bemoaned in many match reports, the essentialist image remains intact. In the preview to the World Cup quarter-final between France and Italy, *El País* notes that 'France and Italy will both try to reach the semi-finals, but each in their own way. Neither will renounce their *traditional* way of playing football in such an important game. The French will attack and attack ... the Italians will defend and look for the counterattack. The *rules* are thus' (3 July; our italics).

Speaking of the role of players from the ethnic minorities in the French team, the Spanish press is initially keen to stress what it sees as the novelty of the introduction of outside elements into French football: 'Certainly what has inspired French football comes from an external vitality and it can almost be said that French football dances to the sound of French rap coming from the *banlieues*, played among young *Maghrebis*' (*El País*, 8 June 1998). The same article then mentions how France's 'immigrant footballers' are 'privileged lads, educated within the French system and, therefore, integrated but not assimilated [into French society] and who display from time to time evidence of the extravagances of another culture'.[10] The coverage of France's black players is, though, treated uniquely in the

Spanish press. A similar theme is, of course, covered extensively and somewhat extravagantly in the French press where France's fraternal teamwork ethic is portrayed as a metaphor for an ideal society (see Chapter 4). It is also touched upon in the German print media, too, where the inclusion of representatives and descendants of France's immigrant populations is also portrayed positively as an example of that country's successful multicultural society (see the *Süddeutsche Zeitung*, for instance). In the Spanish data examined, however, the reaction is rather different. France's black players inspire a range of (often racist) remarks as the French team is compared to Cameroon of the 1990 World Cup and Nigeria of the 1994 World Cup 'except with the Latin instinct' (*ABC*, 12 June 1996). 'Africans play a naïve style of football, take true pleasure in playing and the support is fanatical' is just one comment directed at the French team. This report ends in a rather blunt reference to the colour of some of the French players, which the writer uses with the singularly misguided intention of making an amusing pun: 'I'd like to see Spain beat France, but I see that as being difficult. I see black' (ibid.).

Descriptions of Zinedine Zidane, the French midfielder of North African origin, share much in common with those of other African players: 'His style of play is so *natural* that he makes football seem supernatural' (*El País*, 19 June 1998; our italics). The reader is never allowed to forget Zidane's origins: 'One minute he is God and is everywhere at once, the next minute he is human, remembers his difficult years spent in the immigrant ghetto of La Castellane and loses his temper, stamps on his marker and is sent off' (ibid.). While Zidane 'represents the best traditions of French football, always classy' (*El País*, 13 July 1998), his temper is put down to a flaw in his character that is seemingly, for the Spanish press, inevitable given his ethnic background.

Despite the claims in the Spanish print media that France is a 'country which has maintained its identity' (*El País*, 6 June 1996), what seems to be emerging from the Spanish data is evidence of an evolution in France's imagined identity. By the time of the 1998 World Cup finals it is hinted that the French team might be a catalyst for the incorporation into one society of many ethnic groups: '[For one night] children of Maghrebis, black Africans and West Indians, even Orientals, shared the same emotion and the same fraternal effect that the players had shown on the pitch in the form of many demonstrative collective embraces' (*El País*, 10 July). Similarly, 'There is also a social message in this French match. France is a country of integration, of asylum, represented by a team that corresponds perfectly to the melting pot of a nation which is suffering the sectarian discourse of the ultra-right wing in some regions' (*El País*, 12 July). In short, displaying similar idealism to that witnessed in France itself, the Spanish press concludes that football has 'united the French of all races' (ibid.).

While images remain, then, of the French playing attractive, 'æsthetically pleasing' football as a team, the incorporation of the new ethnic element into France's identity has posed some difficulties for Spanish writers who prefer at times to adhere to facile stereotyping. The communication of the new type of French football has been dealt with rather clumsily and this is partly because of a certain reluctance to compromise on what is the essence of French identity. In some ways the images of the French in the Spanish press are as contradictory as those of the English. While on the one hand the French style of flair football reflects the very essence of what it is to be French, and this identity is never-changing, on the other, the black players are seen as adding a new dimension to French football, a certain brashness and power, surely, then, affecting the unchanging model of the French way of playing.

Stereotypes of the German character pervade all references to the German team and the images portrayed in Spanish football writing replicate to a considerable extent those offered in the press in Britain and in France. The same themes of strength, efficiency and self-belief are evident and the words most used to described Germans in the lexis of Spanish print media discourse include 'discipline', 'order', 'machine' and 'belief'. Many reports refer to the Germans' 'machine-like efficiency' and their 'domination'. For example, 'Then the Teutonic machine began to work' (*ABC*, 10 June 1996); '[We expect Germany] to come out and dictate the game to the Czechs' (*El País*, 9 June 1996); the Germans are credited with 'Order, control, sangfroid'(*El País*, 27 June 1996).

German discipline and efficiency are rarely, if ever, in doubt. Moreover, Spanish football writing mirrors that in Britain and France in its communication of these supposedly typical qualities through the use of imagery comparing Germans to machines, thereby linking once again with the recent successes of the German economy which have been largely built on technological prowess. Thus 'German football is disciplined, physical and efficient' (*El País*, 8 June 1998); 'the German piston [is] vulgar but mechanical' (*ABC*, 26 June 1998); 'Without lifting a finger Germany threw coal on the machine and moved ... [There is] something dangerous in the way they roam about, a regular mechanical rhythm, cold as ice and steel' (*ABC*, 30 June 1998); 'Germany is a winning machine. And when they don't win they are a losing machine. But they are always a machine' (*El País*, 23 June 1998). There is even a conscious awareness among Spanish journalists that they are actually in the process of (re)constructing the typical German stereotype but, rather than engage in a debate about its validity or function, they simply prefer to recycle it. For instance, under the headline 'The great German stereotype', one report explains that 'Germany is a side full of stereotypes. *All true*. Reliability, mechanical tendencies, lack of flair, unattractive goals' (*El País*, 22 June 1998; our italics).

Another important feature of the German stereotype is aggression and, once again, the Spanish press plays its part in reaffirming this as an essentialist quality of German identity. There are references to the 'physical strength' of the Germans (*ABC*, 30 June 1998), for instance, as well as to the fact that 'Germany is muscular and obsessed with winning' (*El País*, 8 June 1998). Indeed, Germany's role in European print media texts is frequently seen as threatening. Real menace oozes from the page of one match report in *ABC* as the reader is told that the Germans 'looked fixedly at their rivals with an icy stare ... and set about their task' (30 June 1998). A complete stylostatistical analysis of the Spanish press would probably reveal fewer recourses to military terminology to describe Germans than in Great Britain or France, though, which might derive from the fact that Spain, unlike the other countries, did not directly experience German belligerence or invasion during either World War.[11] None the less, military metaphors are still present as, for example, when '[manager] Vogts got serious his troops stepped into motion and began to dominate' (*ABC*, 10 June 1996). Moreover, Germany's wartime involvement is itself by no means absent from Spanish match reports. Indeed, it is explicitly referred to by *ABC*'s discussion of the France 98 game against Croatia (30 June). Football, politics and military history are inextricably linked by the piece which mentions several times that Germany and Croatia are old friends because they were allies during the Second World War.

Strong self-belief is another trait customarily attributed to Germans by the Spanish (and other Europeans) who, in awe, generally expect Germany to be always successful. German teams are, therefore, always rated highly, even if the present side is poor, partly because of the fear they inspire by their traditional self-confidence and partly because of their record. 'The Germans can play awful football, be inferior on the pitch, roam about aimlessly, employ the tactic of floating in long balls, but it doesn't matter. They will always be among the favourites in any international tournament' (*El País*, 8 June 1998). Historical successes provide the key to the present. Opposing teams are, apparently, scared of the Germans' reputation. For example, against the USA in the 1998 World Cup 'The German side won because of the power of their history' (*El País*, 16 June). The Germans win because everyone is used to losing to them. In this sense, 'Perhaps football is a prisoner of its past' (*El País*, 22 June 1998). In short, because of 'the winning character of the Germans' (ibid.) their ultimate victory is virtually predestined: 'There is nothing new about the Germans. They win because they have to win. It is written in the history of the World Cup' (*ABC*, 2 July). As far as the Germans are concerned, past performance is, it would seem, always an indication of future value.

At France 98, though, the Spanish press, in common with other European media,[12] had to cope with what it would consider to be a somewhat unexpected, even unpredictable situation, Germany's relatively early elimination from the tournament. The way it did so says much about the tenacity and powers of survival of national stereotypes in European print media sports texts. One writer, for instance, felt it necessary to qualify an apparent lack of confidence among the German team competing in the World Cup as 'surprising' (*El País*, 25 June) thereby implicitly reinforcing the myth that self-belief is usually a typical German trait. Similarly, and somewhat paradoxically, another journalist still noted after Germany's quarter-final defeat by Croatia that they had played with 'boring efficiency' (*El País*, 5 July). So strong are the ties that bind the notion of efficiency with the imagined identity of Germans that even the most inefficient of outcomes, a 3–0 defeat, cannot loosen them. Indeed, Germany's failure to win the tournament is so unexpected that the Spanish press simply has to refer to it as a 'surprise' (ibid.). In the real world of football, that Germany failed should not have been too surprising given its deficiencies in tactics and talent; in the discursive world of media sport, however, it is a surprise when Germans fail to live up to their stereotype and this has to be recorded as such.

Spanish football writing on Germany differs just in one key aspect from that of the rest of the data. Underlying the British and the French reporting there can be sensed a certain (sometimes begrudging) admiration. In the Spanish press, however, there is little trace of this respect. Perhaps the fact that the Spanish value style more highly than results contributes to the failure to be impressed. As we have seen, in Spain boring football is not lauded, no matter how effective it is. There is no disguising the derogatory terminology employed at every opportunity to describe German football and wholehearted credit is rarely given to German victories. Monotony is often associated with German football. 'Germany wins by boring the opposition' (*ABC*, 26 June 1998) is one headline while other articles pick up the theme: Germany is criticised for playing 'always with the same rhythm, like a heavy machine' (*El País*, 5 July1998) and frequently denigrated as 'boring' (ibid.). Moreover, self-belief becomes simple 'German arrogance' (*ABC*, 30 June 1998). '[They] played without concerning themselves with their rivals, and their pride in only thinking about themselves allowed the Czechs to create some problems for a while' (*ABC*, 10 June 1996). The German players are unflatteringly qualified as 'workhorses ... who cover a lot of ground but who play little football' (*ABC*, 27 June 1996). Even towards the end of the 1996 European Championships, which Germany won, they are described as, 'Consistent, rudimentary, granite-like, competitive, strong, brave, resistant. This time at Wembley. Germans, the same as ever ... Boring, monotonous. In short, Germany' (*El País*, 28 June).

Finally, the ultimate condemnation is to attribute the Germans' successes not to their traditional virtues of self-confidence, strength and efficiency but rather to good fortune: 'They usually get results they don't deserve', notes

El País (6 June 1996). Two years later the same newspaper reinforced the point during the 1998 World Cup: 'It is strange how often the Germans are blessed with luck' (*El País*, 22 June) while *ABC* remarked, following Germany's elimination from the tournament, that after '12 years of fortune ... The Germans have finally used up all their luck' (*ABC*, 5 July).

Finally, turning to Italy, there is no doubt that this country has a very well-defined and long-standing identity in the Spanish press. There are references to 'the Italy of old' (*El País*, 18 June 1998), to an Italy that 'played like Italy' (*El País*, 19 June 1998), to a nation 'that doesn't change its identity' (*El País*, 1 July 1998), to an Italy that 'can't and won't change its style' (ibid.) and, in short, to the fact that 'Italy was Italy' (*ABC*, 2 July 1998). What are the principal features of this perennial Italian identity?

First, as in the British media (see Chapter 3), there is an affirmation that Italians are gifted footballers with considerable artistic potential and 'individual talent' (*ABC*, 24 June 1998). Theirs is, apparently, 'a country of æsthetics' (*El País*, 24 June 1998) that has produced footballers with 'great abilities as maestros' (*ABC*, 28 June 1998), led by a manager, Maldini, who 'had the good fortune to be born in Italy, so into his hands fell *naturally* competent teams, *whoever plays in them*' (*ABC*, 24 June 1998; our italics). The Spanish press, however, is perplexed and, no doubt, not a little disappointed that for the most part Italian football teams choose to put the accent on defence, caution and containment ('sterile football' [*El País*, 23 February 1998]) rather than on being bold. Indeed, in a Spain that aspires to style itself (see Chapter 7), little credit is given for a lack of adventure. Italian football is frequently termed 'poor', then, even when it gets results (as in *El País*, 18 June, 24 June 1998; *ABC*, 24 June 1998). Similarly, it is felt noteworthy that Italy beat Cameroon at France 98 by playing 'precisely calculated football [doing] as little as possible ... [and giving] nothing away' (*El País*, 18 June). Again, Italians are qualified as 'astute ... risking nothing' (*El País*, 19 June), 'risking the minimum to win' (*ABC*, 24 June) and described as careful to be 'organised in order to close gaps in the defence and defend with honour' (ibid.). Indeed, these traits are expected of Italy: 'They have done this so many times that no one is surprised by this method any more' (*El País*, 18 June); this is 'their usual plan' (ibid.), 'The same tactics as ever. As old as the Roman uniforms' worn by some of their more colourful fans (*ABC*, 24 June). In short, 'Score and retreat into defence is what Italians are all about' (ibid.). So potent are these supposedly typical Italian qualities that they can, apparently, rub off on foreigners playing in Serie A. Tabárez, a Uruguayan, returned to Spain after a spell at AC Milan to be described as 'the model Italian, who thinks only about defending' (*El País*, 9 February 1998). To an extent, this absence of audacity is portrayed as deriving from a flaw in the Italian psyche. Ultimately Italians lack confidence: 'To play well, Italy need to be a goal or two up', notes *ABC* (18

June 1998), while *El País* ascribed Maldini's reluctance to play del Piero and Baggio up front not to tactical considerations but to a play safe mentality that is content not to be too daring (24 June 1998).

Next, in descriptions reminiscent of those of Carbone and di Canio found in *The Times* (see Chapter 3), the stereotypical Italian temperament is also given a further airing in the Spanish print media studied: 'Christian Panucci, the Italian', for instance, 'is a temperamental, hot-headed gossip who argues with his team mates' (*El País*, 26 January 1998). Moreover, when Italians fail to conform to the volcanic stereotype, the Spanish media also register surprise which, as has been noted elsewhere, is one way in which such a myth can be perpetuated: '*Strange* Italy. The country where everything is discussed at the top of the voice is about to complete the first phase [of France 98] very quietly. The lack of the *usual* destructive arguments ... has given the squad a *surprisingly* festive atmosphere' (*El País*, 23 June; our italics).

To sum up, portrayals of the foreign Other in Spanish football writing are distinctive and recycle many of the characteristics of national stereotypes that have already been encountered in the British and the French press. Images of the battling English, the stylish French, the dour, mechanical Germans and the gifted but cagey Italians are just as much features of Spanish sports media texts as they are of those produced in other European countries.[13] The treatment of foreigners playing football in the domestic game in Spain itself, though, would appear to differ significantly, especially from the data gathered in the British press. Spain, like Great Britain, might be on the periphery of Europe geographically but, whereas Britain in general and England in particular remains psychologically splendidly isolationist and, therefore, suspicious of the foreign Other 'infiltrating' its shores (see Chapters 1 and 3), Spain would appear to show a greater degree of tolerance to foreigners operating in its football league. Certainly the impact of foreign players on the progress of home-grown talent is debated, as it is in England, but the pejorative – and, occasionally downright hostile – stereotyping of foreigners that is so prevalent in both tabloid and 'quality' newspapers in England is largely absent from *El País* and *ABC*. There are sound historical reasons for this. Professional football in England developed for a hundred years with only a small number of non-British players in its ranks since it was not until the 1980s that the number of foreign footballers began to rise significantly. In Spain, however, an important foreign presence (especially Latin American and west European) has always been a feature of the game and Spanish football as a whole, therefore, does not display the same fearful mistrust and even rejection of foreigners that is so typical of a certain English attitude. Reading football as an extension of society,[14] might it be argued, then, that Spain is, in this respect at least, a rather more open country than Great Britain?

Conclusion: Imagined Identities?

Football unites and divides the continent of Europe. The humble (amateur) and not-so-humble (professional) football ground is, even more so than the outlets of a certain fast-food chain, the one common, even ubiquitous element of Europe's landscape from the Atlantic to the Alps, and from the Mediterranean to the Irish Sea. Indeed, some 20 million men and women come together to play football in Europe on an organised basis while countless millions more attend matches as spectators, watch the sport on television, listen to it on the radio, engage with it on the Internet and read about it in the press. The sport's governing bodies, such as FIFA and UEFA, have set up international tournaments that allow Europeans, whether playing for or supporting national teams or domestic club sides, to meet in competition against each other while the increasing mobility of professional footballers – aided by legislation such as the *Bosman* ruling – has also brought Europeans into much more frequent contact with each other through the sport than at any other period in the game's history.

However, as we have seen, when football is mediated, especially by the 'quality' daily press in Europe and particularly in the categories of sports journalism that might be termed hard news and orthodox rhetoric, the accent is placed upon difference, upon that which divides rather than unites, upon that which is distinctive in terms of identity. The narratives about the game in the European football writing examined anchor discourses of collective identity that favour diversity, that celebrate local, regional and national versions of European culture (even in the face of globalising tendencies). Some of the linguistic and discursive mechanisms at work in these narratives have been identified. The simple repetition of meaningful items of vocabulary within and across sports media texts is a favoured recourse. For instance, frequent use of the term 'gallant' in portrayals of the English or of the adjective 'disciplined' when depicting Germans serves to reinforce essential elements in the identities of these nationalities. Secondly, football writing depends heavily on imagery, particularly metaphors. Much of this is at the level of the cliché with footballers being compared to troops fighting in battles to defeat the enemy. More interesting is the use of imaginative and culture-specific metaphors that provide insights into the different European societies studied. The high incidence of religious imagery in the Spanish case, for example, is unique and reflects the still predominantly Catholic nature of that country. Indeed, European football writing is a highly referential form of discourse. Print media texts in this area frequently refer to wider realities outside the footballing context and build upon certain often ideological presuppositions that underpin Europeans' sense of nationhood. French football writing, for instance, not unsurprisingly makes frequent reference to the symbols, events and values of the French Revolution (the Tricolour flag, the *Marseillaise*, the storming of the Bastille, the overthrowing of tyranny in the name of progress) as the Revolution is very much the foundation stone on which modern France has been built as well as the symbolically highly charged event within which shared notions of Frenchness are enshrined. Powerful references such as these mobilise national feeling and promote a consensual vision of national identity. Finally, European football writing frequently relies on stereotypes. Stereotypes, by nature, generally fail to account for the complexities inherent to the identities they portray and often become paradoxical or oversimple (the English are either hooligans or gentlemen). Also they frequently manipulate reality to make it fit preconceived notions, thereby preserving European myths of essentialist national identity (style when displayed by English footballers is qualified as unusual, a novelty or even un-English because in print media discourse on football – as in other social and cultural arenas – style is not felt to be a typically English trait but a French one).

When the European press reflects upon football, there is little movement away from traditional portrayals that continue to posit the existence of distinctive and, as we have seen, of conflictual European regional and national identities. In terms of the expression of collective identities, there would also appear to be little by way of challenge to the dominant social and cultural attitudes towards, say, women or ethnic minorities. In short, the sports texts examined here, produced by (for the most part) highly-educated newspaper editors, columnists and journalists for consumption by Europe's social and political elites, regenerate the powerful cultural myths of the continent's dominant and most empowered group, prosperous, white males, whose discursive reflexes betray an ideological outlook that is essentially conservative rather than radical.

In terms of the representation of African-Caribbeans in football writing, for instance, our case study suggests that, in Great Britain at least, one of the most enduring myths of white, western civilisation is still perpetuated by media sports texts, albeit through subtle uses of language: namely, that of the naturally athletic, strong and threatening black male. The origins of this myth may be traced to the colonial era when cultural representations of blacks portrayed them as aggressive, potentially savage and uncivilised, providing the spurious moral justification for European colonisation. In a small way, exposing the form taken in the language of the football press by outmoded stereotypes of 'racial' difference is the first step to changing the stereotype in favour of a more rounded, inclusive portrayal of the black communities in Europe. Similarly, on the evidence of our data from France, representations of women in the football context also remain framed in potentially damaging traditionalist terms. Women continue to be portrayed primarily in relation to men as passive, as objects/possessions, as flighty, as unintelligent and as fulfilling submissive sexual and maternal roles. In short, patriarchal values of male dominance and female subordination would appear to be upheld rather than effectively questioned by the print media sports texts examined.

With regard to depictions of local and regional identities we have noted the continuing power of football, as mediated by the press, to promote strong affiliations to a given locality by both the accentuating of the supposedly typical values represented by that locality and by the fostering of a sense of difference from other regions with which the locality in question has more or less inimical relations. In this way some of the key internal dynamics of the nations involved are replayed in football writing. In England, for example, a distinct northern identity has been fashioned, deriving largely from the legacy of the Industrial Revolution, which is involved in a somewhat hostile relationship with the politically and economically dominant South-East. In France the notion of a country of rich diversity is given full expression through typical portrayals of its many regions, but not without also, however, raising once again the spectre of the problematic position occupied by the capital Paris. Finally, in Spain, concepts of regional identity take on an added pertinence given the relatively recently decentralised nature of the state and, indeed, the separatist aspirations expressed in some quarters in its constituent nations. Representations of regional identity here are not merely familiar portrayals based on historical legacies; media depictions of the clashing identities of Madrid and Barcelona, for instance, play a significant part in the important ideological conflict between opposing visions of the (centralist) state and the (autonomous) nation.

Most of our study of the football writing in Europe's 'quality' daily press has concerned the vital question of national identities. Football is an important vector for the transmission of widely held beliefs about the typical characteristics of European nations. In the main, print media discourse on football plays a not insignificant part in perpetuating the consensus that national identity is distinctive and capable of reduction to a limited set of typical characteristics. In the British media studied, for instance, English national identity is represented as grounded in concepts of patriotism, courage, fighting spirit and heroism, while the French self-image revolves around notions of flair, style and quality of life, with considerable focus on the national football team as a symbol of France's ethnic diversity and putative harmony. In both cases, however, these essentialist identities are not necessarily totally static. French identity has, as we have seen, relatively recently acquired a more confident outlook and greater resolution of mind. What is interesting to note is that, initially, the French press reacted strongly against the idea that France should develop a more overtly resolute and practical approach to its football, fearing a loss of the quintessential French characteristics of creativity and inspiration. Indeed, the new approach was accepted only when it became clear that France's (stereo)typical qualities could still be preserved in a more rounded scenario in which French style goes hand-in-hand with dogged determination and pragmatism. With regard to English national identity, change is not merely acceptable, it is beginning to be seen as vital (but, once again, so long as traditional virtues are not lost). The heroic near misses of the England team at both the 1996 European Championships and the 1998 World Cup are praised in the media as symbolically loaded examples of the English determination to fight to the end in adversity against unbearable odds. However, while notions of courage and fighting spirit continue to be lauded, calls are now being made for England to jettison its customary aversion to continental European theories and fancy ways in favour of developing a more sophisticated and tactically-aware side to its footballing nature. A debate has been opened in English football circles, then, that interestingly parallels the wider debate in British society about the need for social and political modernisation as well as the extent to which Great Britain's traditional stance of Euro-scepticism is still valid. The case of Spain with respect to the issue of national identity is unique, though. Whereas England and France have recognisably long-standing national identities based upon a set of traditional qualities which are, none the less, in the process of evolution, in Spain the very notion of national identity is itself contentious. Despite attempts by some monarchs to impose unification on the country, the concept of a single national identity never became as historically entrenched in Spain as it did in England or France. Moreover, in the twentieth century the notion of the unitary nation-state became tarnished by association with the Franco dictatorship's excessive and suppressive centralism. From this historical context derives a fluid approach to national identity. The Spanish press fluctuates between attempts to appeal to a certain vision of Spanishness and lamenting the absence of any simple definition of the nation. Furthermore, the supposed characteristics of Spanishness themselves also fluctuate between, on the one hand, an imagined identity based upon *la furia española*, pride and passion, and, on the other, the promotion of a new identity, one that is more stylish and that would reflect Spain's desire to be seen as a more modern, progressive, mainstream European country. The building of a Spanish national identity is still very much work in progress.

Finally, in terms of heterotypification – here, how Europe's dominant footballing countries are perceived by others – it is has been interesting to note that not only are the principal elements of the national identities represented by the 'quality' daily press in Europe essentially the same from country to country, but that they also connect to a considerable extent with those nations' own self-definitions (or autotypification). The fighting spirit lauded in the English self-image is replicated, with negative as well as positive connotations in French and Spanish print media sports texts, which are also united in highlighting familiar themes of English fair play and sporting conduct. Similarly, England's apparent obsession with tradition and the glorious past is a theme found in both Spain and France. Spain's image is of a tough, harsh and somewhat crude nation yearning to become more modern and progressive. It is also contrary, at once pessimistic and optimistic, and divided by the different components of its politico-administrative make-up. The European football writing studied is almost unanimous in its perception of the French. French style is reflected as artistic flair and brilliant technique in Britain as well as in France itself and as a genetic inheritance in Spain, while both Spanish and French newspapers agree on the notion of France's fraternal teamwork ethic even if its 'multiracial' element is viewed negatively by the former and (obviously, as a powerful metaphor) positively by the latter. Italians are portrayed by British and Spanish football writing as gifted and potentially highly artistic characters. They are, though, also expected to be theatrical, volcanic of temperament and suspect in terms of morale, favouring a cautious, cagey or overtly negative approach to their football which is felt to be indicative of this long-standing element in Italy's identity. The greatest convergence in perceptions of national identity is to be found when European football writing focuses on Germany. The British, the Spanish and the French texts all construct German national identity in the same stereotypical terms: aggressive strength, dull efficiency and arrogant self-belief (although these attributes are almost admired in Great Britain and France but denigrated in Spain). Self-glorification and militarism might still be taboo in public discourse in Germany but they continue to be widely attributed to Germans by other Europeans.

It seems, then, that one of the roles played by European print media discourse on football is to reinforce if not inculcate myths of national character which are rooted in wider politico-diplomatic and socio-economic objective realities. Football writing in Britain, France and Spain constantly plays the identity card and, in so doing, strengthens rather than questions notions of collective identity generated by sport and media reflections of sport. The stereotypes of Europeans presented in the texts analysed do not wholly derive from a uniquely English (or, for that matter, French or Spanish) view of the world. There are certainly culture-specific nuances that are noteworthy. England's obsession with its own heroism in the war leads it to portray itself as superior to its foreign neighbours, who are readily depicted as inferior (Italians or Latins in general) or the enemy (Germany). France's obsession with protecting the quality of its own way of life leads it to represent itself as an oasis of civilisation surrounded by barbarous neighbours (principally England and Germany). Spain's obsession with progress and modernity leads to its depicting itself as aspiring to mainstream European qualities of skill and creativity and, therefore, to its denigration of other countries who fail to display these virtues (Germany, England and, occasionally, Italy). However, similar portrayals of the English, the French, the Germans, the Italians and the Spanish are none the less apparent in broadly the same guises across the continent as a whole and are, therefore, indicative of a common European viewpoint on how we all see each other. In short, as Europeans, the one thing we can apparently all agree upon is precisely how we allegedly all differ from each other. Ultimately, through our analyses we have discovered the considerable extent to which concepts of collective national identity remain integral to European football writing and central to that of which it is undoubtedly an extension: European culture in general.

Research into media sport and particularly into the representation of collective identities in Europe's football writing is a burgeoning field. The present volume is one step into this potentially rich area of enquiry. If questions have been posed and debate stimulated, particularly about print media writing styles and the (re)construction of what are essentially *imagined identities*, then our study will have served its purpose. However the sports pages of Europe's 'quality' daily newspapers evolve in the twenty-first century, we trust that they will continue, in their distinctive way, to capture and to convey to their readers the unique excitement generated by the partisan passion that is football, planet Earth's most popular sport.

Notes

Series Editor's Foreword

1. M. Connelly, *The Concrete Blonde* (London: Orion, 1994), p. 9.
2. S. Collini, R. Whatmore and B. Young (eds), *History, Religion and Culture: British Intellectual Life 1750 – 1950* (Cambridge: Cambridge University Press, 2000), p. 3.
3. R. Vinen, *A History in Fragments: Europe in the Twentieth Century* (London: Little, Brown and Company, 2000), p. 7.
4. Collini, Whatmore and Young, *History, Religion and Culture*, p. 20.
5. J.A. Mangan (ed.), *Tribal Identities: Nationalism, Europe, Sport* (London and Portland, OR: Frank Cass, 1996), Introduction, p. 8.
6. Vinen, *A History in Fragments*, p.628.
7. Mangan, *Tribal Identities*, p. 9.
8. P. Gowan and P. Anderson (eds), *The Question of Europe* (London: Verso in association with *New Statesman*, 1997), p. 15.
9. L. Crolley and D. Hand, *Football, Europe and the Press* (London and Portland, OR: Frank Cass, 2002), p. 157.
10. Ibid., p. 161.
11. As I write a vitriolic slanging match is going on in the English and German newspapers following England's defeat of Germany 5–1 in Munich!

Introduction

1. See, for example, R. Boyle and R. Haynes, *Power Play: Sport, the Media and Popular Culture* (Harlow: Pearson Education, 2000); D. Conn, *The Football Business: Fair Game in the 90s?* (Edinburgh: Mainstream, 1997); D. Russell, *Football and the English: A Social History of Association Football in England: 1863–1995* (Preston: Carnegie Publishing, 1997); G. Whannel, *Fields in Vision – Television Sport and Cultural Transformation* (London: Routledge, 1992) and 'Reading the Sports Media Audience', in L. Wenner (ed.), *MediaSport* (London: Routledge, 1998), pp. 119–33. The work of Whannel in particular is a useful lead-in to the study of the interface between sport, media texts, politics and economics.
2. Technically, the terms 'representation' and 'construction' belong to different and opposing schools of discourse analysis, the realist and the post-structuralist, respectively. We, however, are content to use both because media sport does not only create or construct versions of reality, it also cannot be dissociated from its context of wider historical, social and cultural circumstances which it represents. See N. Blain, R. Boyle and H. O'Donnell, *Sport and National Identity in the Media* (Leicester: Leicester University Press, 1993), Ch. 1.
3. For further discussion, see Boyle and Haynes, *Power Play*, pp. 24–9, 171–6; R. Giulianotti, 'Football Media in the UK: A Cultural Studies Perspective' (Buenos Aires, 1997), conference paper; S.F. Kelly, *Back Page Football: A Century of Newspaper Coverage* (Harpenden: Aurora/Queen Anne Press, 1996), pp. 7–9; T. Mason,

Association Football and English Society 1863–1915 (Brighton: Harvester Press, 1981), pp. 188–91; and Russell, *Football and the English*, pp. 103–6, 140–1, 197.

4. E. Saccomano (ed.), *Larousse du football* (Paris: Larousse/Bordas, 1998), pp. 300, 409–10.

5. A. Wahl, 'Pour une histoire du jeu', in H. Hélal and P. Mignon (eds), *Football, jeu et société* (Paris: Cahiers de l'INSEP, no. 25, 1999), pp. 40–1; and A. Wahl, *Les Archives du football. Sport et société en France (1880–1980)* (Paris: Gallimard/Julliard, 1989).

6. G. Mermet, *Francoscopie 1997: Comment vivent les Français* (Paris: Larousse-Bordas, 1996), p. 387 and *Le Monde* (27 June 1998).

7. L. McKeever, 'Reporting the World Cup: Old and New Media', in H. Dauncey and G. Hare (eds), *France and the 1998 World Cup: The National Impact of a World Sporting Event* (London and Portland, OR: Frank Cass, 1999), p. 165.

8. J. Altabella, 'Historia de la prensa deportiva madrileña', in *Orígenes del deporte madrileño* (Madrid: Dirección General de Deportes de la Comunidad Autónoma de Madrid, 1987).

9. D. Jones and J. Baró i Queralt, 'La prensa', in D. Jones (ed.), *Sport i mitjans de comunicació a Catalunya* (Barcelona: Generalitat de Catalunya, 1996), pp. 19–52.

10. Ibid. See this article also for a comparative analysis of sports coverage in general and specialist publications in several European countries.

11. For more on the role of *Marca*, see M. Gutiérrez, '*Marca*: bodas de oro con el periodismo deportivo', in *Periodistas*, 34 (May 1990), pp. 83–5 and, on *El Mundo Deportivo*, Gutiérrez, '*El Mundo Deportivo*: ochenta y cuatro años de historia', *Periodistas*, 32 (April 1990), pp. 93–7.

12. For more on the importance of football to the Spanish press see P. Ball, 'Patriot Games', in A. Lyons and M. Ticher (eds), *Back Home: How the World Watched France 98* (London: WSC Books, 1998), pp. 69–75.

13. See Kelly, *Back Page Football*, p. 9 and A. Hopcraft, *The Football Man* (London: Simon & Schuster, 1988), Ch. 7.

14. Hopcraft, *The Football Man*, Ch. 7.

15. L. Crolley, D. Hand and R. Jeutter, 'National Obsessions and Identities in Football Match Reports', in A. Brown (ed.), *Fanatics! Power, Identity and Fandom in Football* (London: Routledge, 1998), pp. 173–85.

16. See, for instance, J. Garland and M. Rowe, *War Minus the Shooting? Jingoism, the English Press and Euro 96* (Leicester: Scarman Centre, Crime, Order and Policing Series Occasional Paper no. 7, 1997); Hopcraft, *The Football Man*; E. Poulton, 'Fighting Talk from the Press Corps', in M. Perryman (ed.), *The Ingerland Factor: Home Truths from Football* (Edinburgh: Mainstream, 1999), pp. 119–35; I. Ramonet, 'Football et passions nationales', in P. Boniface (ed.), *Géopolitique du football* (Brussels: Editions complexe, 1998), pp. 55–62; and G. Reid, *Football and War* (Wilmslow: Sigma Press, 2000).

17. J. Sugden and A. Tomlinson (eds), *Hosts and Champions. Soccer Cultures, National Identities and the USA World Cup* (Aldershot: Arena, 1994), p. 3.

18. See Conn, *The Football Business*; S. Hamil, J. Michie, C. Oughton and S.Warby (eds), *The Changing Face of the Football Business: Supporters Direct* (London and Portland, OR: Frank Cass, 2000) and Russell, *Football and the English*.

19. See C. Bromberger, 'Football Passion and the World Cup: Why so Much Sound and Fury?', in Sugden and Tomlinson, *Hosts and Champions*, pp. 281–90; id., *Le Match de football. Ethnologie d'une passion partisane à Marseille, Naples et Turin* (Paris: Maison des sciences de l'homme, 1995) and id., 'Le Football, phénomène de représentation collective', in Boniface, *Géopolitique du football*, pp. 41–8.

20. Boyle and Haynes, *Power Play*, p. 13.

21. N. Blain and R. Boyle, 'Sport as Real Life: Media Sport and Culture', in A. Briggs and P. Cobley (eds), *The Media: An Introduction* (London: Longman, 1998), p. 369.

22. Ibid., p. 370.

23. A. Higson, 'National Identity and the Media', in Briggs and Cobley, *The Media*, p. 354.

24. R. Debray, *Transmettre* (Paris: Odile Jacob, 1997). By way of example, see the penetrating analysis of the way in which many of the traditional features of French national identity have been transmitted by successive educational systems in France in S. Citron, *Le Mythe national: l'histoire de France en question* (Paris: Editions ouvrières/EDI, 1991).

25. B. Anderson, *Imagined Communities: Reflections on the Origin and Spread of Nationalism* (London: Verso, 1983).

26. P. Mignon, *La Passion du football* (Paris: Odile Jacob, 1998), p. 37 and C. Bromberger, *Football, la bagatelle la plus sérieuse du monde* (Paris: Bayard, 1998), p. 59.

27. Bromberger, *Football, la bagatelle*, p. 78.

28. Ibid., p. 77. See also J.N. Coelho, 'On the Border: Some Notes on Football and National Identity in Portugal', in Brown, *Fanatics!*, p. 168.

29. Although not exclusively since players and managers contribute to the process, too. The former national team manager of France, Michel Hidalgo, for instance, sagely explains that 'the characteristics of each nation may be seen through its football: skill and magic with the Brazilians, discipline and mental strength with the Germans, spirited enthusiasm with the Japanese, power and skill with the Africans', M. Hidalgo, 'Le Football au mondial: jeu et enjeux' in Hélal and Mignon, *Football, jeu et société*, pp. 20–1.

30. Higson, 'National Identity and the Media', p. 360.

31. P. Anderson and A. Weymouth, *Insulting the Public? The British Press and the EU* (London: Longman, 1999), p. 3.

32. A. Sonntag, 'Le Football, image de la nation', in Boniface, *Géopolitique du football*, p. 33.

33. D. Rowe, J. McKoy and T. Miller, 'Come Together: Sport, Nationalism and the Media Image', in Wenner, *MediaSport*, p. 133. We interpret the use here of 'imaginary' to mean 'imagined' or 'in the imaginary' and certainly not in the sense of 'fictitious'. See also Boyle and Haynes, *Power Play*, pp. 161–4; J. Sugden and A. Tomlinson, *FIFA and the Contest for World Football. Who Rules the People's Game?* (Cambridge: Polity Press, 1998), pp. 208–9, 219–20, 227–8 and Bromberger, *Football, la bagatelle*, pp. 74–5.

34. E.P. Archetti, 'In Search of National Identity: Argentinian Football and Europe', in J.A. Mangan (ed.), *Tribal Identities: Nationalism, Europe, Sport* (London and Portland, OR: Frank Cass, 1996), pp. 201–19.

35. For further discussion see S. Hall and P. du Gay, *Questions of Cultural Identity* (London: Sage, 1996).

36. Blain, Boyle and O'Donnell, *Sport and National Identity in the Media*, Ch. 4.

37. Ibid.

38. *Le Monde électronique* (15 Nov. 2000).

39. See, for instance, Blain, Boyle and O'Donnell, *Sport and National Identity in the Media*; N. Blain and H. O'Donnell, European Sports Journalism and its Readers', in M. Roche (ed.), *Sport, Popular Culture and Identity* (Aachen: Meyer u. Meyer, 1998); Garland and Rowe, *War Minus the Shooting?*; S. Orakwue, *Pitch Invaders. The Modern Black Football Revolution* (London: Victor Gollancz/Cassell, 1998) and Poulton, 'Fighting Talk from the Press Corps'.

40. Boyle and Haynes, *Power Play*, p. 172.

41. Figures based on earlier calculations made by Saccomano, *Larousse du football* and *Four Four Two* (Aug. 1999).

42. Cited by Boyle and Haynes, *Power Play*, pp. 174–6.

43. Russell, *Football and the English*, p. 237.

44. Anderson and Weymouth, *Insulting the Public?*, pp. 5–6.

Chapter 1

1. For more on the history and development of the game see V. Duke and L. Crolley, *Football, Nationality and the State* (London: Longman, 1996); R. Holt, *Sport and the British: A Modern History* (Oxford: Oxford University Press, 1989); T. Mason, *Association Football and English Society 1863–1915* (Brighton: Harvester Press, 1981); T. Mason, *Sport in Britain* (London: Faber, 1988) and D. Russell, *Football and the English: A Social History of Association Football in England: 1863–1995* (Preston: Carnegie Publishing, 1997). A not entirely trivial indication of how important football had become in the national psyche by the late twentieth century is provided by a survey of *Daily Telegraph* readers (6 Oct. 1995), which placed the FA Cup final among the top ten annual events regarded as typifying 'Englishness'. Admittedly, the 540 respondents could not be said to be representative of the nation as a whole, but the results are not without worth. For the record, the other events cited were: Wimbledon, Henley, the Grand National, Cruft's, the Oxford and Cambridge boat race, the Chelsea Flower Show, Trooping the Colour, Remembrance Day and the broadcast of the Festival of Nine Lessons and Carols from King's College Chapel on Christmas Eve.

2. See above, Introduction and N. Blain and R. Boyle, 'Sport as Real Life: Media Sport and Culture', in A. Briggs and P. Cobley (eds), *The Media: An Introduction* (London: Longman, 1998), p. 365.

3. *Brewer's Dictionary of Phrase and Fable* (London: Cassell, 1990), p. 166. The term 'bulldog' serves to describe 'a tenacious and courageous person', *Oxford English Reference Dictionary* (Oxford: Oxford University Press, 1996), p. 192.

4. See P. Broussard, *Génération supporter: enquête sur les ultras du football* (Paris: Robert Laffont, 1990), pp. 13, 28–9.

5. Cited by B. Carrington, ' "Football's Coming Home" but Whose Home? And Do We Want It? Nation, Football and the Politics of Exclusion', in A. Brown (ed.), *Fanatics! Power, Identity and Fandom in Football* (London: Routledge, 1998), p. 102.

6. ITN News (15 June 1998).

7. S.F. Kelly, *Back Page Football: A Century of Newspaper Coverage* (Harpenden: Aurora/Queen Anne Press, 1996), p. 8.

8. For a fuller discussion of this topic see J. Garland and M. Rowe, *War Minus the Shooting? Jingoism, the English press and Euro 96* (Leicester: Scarman Centre, Crime, Order and Policing Series Occasional Paper no. 7, 1997) and E. Poulton, 'Fighting Talk from the Press Corps', in M. Perryman (ed.), *The Ingerland Factor: Home Truths from Football* (Edinburgh: Mainstream, 1999), pp. 119–35.

9. PCC statement, 'France 98 – The World Cup' (13 May 1998).

10. P. Anderson and A. Weymouth, *Insulting the Public? The British Press and the EU* (London: Longman, 1999), p. 176.

11. Ibid.

12. B. Carrington, 'Too Many St. George Crosses to Bear', in Perryman, *The Ingerland Factor*, p. 85. For further discussion of how media sport can become an arena for promoting the supposed superiority of one nation over others see H. O'Donnell, 'Mapping the Mythical: A Geopolitics of National Sporting Stereotypes', *Discourse and Society*, 5, 3 (1994), pp. 345–80.

13. C. Critcher, 'England and the World Cup: World Cup Willies, English Football and the Myth of 1966', in J. Sugden and A. Tomlinson (eds), *Hosts and Champions: Soccer Cultures, National Identities and the USA World Cup* (Aldershot: Arena, 1994), p. 90.

14. N. Blain, R. Boyle and H. O'Donnell, *Sport and National Identity in the European Media* (Leicester: Leicester University Press, 1993), Ch. 4.

15. S. Orakwue, *Pitch Invaders: The Modern Black Football Revolution* (London: Victor Gollancz/Cassell, 1998), p. 28.

16. This English model of 'heroic failure' is not necessarily shared by other countries; see Ch. 4.

17. Despite *The Times*'s wishful thinking in using the term 'British' here, which is, itself, reflective of a certain type of English attitude, England's being part of Britain does not automatically mean that all non-English Britons support the England football team.
18. ITV broadcast of England v. Argentina (30 June 1998).
19. A. Isaacs and J. Monk, *The Illustrated Dictionary of British Heritage* (Cambridge: Market House, 1986), pp. 370–1; *Brewer's Dictionary of Phrase and Fable*, p. 667.
20. For a penetrating analysis of the Anglocentric, imperialistic and racist lyrics and video of *Three Lions* see Carrington, ' "Football's Coming Home" ', pp. 110–14.
21. J.A. Mangan, 'Duty unto Death: English Masculinity in the Age of the New Imperialism', in J.A. Mangan (ed.), *Tribal Identities: Nationalism, Europe, Sport* (London and Portland, OR: Frank Cass, 1996), p. 12.
22. Ibid., p. 11.
23. Ibid., p. 18.
24. Ibid., p. 17.
25. For more on the tabloids' use of military imagery, particularly with reference to Euro 96, see B. Bragg, 'Two World Wars and One World Cup', in Perryman, *The Ingerland Factor*, pp. 39–41 and Poulton, 'Fighting Talk from the Press Corps', in ibid., pp. 125–30.
26. And British, to the extent that the terms 'British' and 'English' are often anomalously interchangeable in sports media discourse.
27. Perryman, *The Ingerland Factor*, p. 28.

Chapter 2

1. The Industrial Revolution of the late eighteenth century was driven by the power and success of the rapidly developing transport and textile industries of northern England, notably the cotton mills of Manchester and Lancashire.
2. It is also not without significance, of course, that the obligatory song adopted to accompany England's campaign at Euro 2000 was a rendering of 'Jerusalem' (performed by Fat Les). Note also the use of the hymn's music during the television coverage of France 98; see Ch. 1.
3. For more on the importance of nostalgia, 1966 and how English nationalism is rooted in past glories see C. Critcher, 'England and the World Cup: World Cup Willies, English Football and the Myth of 1966', in J. Sugden and A. Tomlinson (eds), *Hosts and Champions: Soccer Cultures, National Identities and the USA World Cup* (Aldershot: Arena, 1994), pp. 77–92.
4. J. Hill and J. Williams (eds), *Sport and Identity in the North of England* (Keele: Keele University press, 1996), p. 5.
5. Ibid., p. 4.
6. A. Miall, *Xenophobe's Guide to the English* (Horsham: Ravette, 1993), pp. 7–8.
7. Hill and Williams, *Sport and Identity*, p. 5.
8. Cited by D. Russell, *Football and the English: A Social History of Association Football in England 1863–1995* (Preston: Carnegie Publishing, 1997), p. 68. As Russell points out, some caution needs to be exercised when reading this somewhat ironic example of early print media discourse. From the perspective of the present volume, though, images of rough and ready northerners such as this are not without interest.
9. A. Thompson, 'From Teaching to Coaching: Gérard Houllier', in C. Rühn, *Le Foot: The Legends of French Football* (London: Abacus, 2000), p. 222.
10. See, for instance, C. Bromberger, *Football, la bagatelle la plus sérieuse du monde* (Paris: Bayard, 1998), p. 45; P. Broussard, *Génération supporter: enquête sur les ultras du football* (Paris: Robert Laffont, 1990), pp. 33–58; Russell, *Football and the English*, pp. 67, 205. The slogan is actually the title of a song from the 1945 musical *Carousel*, revived in 1963 by the Merseybeat group Gerry and the Pacemakers.

11. Thompson, 'From Teaching to Coaching', p. 222. Interestingly, the team enthused with this local spirit is an assortment of Dutchmen, Germans, Frenchmen, Czechs, Scandinavians and Scots.

12. R. Boyle and R. Haynes, *Power Play: Sport, the Media and Popular Culture* (Harlow: Pearson Education, 2000), p. 202.

13. See Russell, *Football and the English*, p. 67.

14. Many Manchester City supporters would, of course, argue that such feelings are inappropriate anyway given that City's Maine Road is the only professional football ground actually located in the city of Manchester proper. See D. Hand, 'City 'til I Die? Recent Trends in Popular Football Writing', *Soccer and Society*, 2, 1 (Spring 2001).

15. Cited by S.F. Kelly, *Back Page Football: A Century of Newspaper Coverage* (Harpenden: Aurora/Queen Anne Press, 1996), p. 137.

16. There are many who wish he had kept his promise. He did, and missed.

17. For further discussion see J. Hill, 'Cup Finals and Community in the North of England', in Hill and Williams, *Sport and Identity*, pp. 85–111 and J. Bale, 'Playing at Home: British Football and a Sense of Place', in J. Williams and S. Wagg (eds), *British Football and Social Change* (Leicester: Leicester University Press, 1991).

18. See P. Vasili, *The First Black Footballer – Arthur Wharton 1865–1930: An Absence of Memory* (London and Portland, OR: Frank Cass, 1998).

19. See B. Carrington, ' "Football's Coming Home" but Whose Home? And Do We Want It? Nation, Football, and the Politics of Exclusion', in A. Brown (ed.), *Fanatics! Power, Identity and Fandom in Football* (London: Routledge, 1998), p. 114.

20. S. Orakwue, *Pitch Invaders: The Modern Black Football Revolution* (London: Victor Gollancz/Cassell, 1998), p. 29.

21. See L. Back, T. Crabbe and J. Solomos, 'Racism in Football: Patterns of Continuity and Change', in Brown, *Fanatics!*, pp. 77–80. Additionally, for a depressing catalogue of the racism suffered throughout a career by a professional footballer, see R. Moran, 'You Send Me Bananas', in M. Perryman (ed.), *The Ingerland Factor: Home Truths from Football* (Edinburgh: Mainstream, 1999).

22. S. Lyle, 'Racism, Football and the Media', paper presented to the conference 'Challenging Racism in Football. New Solutions to Old Problems?', University of Leicester (4 Sept. 1997).

23. Orakwue, *Pitch Invaders*, p. 7.

24. Ibid., p. 9.

25. Ibid., p. 73. For further discussion, see also Boyle and Haynes, *Power Play*, pp.111–26.

26. In this respect at least, the discourse of newspaper articles on football neatly side-steps the issue of the disparity between the origins of football clubs' players and the locality they are deemed to represent and from which – in most cases – they draw most of their support. For instance, the fact that the successful Chelsea team of the mid 1990s rarely fielded an Englishman let alone a Londoner (Denis Wise excepted) did not prevent their being qualified as 'the west London team' (*The Times*, 14 May 1998) so strong are the discursive and representational links between a football club and the locality in which it is situated.

27. Russell, *Football and the English*, p. 235.

28. *Soccer Star* [magazine], 1953, cited by Russell, *Football and the English*, p. 172. The players referred to in these two examples were Eusebio and Delapena, respectively.

29. Orakwue, *Pitch Invaders*, p. 10. See also, Back, Crabbe and Solomos, 'Racism in Football'.

30. Moran, 'You Send Me Bananas', p. 162.

Chapter 3

1. A. Miall, *Xenophobe's Guide to the English* (Horsham: Ravette, 1993), p. 5 and M. Perryman (ed.), *The Ingerland Factor: Home Truths from Football* (Edinburgh: Mainstream, 1999), p. 24. The broadcaster and writer Jeremy Paxman is another who has noted that one of the aspects of Englishness is 'finding foreigners funny'; see J. Paxman, *The English: A Portrait of a People* (London: Penguin, 1999), p. 23.
2. *The Guinness Book of Football* (London: Guinness Publishing, 1998), p. 58.
3. For the record, they were: Harry Dowd, Tony Book, Glyn Pardoe, Mike Doyle, George Heslop, Alan Oakes, Mike Summerbee, Colin Bell, Francis Lee, Neil Young and Tony Coleman.
4. Channel 5, 'Football's Foreign Legion' (John Salthouse, narrator; Richard Stafford, producer/director, 4 March 1999).
5. *Guinness Book of Football*, pp. 58, 61.
6. Foreign players in the top division of each country surveyed during the 1999/2000 season accounted for the following percentage totals: England 50, France 18, Germany 42, Italy 32 and Spain 36 (*France Football*, 18 January, 25 January, 1 February, 8 February, 15 February 2000). Admittedly, stripping out the Scots, the Welsh and the Irish from the figure for England would reduce the percentage of foreigners to 36 but would still place England joint second in the list.
7. *Guinness Book of Football*, p. 50. Indeed, the vocabulary employed by supposedly neutral observers often reveals implicit (and traditionally English) fears in this respect. The narrator of a television treatment of the subject, for instance (Channel 5, 'Football's Foreign Legion'), also used as presuppositions rather than as debatable concepts the pejorative and menacing terms 'the foreign invasion' and 'the floodgates [being] opened', while the title of the programme itself suggests hostility with its militaristic connotations.
8. ITV, Italy v. Chile (11 June 1998).
9. Cited by G. Mermet, *Francoscopie 1997: Comment vivent les Français* (Paris: Larousse/Bordas, 1996), pp. 39–41.
10. BBC 1, Germany v. Croatia (4 July 1998).
11. BBC 2, Germany v. Romania (12 June 2000).
12. N. Seitz, *Doppelpässe: Fußball und Politik* (Frankfurt: Eichborn, 1997).
13. ITV, Germany v. Mexico (29 June 1998).
14. BBC 1, Germany v. Croatia (4 July 1998).
15. See A. Lyons and M. Ticher (eds), *Back Home: How the World Watched France 98* (London: WSC Books, 1998), pp. 66–8, 83, 92–3, 95–6, 122–3, 145, 186–8.
16. Cited by C. Connelly, *Spirit High and Passion Pure: A Journey through European Football* (Edinburgh: Mainstream, 2000), pp. 187–8.
17. Ginola has been described on television, for example, as 'the glamour boy winger' and 'the flamboyant Frenchman' (Channel 5, 'Football's Foreign Legion'). For further discussion of the mediation of Frenchness in the football context see S. Gardiner, 'The Law and Hate Speech: "Ooh, aah, Cantona" and the Demonisation of "the Other"', in A. Brown (ed.), *Fanatics! Power, Identity and Fandom in Football* (London: Routledge, 1998), pp. 249–64.
18. ITV, France v. South Africa (12 June 1998).
19. R. Holt, 'Contrasting Nationalisms: Sport, Militarism and the Unitary State in Britain and France before 1914', in J.A. Mangan (ed.), *Tribal Identities: Nationalism, Europe, Sport* (London and Portland, OR: Frank Cass, 1996), pp.39–54; A. Wahl, *Les Archives du football. Sport et société en France (1880–1980)* (Paris: Gallimard/Julliard, 1989). For further discussion see Chapter 4.
20. BBC 1, France v. Paraguay (28 June 1998).
21. ITV, France v. Italy (3 July 1998).
22. BBC 1, France v. Croatia (8 July 1998).

23. *Athletic News*, 20 May 1929, cited by S.F. Kelly, *Back Page Football: A Century of Newspaper Coverage* (Harpenden: Aurora/Queen Anne Press, 1996), p. 65.
24. See Gardiner, 'The Law and Hate Speech'.
25. P. Davies, 'Look at the State of Us' in Perryman, *The Ingerland Factor*, p. 178.
26. BBC 2, 'Best of Enemies' (Kenneth Baker, presenter; Alison Cahn, producer; Anne Tyerman, editor, 12 January 2000).

Chapter 4

1. A. Wahl, *Les Archives du football. Sport et société en France (1880–1980)* (Paris: Gallimard/Julliard, 1989), pp. 159–60.
2. For more on the symbolism of colour in football see M. Pastoureau, 'Les Couleurs du stade', *Vingtième siècle*, 26 (1990), pp. 11–18; and for a discussion of the tricolour and the *Marseillaise* in the national context see P. Nora (ed.), *Les Lieux de mémoire* (Paris: Gallimard, 1997), Vol. 1, pp. 49–66, 107–54. For an in-depth analysis of the role of the cockerel symbol in a French football context see D. Hand, 'Footix: the History behind a Modern Mascot', *French Cultural Studies*, 9 (1998), pp. 239–47; and for a study of the cockerel as a national symbol see Nora, *Les Lieux de mémoire*, Vol. 1, pp. 4297–320.
3. N. Blain and H. O'Donnell, 'European Sports Journalism and its Readers', in M. Roche (ed.), *Sport, Popular Culture and Identity* (Aachen: Meyer u. Meyer, 1998). The authors posit three possible relationships between football and society: football is a sign of society (a facet of a country's identity), an extension of society (so sporting failure would represent the nation's failure) and a simulacrum of society (where football refers only to itself). Clearly the boundaries between these possibilities cannot be so rigid and, most importantly, we would nuance the authors' opinions and contend that the second relationship is clearly identifiable in mainland Europe as well as in England.
4. Wahl, *Les Archives*, pp. 159–60.
5. J. Rigaud, *L'Exception culturelle. Culture et pouvoirs sous la Ve République* (Paris: Grasset, 1995), p. 17, cited by S. Collard, 'French Cultural Policy: the Special Role of the State', in W. Kidd and S. Reynolds, *Contemporary French Cultural Studies* (London: Arnold, 2000), pp. 38–50; J. Michelet, *Le Peuple* (Paris: Comptoir des imprimeurs unis, 1846); M. Thorez, *Fils du peuple* (Paris: Editions sociales, 1949), p.118; Charrat, cited in J. Favier (ed.), *Chronique de la France et des Français* (Paris: Jacques Legrand/Larousse, 1987), p. xii and J.-M. Le Pen, 1988 Presidential election campaign leaflet.
6. For example, C. Bromberger, *Football, la bagatelle la plus sérieuse du monde* (Paris: Bayard, 1998), pp. 77–85; A. Greaves, 'Sport in France', in M. Cook (ed.), *French Culture since 1945* (London: Longman, 1993), pp.130–2 and J. Marks, 'The French National Team and National Identity: Cette France d'un "bleu métis"', in H. Dauncey and G. Hare (eds), *France and the 1998 World Cup: The National Impact of a World Sporting Event* (London and Portland, OR: Frank Cass, 1999), pp. 44–5.
7. See E. Saccomano (ed.), *Larousse du football* (Paris: Larousse-Bordas, 1998), pp. 52–3, 152–3.
8. For an overview and discussion of the 'Jacquet affair', see L. McKeever, 'Reporting the World Cup: Old and New Media', in Dauncey and Hare, *France and the 1998 World Cup*, pp. 164–6 and P. Tournon, 'The Right Man: Aimé Jacquet', in C. Rühn (ed.), *Le Foot: The Legends of French Football* (London: Abacus, 2000). Jacquet recounts his own story in his autobiography, A. Jacquet, *Ma Vie pour une étoile* (Paris: Laffont/Plon, 1999). In a later work he describes his journalist critics at *L'Equipe* as 'those incompetent, irresponsible, arrogant and wicked people' (Jacquet, *C'est quoi le foot?* [Paris: Albin Michel, 2000], p. 13).

9. See *Le Monde* (14 July 1998) which elevates Jacquet's story to the status of 'parable'.
10. Dauncey and Hare, *France and the 1998 World Cup*, p. 208.
11. M. Agulhon and P. Oulmont, *Nation, patrie, patriotisme* (Paris: La Documentation française, 1993), p. 1.
12. See S. Citron, *Le Mythe national: l'histoire de France en question* (Paris: Editions ouvrières/EDI, 1991).
13. Ibid.
14. 14 July is, of course, France's national day, commemorating the storming of the Bastille in 1789, the symbolic starting point of the Revolution. France's triumph over Brazil took place on 12 July 1998 and 13 July was made a one-off national holiday, thereby effectively linking the jubilation expressed in the football context to the celebration of the founding moment of contemporary France's political identity. Indeed, the organisers of the tournament, the Comité français d'organisation, had wanted the final to be played on Bastille Day but the idea was refused by FIFA who preferred the traditional Sunday date.
15. For a historical overview of the phenomenon see Marks, 'The French National Team and National Identity', pp. 47–54.
16. B. Stasi, 'Le Football: aventure personnelle et phénomène de société', in P. Boniface (ed.), *Géopolitique du football* (Brussels: Editions complexe, 1998), p. 130.
17. P. Mignon, *La Passion du football* (Paris: Odile Jacob, 1998), p. 264.
18. D. Bernard, 'The New Ambassadors, or the Reincarnation of the Temple Money Changers?', in Rühn, *Le Foot*, p. 286.
19. That is, blacks, whites and second-generation North Africans. The phrase's punchiness, alliteration and word play on the colours of the national flag (*bleu, blanc, rouge* – blue, white, red) are, of course, all woefully lost in translation.
20. 'Did We therefore Have a Celebration of Multicultural France, or the Celebration of a France of Integration, or Even of Assimilation?', P. Mignon, 'Fans and Heroes', in Dauncey and Hare, *France and the 1998 World Cup*, p. 95.
21. J.N. Coelho, 'On the Border: Some Notes on Football and National Identity in Portugal', in A. Brown (ed.), *Fanatics! Power, Identity and Fandom in Football* (London: Routledge, 1998), p. 159.
22. Mignon, 'Fans and Heroes', p. 96. See also P. Mignon, 'France: A Beautiful World', in A. Lyons and M. Ticher (eds), *Back Home: How the World Watched France 98* (London: WSC Books, 1998), pp. 206–7.
23. A. Sonntag, 'Le Football, image de la nation', in Boniface, *Géopolitique du football*, p. 32. For the controversial view that France 98 might have done precisely the opposite and actually served the ideas of the extreme right, see the highly polemical discussion provided by M. Perelman, *Les Intellectuels et le football: montée de tous les maux et recul de la pensée* (Paris: Les Editions de la passion, 2000), pp.13–17.
24. E. Renan, *Qu'est-ce qu'une nation? Conférence faite en Sorbonne, le 11 mars 1882* (Paris: Imprimerie nationale, 1996 [C. Lévy, 1882]).

Chapter 5

1. G. Michaud and A. Kimmel, *Le Nouveau guide France* (Paris: Hachette, 1996), p. 9.
2. V. Duke and L. Crolley, *Football, Nationality and the State* (London: Longman, 1996), pp. 4, 25–6, 36–7, 40–3, 47–8.
3. *France Football*, 13 June 2000.
4. For further discussion see L. Ravenel, *La Géographie du football en France* (Paris: PUF, 1998), pp. 122–8 and P. Mignon, *La Passion du football* (Paris: Odile Jacob, 1998), pp. 209, 224, 257.

Football, Europe and the Press

5. Ravenel, *La Géographie du football*, p. 125.
6. A. Wahl, 'Pour une histoire du jeu', in H. Hélal and P. Mignon (eds), *Football, jeu et société* (Paris: Cahiers de l'INSEP, no. 25, 1999), pp. 40–1.
7. J. Favier (ed.), *Chronique de la France et des Français* (Paris: Jacques Legrand/Larousse, 1987), p. 1250.
8. See Ravenel, *La Géographie du football*, p. 25; E. Saccomano (ed.), *Larousse du football* (Paris: Larousse/Bordas, 1998), p. 39 and C. Rühn, 'Blood and Gold: The Best Public in France', in C. Rühn, *Le Foot: The Legends of French Football* (London: Abacus, 2000), p. 258.
9. C. Bromberger, *Football, la bagatelle la plus sérieuse du monde* (Paris: Bayard, 1998), p. 80. A survey of some 300 Lens fans was carried out in 1994 with the help of J.-M. Mariottini.
10. See Saccomano, *Larousse du football*, p. 392.
11. Michaud and Kimmel, *Le Nouveau guide France*, pp. 27, 92. The pen portraits provided by introductory guides to France such as Michaud and Kimmel's are revealing in this respect in that they supposedly focus on the essential summary characteristics of the cities and regions they describe and, in so doing, recycle rather than challenge traditional perceptions.
12. Ravenel, *La Géographie du football*, pp. 40, 45. In May 1992, a temporary stand at the Furiani stadium collapsed before the French FA Cup semi-final against Olympique de Marseille resulting in the death of 17 spectators.
13. J. Gritti, *Sport à la une* (Paris: Armand Colin, 1975), p. 144, cited by Ravenel, *La Géographie du football*, p. 22.
14. Conseil Constitutionnel, www.conseil-constitutionnel.fr/n/91290dc.htm
15. For example, see *France Football*, 19 Jan. 1999, p. 48.
16. *France Football*, 29 Aug. 2000. For further material on Corsican football see V. Sinet, *La Fabuleuse histoire du football corse* (Ajaccio: Editions Albiana, 2000).
17. See Ravenel, *La Géographie du football*, p. 36.
18. Favier, *Chronique de la France*, p. 1262.
19. For more on Lugdunum's and, indeed, on Lyon's other main supporters' club, the Bad Gônes see *France Football*, 14 Dec. 1999.
20. A. Pecheral, 'Olympique Marseille: The First French European Cup Victory', in Rühn, *Le Foot*, p. 15 and J. Carlin, 'Brothers in Arms: Les Bleus Win the World Cup, 1998', in ibid., p. 60.
21. C. Bromberger, *Le Match de football. Ethnologie d'une passion partisane à Marseille, Naples et Turin* (Paris: Maison des sciences de l'homme, 1995), p. 124 and Bromberger, *Football, la bagatelle*, pp. 80–5.
22. Ravenel, *La Géographie du football*, p. 38.
23. Bromberger, *Football, la bagatelle*, p. 85, quoting an OM supporter.
24. Pecheral, 'Olympique Marseille', p. 15.
25. See, for instance, P. Broussard, *Génération supporter: enquête sur les ultras du football* (Paris: Robert Laffont, 1990), pp. 159, 174–6, 179 and Bromberger, *Football, la bagatelle*, pp. 69–72.
26. C.-F. Ramuz, cited by Michaud and Kimmel, *Le Nouveau guide France*, p. 31.
27. Favier, *Chronique de la France*, p. 1252.
28. A.S. Fell and C. Tinker, 'Representing Paris', in *Modern and Contemporary France*, 8, 3 (2000), pp. 301–3.
29. Broussard, *Génération supporter*, pp. 174–6; see also Pecheral, 'Olympique Marseille', p. 15.
30. Jacques Chirac was Mayor of Paris between 1977 and 1995; Canal Plus, the television station, bought into PSG in May 1991.
31. Michaud and Kimmel, *Le Nouveau guide France*, p. 19.
32. Ibid., p. 64.

Chapter 6

1. Larousse, *Larousse multimédia encyclopédique*, CD Rom (Paris: Larousse/Liris Interactive, 1997).
2. See, for instance, N. Yapp and M. Syrett, *The Xenophobe's Guide to the French* (Horsham: Ravette, 1993), pp. 5–9.
3. Canal Plus, 'Ecosse-Maroc' (23 June 1998).
4. D. Jeandupeux, 'Le Style d'un club', in H. Hélal and P. Mignon (eds), *Football, jeu et société* (Paris: Cahiers de l'INSEP, no. 25, 1999), p. 125.
5. For further discussion see G. Armstrong and R. Harris, 'Football Hooligans: Theory and Evidence', *Sociological Review*, 39, 3 (1991), pp. 427–58.
6. The word play is unfortunately not quite so striking in translation. In the original French 'le joyeux [de la Couronne]' (joy) is an effective play on words for 'le joyau' (jewel).
7. See E. Saccomano (ed.), *Larousse du football* (Paris: Larousse/Bordas, 1998), pp. 214–15, for instance.
8. See L. Crolley, D. Hand and R. Jeutter, 'Playing the Identity Card: Stereotypes in European Football', *Soccer and Society*, I, 2 (2000), pp. 107–28 and N. Blain, R. Boyle and H. O'Donnell, *Sport and National Identity in the Media* (Leicester: Leicester University Press, 1993), Ch. 4.
9. R. Holt, 'Contrasting Nationalisms: Sport, Militarism and the Unitary State in Britain and France before 1914', in J.A. Mangan (ed.), *Tribal Identities: Nationalism, Europe, Sport* (London and Portland, OR: Frank Cass, 1996), p. 43.
10. See, for instance, Saccomano, *Larousse du football*, pp. 52–3 which contrasts the 'magical', 'joyful', 'brilliant' French 'geniuses' with the 'mechanical', 'imposing', 'violent' and 'aggressive' Germans.
11. H. Dauncey and G. Hare (eds), *France and the 1998 World Cup: The National Impact of a World Sporting Event* (London and Portland, OR: Frank Cass, 1999), p. 6.
12. A high-ranking military officer, Boulanger, nicknamed General Revenge, made this the central platform of his political career which almost culminated in his seizing power in a *coup d'état* in 1899.
13. Acknowledgement is made to Donald P. Bellisario in whose television programme, 'Quantum Leap' (Universal Television, 1989–94) the phrase appears.
14. Yapp and Syrett, *Xenophobe's Guide*, p. 7.
15. See Ch. 4 and A. Greaves, 'Sport in France', in M. Cook (ed.), *French Culture since 1945* (London: Longman, 1993), pp. 130–2.
16. G. Gebauer, 'Les Trois dates de l'équipe d'Allemagne de football', in Hélal and Mignon, *Football, jeu et société*, pp. 107–10. When Germany fails and the image is, therefore, tarnished, the German press is swift to condemn the team. The magazine *Stern*, for instance, saw the exit from France 98 as a mirror image of Chancellor Kohl's 'worn-out, stolid, uninspiring running of the country', cited by U. Hesse-Lichtenberger, 'National Theatre', in A. Lyons and M. Ticher (eds), *Back Home: How the World Watched France 98* (London: WSC Books, 1998), p. 29.
17. V. Duke and L. Crolley, *Football, Nationality and the State* (London: Longman, 1996), p. 128.
18. From documents kindly supplied by the Fédération française de football.
19. The last World Cup was held in (and won by) the USA in 1999 but France failed to reach the finals.
20. C. Bromberger, *Football, la bagatelle la plus sérieuse du monde* (Paris: Bayard, 1998), p. 94. Mignon's work on Paris Saint-Germain suggests that women consistently accounted for over 10 per cent of crowds there in the early 1990s: P. Mignon, *La Passion du football* (Paris: Odile Jacob, 1998), pp. 229–30.
21. P. Mignon, 'France: A Beautiful World', in Lyons and Ticher, *Back Home*, p. 207.
22. P. Mignon, 'Fans and Heroes', in Dauncey and Hare, *France and the 1998 World Cup*, p. 96 and *Libération*, 10 and 14 July 1998.

23. *France Football*, 2780, 20 July 1999.
24. Ibid., 2768, 27 April 1999.
25. L. McKeever, 'Reporting the World Cup: Old and New Media', in Dauncey and Hare, *France and the 1998 World Cup*, p. 176.
26. *The Times*, 18 June 1998.
27. Dauncey and Hare, *France and the 1998 World Cup*, p. vii (our italics).

Chapter 7

1. For more detailed analysis of the history and recent developments in changing notions of national identities in Spain see C. Mar-Molinero and A. Smith, *Nationalism and the Nation in the Iberian Peninsular* (Oxford: Berg, 1996).
2. F. León Solís, 'El juego de las nacionalidades', *International Journal of Iberian Studies*, 9, 1 (1996), pp. 28–45.
3. Ibid.
4. Mar-Molinero briefly examines how linguistic issues, central to the debates over identity in Spain, are treated in C. Mar-Molinero, 'The Politics of Language: Spain's Minority Languages', in H. Graham and J. Labanyi (eds), *Spanish Cultural Studies: An Introduction* (Oxford: Oxford University Press, 1995), pp. 336–41. See also León Solís, 'El juego de las nacionalidades'.
5. B. Anderson, *Imagined Communities: Reflections on the Origin and Spread of Nationalism* (London: Verso, 1983).
6. Spain has qualified for ten out of the 13 post-war World Cup finals but since 1950, when it finished fourth, it has never progressed beyond the quarter finals (which it reached in 1982, 1986, 1990 and 1994).
7. During the 1998 World Cup finals no fewer than six of the Spanish squad were involved in negotiations involving their contracts with their clubs. This led to some criticism from sections of the media and cynicism from those who believed the players were mercenary and trying to exploit the World Cup for their own personal ends rather than playing for their country.
8. M. Moliner, *Diccionario de uso del español* (Madrid: Editorial Gredos, 1991), p. 1358.
9. The discussion of the term *la furia española* took place in interviews with Catalan football fans conducted during May 1999.
10. *Centro de Investigaciones Sociológicas* (Madrid: 1994).
11. S. Balfour, 'The Loss of Empire, Regenerationism, and the Forging of a Myth of National Identity', in Graham and Labanyi, *Spanish Cultural Studies*, p. 30.
12. Anderson, *Imagined Communities*; A. Higson, 'National Identity and the Media', in A. Briggs and P. Cobley (eds), *The Media: An Introduction* (London: Longman, 1998); E. Renan, *Qu'est-ce qu'une nation?* (Paris: Imprimerie nationale, 1996 [1882]).
13. Clemente was manager of the *Selección* for six years (1992–98), throughout the period when the main database was gathered. Following intense media speculation immediately following the 1998 World Cup, he was replaced as manager of the national side in September 1998 by Camacho.
14. L. Crolley, D. Hand and R. Jeutter, 'National Obsessions and Identities in Football Match Reports', in A. Brown (ed.), *Fanatics! Power, Identity and Fandom in Football* (London: Routledge, 1998), pp. 173–85; L. Crolley, D. Hand and R. Jeutter, 'Playing the Identity Card: Stereotypes in European Football', *Soccer and Society*, 1, 2 (2000), pp. 107–28.
15. S. Lorente (ed.), *Informe sociológico sobre la situación social en España* (Madrid: FOESSA, 1994). There has been a significant decline in the last 20 years with 64 per cent claiming to be practising Catholics in 1970 dropping to 30 in 1993. Additionally, those who claimed to be 'rarely practising Catholics' remained largely unchanged from 23 per cent to 22 (ibid.). For a more detailed analysis of recent trends in religious belief and practice in Spain see T. Lawlor and M. Rigby, *Contemporary Spain: Essays*

and Texts on Politics, Economics, Education and Employment, and Society (London: Longman, 1998), pp. 323–7.

16. J. Hooper, *The Spaniards: A Portrait of the New Spain* (London: Penguin, 1986).
17. Crolley *et al.*, 'National Obsessions and Identities in Football Match Reports'.
18. 64 per cent of young Spaniards believe serving in the armed forces is a vocation and, therefore, that it should not be compulsory for all. Just 12 per cent expressed a wish to become a member of the armed forces, yet military service (or its alternative, a longer period of community service) is obligatory: *Encuesta sobre la defensa nacional y la profesionalización del Ejército* (Madrid: *Centro de Investigaciones Sociológicas*, 2000).
19. G. Orwell, *Homage to Catalonia* (London: Penguin,1938). For a graphic account of life on the front see also I. Puig (ed.), *Personal Memories of the Days of the Spanish Civil War in Catalan and English: Lluís Puig Casas* (Lampeter: Mellen, 1999).
20. D. Rowe, J. McKoy and T. Miller, 'Come Together: Sport, Nationalism and the Media Image', in L. Wenner (ed.), *MediaSport* (London: Routledge, 1998), p. 120.

Chapter 8

1. See J. Solé Tura, *Nacionalidades y nacionalismos en España* (Madrid: Alianza Editorial, 1985) for detailed background on the evolution of nationalisms and regionalisms in Spain.
2. For more on the historical and contemporary links between football and the socio-political fabric of Spain see L. Crolley, 'Real Madrid v Barcelona: The State against a Nation? The Changing Role of Football in Spain', *International Journal of Iberian Studies*, 10, 1 (1997), pp. 33–43.
3. H. Graham and J. Labanyi (eds), *Spanish Cultural Studies: An Introduction* (Oxford: Oxford University Press, 1995), section two provides a useful introduction to the roots and development of nationalism and regionalism at the turn of the twentieth century.
4. S. Balfour, 'The Loss of Empire, Regenerationism, and the Forging of a Myth of National Identity', in Graham and Labanyi, *Spanish Cultural Studies*, p. 29.
5. For more on the development of nationalism in Catalonia and the Basque Country see D. Conversi, *The Basques, the Catalans and Spain: Alternative Routes to Nationalist Mobilisation* (London: Hurst, 1996).
6. S. Segurola (ed.), *Fútbol y pasiones políticas* (Barcelona: Temas de debate, 1996), p. 164.
7. From 1937 onwards *Euskadi* played friendly matches to raise funds for the Basque military and to spread propaganda. For statistical details of games played by *Euskadi* and their results see C. Fernández Santander, *El fútbol durante la guerra civil y el franquismo* (Madrid: Editorial San Martín, 1990).
8. For more on the early development of FC Barcelona as a symbol of Catalonia see Crolley, 'Real Madrid v Barcelona' and also J. Sobrequés i Callico, *Terra Nostra. Un club al servei de Catalunya* (Barcelona: Editorial Labor, 1991) for some interesting anecdotes.
9. J. García Candau, *Madrid – Barça: Historia de un desamor* (Madrid: El País Aguilar, 1996), p. 8 assumes that the hostile relationship between Real Madrid and FC Barcelona that exists today dates only as far back as the Franco period.
10. The proposal has the overwhelming support of nationalist parties in Catalonia, the Basque Country and Galicia (the *Convergencia i Unió*, the *Partido Nacionalista Vasca* and the *Bloque Nacionalista Galego*, respectively).
11. *La Constitución Española* (Madrid: Alianza Editorial, 1978). The Spanish Constitution was approved on 31 October 1978 and ratified by public referendum on 29 December.
12. Ibid.

13. C. Mar-Molinero, 'The Politics of Language: Spain's Minority Languages', in Graham and Labanyi, *Spanish Cultural Studies*, pp. 336–41.

14. See *Anuario El País* (Madrid: 2000) for a breakdown of readership figures for some major national and regional newspapers and for viewing figures for national and local television.

15. See V. Duke and L. Crolley, *Football, Nationality and the State* (London: Longman, 1996) for information on the implicit and explicit links between football and politics in twentieth-century Spain.

16. For instance, it is important to remember that during the early Franco period (1939–43) all Spanish football clubs, even those in areas where anti-Franco feelings were highest, were run by chairmen who were appointed to the position by the state. This was known as the process of *depuración* (cleansing). Even the chairman of FC Barcelona (with the exception of the single month of July 1942) was *un militar franquista*, Enrique Piñeiro. Therefore no football club was allowed to stray far from the policies of the Franco regime.

17. D. Shaw, *Fútbol y franquismo* (Madrid: Alianza Editorial, 1987) and Fernández Santander, *El fútbol durante la guerra civil y el franquismo* provide more detailed accounts of the role of football during the Franco period.

18. See Crolley, 'Real Madrid v Barcelona'.

19. Study carried out by the Centro de Investigaciones Sociológicas (Barcelona, 1995) quoted in *Tiempo* (25 September 1995).

20. J. Hargreaves, 'The Catalanisation of the Barcelona Olympic Games: A Case Study of Nationalism in Contemporary Spain', paper presented at the conference on Nationality and National Identity in the Iberian Peninsula, University of Southampton (March 1995).

21. See, for instance, M. Moragas Spà, 'Esport i mitjans de communicació', in D. Jones (ed.), *Esport i mitjans de communicació a Catalunya* (Barcelona: Generalitat de Catalunya, 1996), pp. 11–18.

22. Not long after Real Madrid had won no fewer than five European Cups, the government minister José Solís declared the club to be 'the best ambassador we have ever sent abroad' (*Boletin del Real Madrid*, 1961) and, indeed, when FC Barcelona knocked them out of the competition in 1961, the media accused the Catalan club of eliminating Spain from Europe (see Crolley, 'Real Madrid v Barcelona').

23. For an extensive treatment see Crolley, 'Real Madrid v Barcelona' and for some fascinating anecdotes consult García Candau, *Madrid – Barça: Historia de un desamor*.

24. FC Barcelona has, for many years, marketed itself using the slogan 'More than a club' thereby drawing attention to its role as representative of the Catalan people.

25. D. Crystal, *The Cambridge Encyclopaedia of Language* (Cambridge: Cambridge University Press, 1992), p. 326.

26. J. Hooper, *The Spaniards: A Portrait of the New Spain* (London: Penguin, 1986), pp. 222–3 outlines some of the main contributions of the Basque Country to sport, including the invention of *pelota* (a game similar to squash), *perratxe* (not unlike golf) and *anikote* (something like cricket).

27. P. Unzueta, 'Fútbol y nacionalismo vasco', in Segurola, *Fútbol y pasiones políticas*, p. 155.

28. In M. Leguineche, P. Unzueta and S. Segurola, *Athletic: 100 Conversaciones en la Catedral* (Madrid: Grupo Santillana de Ediciones, 1998), p. 109.

29. Unzueta, 'Fútbol y nacionalismo vasco', p. 157.

30. Ibid.

31. For more detailed information on the intricate links between football and politics, and, increasingly, the role of the media see B. Calleja, *La Guerra 'Incivil' del Fútbol* (Barcelona: Plaza y Janés Editores, 1997).

Chapter 9

1. P. Unzueta, 'Fútbol y nacionalismo vasco', in S. Segurola (ed.), *Fútbol y pasiones políticas* (Barcelona: Temas de debate, 1999), p. 148.
2. TVE's current affairs television programme *Informe Semanal* (November 1999) ran a report on the difficulties faced by young Spanish players to become successful in the Spanish League.
3. See J. Sobrequés i Callicó, *Terra Nostra: FC Barcelona. Un club al servei de Catalunya* (Barcelona: Editorial Labor, 1991), pp. 19–23. This provides details of how the foreigner debate lay at the heart of some of the original tensions between FC Barcelona and RCD Espanyol, including, for example, one case when FC Barcelona beat Espanyol 3–0 but the result was reversed following an appeal by Espanyol who complained that FC Barcelona had included an ineligible foreigner in their team. Sobrequés's rather biased text includes many examples of FC Barcelona's 'acceptance' and 'welcoming' of foreigners in contrast to RCD Espanyol's 'intolerance' (p. 21).
4. Much of Latin America formed a significant part of the Spanish Empire from the 1550s to the 1890s. In 1999 Latin Americans constituted nearly 20 per cent of Spain's foreign residents (Instituto Nacional de Estadística; in January 2000 Latin Americans were the single biggest group of foreign footballers in the Primera Liga (44 per cent of all foreign players) which might be contrasted with England where European Economic Area nationals are the biggest group (71 per cent of all non-English players in the Premiership) and France where it is Africans (39 per cent of foreign footballers in *Division 1*); see *France Football* (18 January, 25 January and 15 February 2000).
5. D. Hill, 'The Sin of Pride', in A. Lyons and M. Ticher (eds), *Back Home: How the World Watched France 98* (London: WSC Books, 1998), p. 12.
6. The brothers Dougie and Eddy Brimson have written several 'football diaries' in which they draw vivid pictures of life as England followers and where the image of xenophobic, shaven-headed, bare-chested, drunken lager-louts, waving a Cross of Saint George and displaying their intolerance of other cultures features strongly, for instance, *Everywhere We Go: Behind the Matchday Madness* (London: Headline, 1996) and *Capital Punishment* (London: Headline, 1997).
7. C. Ward, *Well Frogged Out: The Fans' True Story of France 98* (Edinburgh: Mainstream, 1998).
8. M. Perryman (ed.), *The Ingerland Factor: Home Truths from Football* (Edinburgh: Mainstream, 1999), p. 22.
9. The TMO/INRA survey of Europeans' perceptions of their neighbours introduced earlier (see Ch. 3) ranks France first out of 14 in the category *quality of life*. Cited by G. Mermet, *Francoscopie 1997: Comment vivent les Français* (Paris: Larousse/Bordas, 1996), pp. 39–41.
10. The reference is to the French goalkeeper Bernard Lama who was punished for drug-taking and defended himself by claiming that it helped his 'interior serenity'.
11. On the contrary, Spain was neutral in both conflicts and Germany was an ally of Franco's in the Spanish Civil War.
12. See Lyons and Ticher, *Back Home*.
13. See L. Crolley, D. Hand and R. Jeutter, 'Playing the Identity Card: Stereotypes in European Football', *Soccer and Society*, 1, 2 (Summer 2000), pp. 107–28 and H. O'Donnell, 'Mapping the Mythical: A Geopolitics of National Sporting Stereotypes', *Discourse and Society*, 5, 3 (1994), pp. 345–80.
14. N. Blain and H. O'Donnell, 'European Sports Journalism and Its Readers', in M. Roche (ed.), *Sport, Popular Culture and Identity* (Aachen: Meyer u. Meyer, 1998).

Select Bibliography

Agulhon, M. and P. Oulmont, *Nation, patrie, patriotisme* (Paris: La Documentation française, 1993)

Anderson, B., *Imagined Communities: Reflections on the Origin and Spread of Nationalism* (London: Verso, 1983)

Anderson, P. and A. Weymouth, *Insulting the Public? The British Press and the EU* (London: Longman, 1999)

Anuario El País (Madrid: *El País*, 2000)

Archetti, E.P., 'In Search of National Identity: Argentinian Football and Europe', in J.A. Mangan (ed.), *Tribal Identities: Nationalism, Europe, Sport* (London and Portland, OR: Frank Cass, 1996), pp. 201–19

Armstrong, G. and R. Harris, 'Football Hooligans: Theory and Evidence', *Sociological Review*, 39, 3 (1991), pp. 427–58

Back, L., T. Crabbe and J. Solomos, 'Racism in Football: Patterns of Continuity and Change', in A. Brown (ed.), *Fanatics! Power, Identity and Fandom in Football* (London: Routledge, 1998), pp. 71–87

Bale, J., 'Playing at Home: British Football and a Sense of Place', in J. Williams and S. Wagg (eds), *British Football and Social Change* (Leicester: Leicester University Press, 1991)

Balfour, S., 'The Loss of Empire, Regenerationism, and the Forging of a Myth of National Identity', in H. Graham and J. Labanyi (eds), *Spanish Cultural Studies: An Introduction*, (Oxford: Oxford University Press, 1995) pp. 25–30

Ball, P., 'Patriot Games', in A. Lyons and M. Ticher (eds), *Back Home: How the World Watched France 98* (London: WSC Books, 1998), pp. 69–75

Bernard, D., 'The New Ambassadors, or the Reincarnation of the Temple Money Changers?', in C. Rühn, *Le Foot: The Legends of French Football* (London: Abacus, 2000), pp. 285–6

Blain, N. and R. Boyle, 'Sport as Real Life: Media Sport and Culture', in A. Briggs and P. Cobley (eds), *The Media: An Introduction* (London, Longman, 1998)

Blain, N. and H. O'Donnell, 'European Sports Journalism and its Readers', in M. Roche (ed.), *Sport, Popular Culture and Identity* (Aachen: Meyer u. Meyer, 1998)

Blain, N., R. Boyle and H. O'Donnell, *Sport and National Identity in the Media* (Leicester: Leicester University Press, 1993)

Boniface, P. (ed.), *Géopolitique du football* (Brussels: Editions complexe, 1998)

Boyle, R. and R. Haynes, *Power Play: Sport, the Media and Popular Culture* (Harlow: Pearson Education, 2000)

Bozonnet, J.-J., *Sport et société* (Paris: Le Monde Editions, 1996)

Bragg, B., 'Two World Wars and One World Cup', in M. Perryman (ed.), *The Ingerland Factor: Home Truths from Football* (Edinburgh: Mainstream, 1999), pp. 37–43

Brewer's Dictionary of Phrase and Fable (London: Cassell, 1990)

Bromberger, C., 'Football Passion and the World Cup: Why So Much Sound and Fury?', in J. Sugden and A. Tomlinson (eds), *Hosts and Champions: Soccer Cultures, National Identities and the USA World Cup* (Aldershot: Arena, 1994), pp. 281–90

Bromberger, C., *Le Match de football. Ethnologie d'une passion partisane à Marseille, Naples et Turin* (Paris: Maison des sciences de l'homme, 1995)

Bromberger, C., 'Le Football, phénomène de représentation collective', in P. Boniface (ed.), *Géopolitique du football* (Brussels: Editions complexe, 1998), pp. 41–8

Bromberger, C., *Football, la bagatelle la plus sérieuse du monde* (Paris: Bayard, 1998)

Broussard, P., *Génération supporter: enquête sur les ultras du football* (Paris: Robert Laffont, 1990)

Brown, A. (ed.), *Fanatics! Power, Identity and Fandom in Football* (London: Routledge, 1998)

Calleja, B., *La Guerra 'Incivil' del Fútbol* (Barcelona: Plaza y Janés Editores, 1997)

Carlin, J., 'Brothers in Arms: Les Bleus Win the World Cup, 1998', in C. Rühn, *Le Foot: The Legends of French Football* (London: Abacus, 2000), pp. 59–70

Carrington, B., '"Football's Coming Home" but Whose Home? And Do We Want It? Nation, Football and the Politics of Exclusion', in A. Brown (ed.), *Fanatics! Power, Identity and Fandom in Football* (London: Routledge, 1998), pp. 101–23

Carrington, B., 'Too Many St. George Crosses to Bear', in M. Perryman (ed.), *The Ingerland Factor: Home Truths from Football* (Edinburgh: Mainstream, 1999), pp. 71–86

Centro de Investigaciones Sociológicas, *Encuesta sobre la defensa nacional y la profesionalización del Ejército* (Madrid, 2000)

Citron, S., *Le Mythe national: l'histoire de France en question* (Paris: Editions ouvrières/EDI, 1991)

Coelho, J.N., 'On the Border: Some Notes on Football and National Identity in Portugal', in A. Brown (ed.), *Fanatics! Power, Identity and Fandom in Football* (London: Routledge, 1998), pp. 158–72

Conn, D., *The Football Business: Fair Game in the 90s?* (Edinburgh: Mainstream, 1997)

Connelly, C., *Spirit High and Passion Pure: A Journey through European Football* (Edinburgh: Mainstream, 2000)

La Constitución Española (Madrid: Alianza Editorial, 1978)

Conversi, D., *The Basques, the Catalans and Spain: Alternative Routes to Nationalist Mobilisation* (London: Hurst, 1996)

Critcher, C., 'England and the World Cup: World Cup Willies, English Football and the Myth of 1966', in J. Sugden and A. Tomlinson (eds), *Hosts and Champions. Soccer Cultures, National Identities and the USA World Cup* (Aldershot: Arena, 1994), pp 77–92

Crolley, L., 'Real Madrid v Barcelona: The State against a Nation? The Changing Role of Football in Spain', *International Journal of Iberian Studies*, 10, 1 (1997), pp. 33–43

Crolley, L., D. Hand and R. Jeutter, 'National Obsessions and Identities in Football Match Reports', in A. Brown (ed.), *Fanatics! Power, Identity and Fandom in Football* (London: Routledge, 1998), pp. 173–85

Crolley, L., D. Hand and R. Jeutter, 'Playing the Identity Card: Stereotypes in European Football', *Soccer and Society* 1, 2 (2000), pp. 107–28

Crystal, D., *The Cambridge Encyclopaedia of Language* (Cambridge: Cambridge University Press, 1992)

Dauncey, H. and G. Hare (eds), *France and the 1998 World Cup. The National Impact of a World Sporting Event* (London and Portland, OR: Frank Cass, 1999)

Davies, P., 'Look at the State of Us', in M. Perryman (ed.), *The Ingerland Factor. Home Truths from Football* (Edinburgh: Mainstream, 1999), pp. 177–83

Debray, R., *Transmettre* (Paris: Odile Jacob, 1997)

Dimeo, P. and G.P.T. Finn, 'Scottish Racism, Scottish Identities: the Case of Partick Thistle', in A. Brown (ed.), *Fanatics! Power, Identity and Fandom in Football* (London: Routledge, 1998), pp. 124–38

Duke, V. and L. Crolley, *Football, Nationality and the State* (London: Longman, 1996)

Favier, J. (ed.), *Chronique de la France et des Français* (Paris: Jacques Legrand/Larousse, 1987)

Fell, A.S. and C. Tinker, 'Representing Paris', *Modern and Contemporary France*, 8, 3 (2000), pp. 301–3

Fernández Santander, C., *El fútbol durante la guerra civil y el franquismo* (Madrid: Editorial San Martín, 1990)

García Candau, J., *Madrid — Barça: Historia de un desamor* (Madrid: El País Aguilar, 1996)

Gardiner, S., 'The Law and Hate Speech: "Ooh, aah, Cantona" and the Demonisation of "the Other" ', in A. Brown (ed.), *Fanatics! Power, Identity and Fandom in Football* (London: Routledge, 1998), pp. 249–64

Garland, J. and M. Rowe, *War Minus the Shooting? Jingoism, the English Press and Euro 96* (Leicester: Scarman Centre, Crime, Order and Policing Series Occasional Paper no. 7, 1997)

Gebauer, G., 'Les Trois dates de l'équipe d'Allemagne de football', in H. Hélal and P. Mignon (eds), *Football, jeu et société* (Paris: Cahiers de l'INSEP, no. 25, 1999), pp. 101–11

Giulianotti, R., 'Football Media in the UK: A Cultural Studies Perspective' (Buenos Aires: 1997), conference paper

Graham, H. and J. Labanyi, *Spanish Cultural Studies: An Introduction* (Oxford: Oxford University Press, 1995)

Greaves, A., 'Sport in France', in M. Cook (ed.), *French Culture since 1945* (London: Longman, 1993), pp. 125–48

Gritti, J., *Sport à la une* (Paris: Armand Colin, 1975)

The Guinness Book of Football (London: Guinness Publishing, 1998)

Gutiérrez, M., '*El Mundo Deportivo*: ochenta y cuatro años de historia', *Periodistas*, 32 (April 1990), pp. 93–7

Gutiérrez, M., '*Marca*: bodas de oro con el periodismo deportivo', *Periodistas*, 34 (May 1990), pp. 83–5

Hall, S. and P. du Gay, *Questions of Cultural Identity* (London: Sage, 1996)

Hamil, S., J. Michie, C. Oughton and S. Warby (eds), *The Changing Face of the Football Business: Supporters Direct* (London and Portland, OR: Frank Cass, 2000)

Hand, D., 'Footix: the History behind a Modern Mascot', *French Cultural Studies*, 9 (1998), pp. 239–47

Hélal, H. and P. Mignon (eds), *Football, jeu et société* (Paris: Cahiers de l'INSEP, no. 25, 1999)

Hesse-Lichtenberger, U., 'National Theatre', in A. Lyons and M. Ticher (eds), *Back Home: How the World Watched France 98* (London: WSC Books, 1998), pp. 21–9

Hidalgo, M., 'Le Football au mondial: jeu et enjeux', in H. Hélal and P. Mignon (eds), *Football, jeu et société* (Paris: Cahiers de l'INSEP, no. 25, 1999), pp. 17–34

Higson, A., 'National Identity and the Media', in A. Briggs and P. Cobley (eds), *The Media: An Introduction* (London: Longman, 1998)

Hill, D., 'The Sin of Pride', in A. Lyons and M. Ticher (eds), *Back Home: How the World Watched France 98* (London: WSC Books, 1998), pp. 11–19

Hill, J., 'Cup Finals and Community in the North of England', in J. Hill and J. Williams (eds), *Sport and Identity in the North of England* (Keele: Keele University Press, 1996), pp. 85–111

Hill, J. and J. Williams (eds), *Sport and Identity in the North of England* (Keele: Keele University Press, 1996)

Holt, R., *Sport and the British: A Modern History* (Oxford: Oxford University Press, 1989)

Holt, R., 'Contrasting Nationalisms: Sport, Militarism and the Unitary State in Britain and France before 1914', in J.A. Mangan (ed.), *Tribal Identities: Nationalism, Europe, Sport* (London and Portland, OR: Frank Cass, 1996), pp. 39–54

Hooper, J., *The Spaniards: A Portrait of the New Spain* (London: Penguin, 1986)

Hopcraft, A., *The Football Man* (London: Simon & Schuster, 1988)

Isaacs, A. and J. Monk, *The Illustrated Dictionary of British Heritage* (Cambridge: Market House, 1986)

Jeandupeux, D., 'Le Style d'un club', in H. Hélal and P. Mignon (eds), *Football, jeu et société* (Paris: Cahiers de l'INSEP, no. 25, 1999), pp. 121–33

Jones, D. (ed.), *Sport i mitjans de comunicació a Catalunya* (Barcelona: Generalitat de Catalunya, 1996)

Jones, D. and J. Baró i Queralt, 'La prensa', in D. Jones (ed.), *Sport i mitjans de comunicació a Catalunya* (Barcelona: Generalitat de Catalunya, 1996), pp. 19–52

Kelly, S.F., *Back Page Football: A Century of Newspaper Coverage* (Harpenden: Aurora/Queen Anne Press, 1996)

Larousse multimédia encyclopédique, CD Rom (Paris: Larousse/Liris Interactive, 1997)

Lawlor, T. and M. Rigby, *Contemporary Spain: Essays and Texts on Politics, Economics, Education and Employment, and Society* (London: Longman, 1998)

Leguineche, M., P. Unzueta and S. Segurola, *Athletic: 100 Conversaciones en la Catedral* (Madrid: Grupo Santillana de Ediciones, 1998)

León Solís, F., 'El juego de las nacionalidades', *International Journal of Iberian Studies*, 9, 1 (1996), pp. 28–45

Lorente, S. (ed.), *Informe sociológico sobre la situación social en España* (Madrid: FOESSA, 1994)

Lyons, A. and M. Ticher (eds), *Back Home: How the World Watched France 98* (London: WSC Books, 1998)

Mangan, J.A. (ed.), *Tribal Identities: Nationalism, Europe, Sport* (London and Portland, OR: Frank Cass, 1996)

Mangan, J.A., 'Duty unto Death: English Masculinity and Militarism in the Age of the New Imperialism', in J.A. Mangan (ed.), *Tribal Identities: Nationalism, Europe, Sport* (London and Portland, OR: Frank Cass, 1996), pp. 10–38

Marks, J., 'The French National Team and National Identity: "Cette France d'un bleu métis" ', in H. Dauncey and G. Hare (eds), *France and the 1998 World Cup: The National Impact of a World Sporting Event* (London and Portland, OR: Frank Cass, 1999), pp. 41–57

Mar-Molinero, C., 'The Politics of Language: Spain's Minority Languages', in H. Graham and J. Labanyi, *Spanish Cultural Studies: An Introduction* (Oxford: Oxford University Press, 1995), pp. 336–41

Mar-Molinero, C. and A. Smith, *Nationalism and the Nation in the Iberian Peninsula* (Oxford: Berg, 1996)

Martialay, F. and B. Salazar, *Las grandes mentiras del fútbol español* (Madrid: Fuerza Nueva Editorial, 1997)

Mason, T., *Association Football and English Society 1863–1915* (Brighton: Harvester Press, 1981)

Mason, T., *Sport in Britain* (London: Faber, 1988)

McKeever, L., 'Reporting the World Cup: Old and New Media', in H. Dauncey and G. Hare (eds), *France and the 1998 World Cup: The National Impact of a World Sporting Event* (London and Portland, OR: Frank Cass, 1999), pp. 161–83

Mermet, G., *Francoscopie 1997: Comment vivent les Français* (Paris: Larousse/Bordas, 1996)

Miall, A., *Xenophobe's Guide to the English* (Horsham: Ravette, 1993)

Michaud, G. and A. Kimmel, *Le Nouveau guide France* (Paris: Hachette, 1996)

Mignon, P., *La Passion du football* (Paris: Odile Jacob, 1998)

Mignon, P., 'France: A Beautiful World', in A. Lyons and M. Ticher (eds), *Back Home: How the World Watched France 98* (London: WSC Books, 1998), pp. 199–207

Mignon, P., 'Fans and Heroes', in H. Dauncey and G. Hare (eds), *France and the 1998 World Cup: The National Impact of a World Sporting Event* (London and Portland, OR: Frank Cass, 1999), pp. 79–97

Moliner, M., *Diccionario de uso del español* (Madrid: Editorial Gredos, 1991)

Moragas Spà, M., 'Esport i mitjans de communicació', in D. Jones (ed.), *Esport i mitjans de communicació a Catalunya* (Barcelona: Generalitat de Catalunya, 1996), pp. 11–18

Moran, R., 'You Send Me Bananas', in M. Perryman (ed.), *The Ingerland Factor: Home Truths from Football* (Edinburgh: Mainstream, 1999), pp. 157–64

Nora, P. (ed.), *Les Lieux de mémoire* (Paris: Gallimard, 1997)

O'Donnell, H., 'Mapping the Mythical: A Geopolitics of National Sporting Stereotypes', *Discourse and Society*, 5, 3 (1994), pp. 345–80

Orakwue, S., *Pitch Invaders: The Modern Black Football Revolution* (London: Victor Gollancz/Cassell, 1998)

Orwell, G., *Homage to Catalonia* (London: Penguin, 1938)

The Oxford English Reference Dictionary (Oxford: Oxford University Press, 1996)

Pastoureau, M., 'Les Couleurs du stade', *Vingtième siècle*, 26 (1990), pp. 11–18

Paxman, J., *The English: A Portrait of a People* (London: Penguin, 1999)

Pecheral, A., 'Olympique Marseille: The First French European Cup Victory', in C. Rühn, *Le Foot: The Legends of French Football* (London: Abacus, 2000), pp. 13–17

Perelman, M., *Les Intellectuels et le football: montée de tous les maux et recul de la pensée* (Paris: Les Editions de la passion, 2000)

PCC, 'France 98 – The World Cup' (13 May 1998), press statement

Perryman, M. (ed.), *The Ingerland Factor: Home Truths from Football* (Edinburgh: Mainstream, 1999)

Pickup, I., 'French Football from its Origins to Euro 96', in H. Dauncey and G. Hare (eds), *France and the 1998 World Cup: The National Impact of a World Sporting Event* (London and Portland, OR: Frank Cass, 1999), pp. 22–40

Poulton, E., 'Fighting Talk from the Press Corps', in M. Perryman (ed.), *The*

Ingerland Factor: Home Truths from Football (Edinburgh: Mainstream, 1999), pp. 119–35

Puig, I. (ed.), *Personal Memories of the Days of the Spanish Civil War in Catalan and English: Lluís Puig Casas* (Lampeter: Mellen, 1999)

Ramonet, I., 'Football et passions nationales', in P. Boniface (ed.), *Géopolitique du football* (Brussels: Editions complexe, 1998), pp. 55–62

Ravenel, L., *La Géographie du football en France* (Paris: PUF, 1998)

Reid, G., *Football and War* (Wilmslow: Sigma Press, 2000)

Renan, E., *Qu'est-ce qu'une nation? Conférence faite en Sorbonne, le 11 mars 1882* (Paris: Imprimerie nationale, 1995 [C. Lévy, 1882])

Rowe, D., J. McKoy and T. Miller, 'Come Together: Sport, Nationalism and the Media Image', in L. Wenner (ed.), *MediaSport* (London: Routledge, 1998), pp. 119–33

Rühn, C., *Le Foot: The Legends of French Football* (London: Abacus, 2000)

Russell, D., *Football and the English: A Social History of Association Football in England: 1863–1995* (Preston: Carnegie Publishing, 1997)

Saccomano, E. (ed.), *Larousse du football* (Paris: Larousse/Bordas, 1998)

Segurola, S. (ed.), *Fútbol y pasiones políticas* (Barcelona: Temas de debate, 1999)

Seitz, N., *Doppelpässe: Fußball und Politik* (Frankfurt: Eichborn, 1997)

Shaw, D., *Fútbol y franquismo* (Madrid: Alianza Editorial, 1987)

Sobrequés i Callico, J., *Terra Nostra: Un club al servei de Catalunya* (Barcelona: Editorial Labor, 1991)

Solé Tura, J., *Nacionalidades y nacionalismos en España* (Madrid: Alianza Editorial, 1985)

Sonntag, A., 'Le Football, image de la nation', in P. Boniface (ed.), *Géopolitique du football* (Brussels: Editions complexe, 1998), pp. 31–40

Stasi, B., 'Le Football: aventure personnelle et phénomène de société', in P. Boniface (ed.), *Géopolitique du football* (Brussels: Editions complexe, 1998), pp. 127–31

Sugden, J. and A. Tomlinson (eds), *Hosts and Champions: Soccer Cultures, National Identities and the USA World Cup* (Aldershot: Arena, 1994)

Sugden, J. and A. Tomlinson, *FIFA and the Contest for World Football: Who Rules the People's Game?* (Cambridge: Polity Press, 1998)

Thompson, A., 'From Teaching to Coaching: Gérard Houllier', in C. Rühn, *Le Foot: The Legends of French Football* (London: Abacus, 2000), pp. 216–22

Unzueta, P., 'Fútbol y nacionalismo vasco', in S. Segurola (ed.), *Fútbol y pasiones políticas* (Barcelona: Temas de debate, 1999), pp. 147–68

Vasili, P., *The First Black Footballer – Arthur Wharton 1865–1930: An Absence of Memory* (London and Portland, OR: Frank Cass, 1998)

Wahl, A., *Les Archives du football. Sport et société en France (1880–1980)* (Paris: Gallimard/Julliard, 1989)

Wahl, A., 'Pour une histoire du jeu', in H. Hélal and P. Mignon (eds), *Football, jeu et société* (Paris: Cahiers de l'INSEP, no. 25, 1999), pp. 35–45

Wenner, L. (ed.), *MediaSport* (London: Routledge, 1998)

Whannel, G., *Fields in Vision – Television Sport and Cultural Transformation* (London: Routledge, 1992)

Whannel, G., 'Reading the Sports Media Audience', in L. Wenner (ed.), *MediaSport* (London: Routledge, 1998), pp. 119–33

Yapp, N. and M. Syrett, *The Xenophobe's Guide to the French* (Horsham: Ravette, 1993)

Index